# The Shell Book of
# CURIOUS BRITAIN

# The Shell Book of
# CURIOUS BRITAIN

Anthony Burton

**DAVID & CHARLES**
Newton Abbot   London

**British Library Cataloguing in Publication Data**
Burton, Anthony
The Shell book of curious Britain.
1. Great Britain — Description and travel —
1971-
I. Title
914.1'0485'8        DA632

ISBN 0-7153-8083-4

Typeset by Typesetters (Birmingham) Ltd
and printed in Great Britain
by the Alden Press, Oxford
for David & Charles (Publishers) Limited
Brunel House   Newton Abbot   Devon

# Contents

*For Pip,*
*who did most of the hard work*

# Ordinary and Extraordinary:
# An Introduction

Everyone must, I imagine, at some time or other have had the experience of walking down a street or along a country lane and suddenly being confronted by something that stops you in your tracks. 'Good lord,' you exclaim, 'what an extraordinary object.' This book is about just such extraordinary objects. Having said that, we are not very much nearer to an idea of what such objects might be. So, before beginning our tour round some of the odder places in these islands, perhaps it would be as well to have some notion of the sort of things we shall be meeting.

The most obvious category of extraordinary objects is that of things deliberately designed to attract attention, things indeed which have no other object in life. Until recently, I had a regular Saturday morning occupation: driving my daughter to a riding school in the Oxfordshire village of Steeple Aston. One of those mornings was too bright, too perfect to be wasted so I wandered off through the village and out along a footpath across the fields. And there it was: one of those 'good lord, how extraordinary' things. In the middle of a field stood a high wall, heavily buttressed on one side and punctured by three tall arches. Was it part of some monstrously large barn or the sole remains of a great medieval foundation? Neither explanation seemed the least bit likely, as there was not a trace to suggest there might have been more bits to the building. Was it perhaps a monumental entrance? If so, an entrance to what? All one could say, quite positively, was that it was an undeniably dominant feature in the landscape: it caught the eye. And that, indeed, is just what it was built to do, and that gives it a name. It is an eye catcher, designed by William Kent in the 1740s.

Eye catchers, like follies, were among the products of the great landscape artists of the eighteenth century, the men such as Kent and Capability Brown. Unlike conventional landscape artists who made a

The Rousham eye catcher (at Steeple Aston), a great wall which has only one function to perform — to stand and be looked at *(National Monuments Record)*

picture of the landscape with brush, paint and canvas, they made the landscape itself look like a picture. The Steeple Aston wall, with its vaguely medieval style, was put there for the gentry to look at. Nature had provided green, gently sloping land: man, the improver, added a dramatic focal point. If eye catchers such as this stop us in our tracks, then they are doing no more than fulfilling their true function. But what other things and places have the same effect? Only a few of the places we shall be looking at were built solely to attract attention.

In many cases, the extraordinary turns out to be no more than the ordinary of yesterday. Ivinghoe, in Buckinghamshire, apart from possessing a splendid seventeenth-century windmill — and windmills are, happily, still sufficiently common not to merit an inclusion in a book of oddities — does have a genuine curiosity. Hung on the church wall is a device consisting of a 14ft rough wooden pole with a huge iron hook at the end of it, looking rather like a gargantuan shepherd's crook. Those who have never seen such an object before – and I have not seen another – might well spend some time pondering over its possible uses. It is, in fact, a fire-fighting device. Thatched roofs were, and are, common in the region. They can be very beautiful, but if a roof catches fire there is the great danger that bunches of burning thatch will be blown away to set fire to neighbouring roofs. To prevent the fire spreading, the hook was used to pull the burning thatch to the ground. Extraordinary it might seem to us now until we know its use, but a hundred years ago it would have excited as much interest as a fire extinguisher attached to a wall does today. Its present extraordinariness derives also in part from the fact that it is put on public display. The most commonplace object can appear interesting if taken out of context and displayed to the public – a notion that has been taken to extremes in recent years by artists who have placed, for example, piles of bricks in art galleries.

Similar objects which baffle and intrigue us can be found in many places. John Hopkins, the former landlord of my village local, acquired a strange device, consisting of a wooden cylinder which splits longitudinally. Inside are two wooden screws, which fit through holes

Ivinghoe's ancient thatch hook *(National Monuments Record)*

in the cylinder. As the screws are turned, so the two halves of the cylinder are forced apart. It is beautifully made, but none of us had the least idea of how it was used. The local museum had no notion; the oldest village inhabitants could recall nothing like it. Then one day someone came by who knew exactly what it was, and our mysterious object became a commonplace, brought out occasionally to test the ingenuity of visitors. Now that the landlord has retired taking the cylinder with him, the answer can be revealed. It is a purse stretcher, dating back to the days when purses were themselves made in cylindrical form. It was quite a disappointment, in a way, to solve the puzzle, for one of the delights of hunting out the extraordinary is that one frequently ends up with at least as many questions as answers – though that might appear merely frustrating for those who prefer the ordered life, with everything filed away in the correctly labelled compartment.

One area of surprise and delight appears when we come across places and things which manage to fall outside the slots into which they are supposed to fit. We live in an age which places a high priority on standardisation and regulation. Houses, for example, must conform to certain rules. This is fine when the rules are designed to cover such matters as safety, but too often they can be used to produce mere conformity, for the sake of conformity. It can be, and indeed is, claimed that such rules prevent the construction of 'eyesores', though when such claims are put forward by those bodies which actively encourage the construction of tower blocks they need not be taken too seriously. But what is an eyesore? To some the mock Gothic so beloved of Victorian builders is simply hideous – for others the Gothic cottage is a home of character and individuality. Certainly, some of the bizarre buildings that we shall see later would never get past the local planning committee. Many people find this rather sad, and as there is a limited stock of 'houses of character' – there are far fewer than one is led to believe by the claims of estate agents – people look to other buildings. Chapels, village schools, disused railway stations, barns and mills; all have been converted into homes by enthusiastic owners looking for something different. Such schemes often prove very successful, achieving effects of great exuberance which high costs and rigid rules make all but impossible in the more ordinary house.

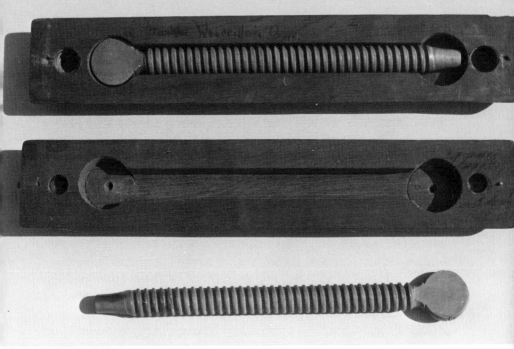

John Hopkins' mystery object from Islip *(Richard Garratt)*

Other houses which, a century ago, could be a riot of elaboration —
the houses for the dead — have all but vanished. No mausoleum is
needed to hold a spoonful of ashes. There have even been cases in
recent years where families have been forbidden to erect grandiose
graveside monuments because the local vicar thought them
undignified. Perhaps he thought the neighbours might complain.
There are a great many who think it quite proper that they should
impose their standards of respectability and propriety on the rest of
the community. Happily, for every Jack in office with a rule book,
there is always an individual determined to go his or her own way.
Such individualists have plenty of good, historical precedent on their
side.

Old traditions are untidy anachronisms to some, living links with
the past to others. I once took a Swedish friend down to my local for a
pint, where we were greeted by the sight of a troop of Morris Men. It
was difficult to tell whether he was delighted or merely astonished. He
had never, he declared, seen anything so bizarre. What then would he
have made of the Coconut Dancers of Bacup, stout Lancashire men

who black-up their faces, don outlandish costumes and then proceed to clog dance through the streets? Or what of such strange customs as 'Bottle Kicking and Hare Pie Scrambling'? Every Easter at Hallaton in Leicestershire, a hare pie is carried to the top of Hare Pie Hill and then scattered over the ground in what one might assume is a survivor of an old fertility rite. After that comes the battle of the bottles which, to add to the confusion, are not bottles at all but three barrels, one of which is empty. The residents of Hallaton do battle with the neighbouring village of Medbourne, the object being to get the empty barrel back to within one's own parish boundary. At that point the victors can claim and consume the contents of the full barrels.

This country has a multitude of such customs and rites which have survived even though their origins might now be obscure. Without exception, however, they did not begin as quaint and jolly pastimes, but as serious rituals which were considered important to the well-being of the community. No dedicated hunter after the curious will ever be able to resist the lure of these ancient customs which have survived for so long. We shall be getting some idea of just where and how long ago they started when we come to look at some of the very ancient and very strange British monuments.

If the extraordinary so often turns out to be the commonplace of yesterday or to have some quite rational explanation, can the extraordinary be said to exist at all? Strictly speaking, one could say not. But we exist in a particular slot in time and space and if we can accept that the definition of what is extraordinary is purely subjective and always changing, then we can quite happily continue exclaiming with astonishment and delight at whatever takes our fancy. But it is as well to remember that our responses are very much of our own time, and it makes an entertaining game to draw up a list of objects which seem commonplace to us but which will seem scarcely credible a century from now. When the last motor car and the last lorry have used the last drop of petrol what will our successors make of the ruins of Spaghetti Junction? Telecommunication must surely change, so what of London's Post Office Tower? Will we still be writing letters, and if not what strange anachronisms post boxes will appear. How long before the first Tower Block Preservation Society is formed? It might seem impossible, but who would have believed even twenty years ago that Battersea Power Station would be placed under a preservation order in 1980?

If the dividing line between ordinary and extraordinary is so thin and arbitrary, then at least I have no need to apologise for what follows in the rest of the book. It is an entirely personal selection of those places and things which amuse, delight or amaze me. I hope it will prove equally interesting to others, but in such an area where subjectivity is all, one can be quite certain that some things I find fascinating will seem pedestrian and dull to others, while places that I have left out because they failed to arouse my interest will turn out to be someone else's favourites. All I can hope is that the reader will discover in these pages some spot that he did not know about, and that the discovery will give him as much pleasure as it has already given me.

# 1
# Ancient Mysteries

The sight of a large stone, standing aloof on the skyline, can be strange and mysterious. We see, or fancy we see, the shape of a man's head or some great beast. Well-known examples can be found among the moorland tors of Devon and Cornwall, where erosion produces such odd effects as the stones that make up the Cheesewring. Here the appearance is of a massive balancing act of giant, petrified cheeses, piled one on top of the other. Even more bizarre shapes appear at places such as Brimham rocks in Yorkshire. As a child, this was one of my favourite spots for an outing. I could clamber over the Pulpit and the Devil's Anvil, or stare at the Dancing Bear, agreeing, Polonius-like, that it was indeed a fair representation of a cavorting animal. The Yoke of Oxen remained and remains, however, totally unconvincing.

Sometimes such large stones break and the parts are smoothed by the weather, so that one part actually moves on top of the other. Elsewhere large boulders have been carried down hillsides by long-departed glaciers to take up equally precarious positions. Such stones are known as rocking stones or logans, and people used to be rather unwilling to accept the idea that such odd phenomena could have perfectly natural explanations, so the supernatural was invoked. Isolated pillars of rock, such as that at the edge of the Cotswold scarp at Leckhampton, were given fanciful names like 'Devil's Chimney'. The Devil, one soon discovers, was a busy character, depositing all manner of stones in all manner of places. Later, in the 'rational' age of the eighteenth century, less fanciful, but no more accurate, explanations were put forward. Travellers described logans as the work of Druids, and those same gentlemen were said to have

*(opposite)* The Devil's Chimney at Leckhampton owes rather more to quarrymen than to diabolic practices *(British Tourist Authority)*

constructed the whole of Brimham rocks, which was in fact a Druidic temple. They manufactured mysteries where none exist – but among the standing stones there are genuine mysteries in plenty and, in many cases, a good many unanswered questions. Take, for example, the standing stones near Boroughbridge in North Yorkshire.

Three slender stones, ranging in height from 18ft to over 20ft stand in fields near the village. There is certainly no question of their being natural phenomena, produced by erosion or the like. They were quarried some miles away, near Knaresborough, and brought here to be set up in a straight line. There were originally four stones, but the fourth was pulled down by locals in the sixteenth century, either through superstition or because of rumours that treasure was to be found underneath. That much we know for certain. But what should we make of the long, vertical grooves which are such a feature of the stones? Were they cut by men or formed by natural forces? Certainly

Visitors to Brimham rocks are invited to see a dancing bear and the Devil's anvil in these weathered stones *(National Trust: photo Derek G. Widdicombe)*; *(opposite)* these ancient stones near Boroughbridge, known as the Devil's Arrows, were placed there by man, but no one knows why *(Reece Winstone)*

another outcrop of the same rock, millstone grit, at Armscliffe Crag near Harrogate, shows a similar pattern and that is certainly due to natural weathering. On the other hand, the 'Nine Stones' on Harthill Moor, Derbyshire show grooves which are certainly man made. Natural or unnatural patterning – no one seems quite sure. Local legend, however, has its own explanation. These are Devil's Arrows. Satan took a dislike to the local population who had turned to Christianity, and he fired off these missiles from nearby Howe Hill. Either his aim was poor – and in most of such legends the Devil comes across as remarkably myopic – or else the forces of virtue were too strong for him. In either event he missed, and the arrows stand today, safely embedded in open ground. So, in this one simple story we have three elements – the works of man, natural forces, and super-natural powers. The same three elements tend to recur whenever we look at these most strange and mysterious sites.

The supernatural element is always strong in these stories. Over at Rudston on Humberside, there is a huge standing stone, rising nearly 26ft above ground and very similar to the stones which make up the Devil's Arrows. Its home is now within the churchyard of Rudston parish church. Inevitably, its presence is attributed by local legend to the bad temper, not to mention the bad aim, of the Devil, who wanted to destroy the church. What seems much more likely is that historical events were precisely the reverse of the legend. To the early Christians, the old religions of the country were the work of the Devil, which it was their duty to destroy. It seems very probable that the great stone, which has certainly stood on its present site since at least 2000 BC, was a sacred place. The Christians sought to de-paganise it by bringing it within the confines of the church. By incorporating the stone into consecrated ground, the Devil's church was destroyed as effectively as legend has it the Devil had hoped to destroy the Christian church. But what are such stones? Why were they erected in the first place? These are questions for which there is no ready answer, and the more one investigates ancient stones, the odder they seem to become and the more the mysteries multiply.

*(opposite)* The monolith safely enclosed within the holy ground of the churchyard at Rudston *(BBC Hulton Picture Library)*

Men-an-Tol in Cornwall. Miraculous cures are said to be effected by passing the invalid through the circular stone *(Batsford: supplied by National Monuments Record)*

The Devil puts in an appearance in many stone legends. In Cornwall you may come across the Devil's Eye. It is more properly known as the Men-an-Tol, and stands on the White Downs, near Morvah, on the north coast. It too is a standing stone, long established as a Bronze Age monument, but one with a weird set of attached legends. Those who speak the ancient language of the region will know that its name means 'stone with a hole'. It is in fact circular, looking rather like an upended doughnut. There are two other, conventional, stones associated with it. The fascination of such groups lies in good measure with the stories of supernatural powers that surround them, and such stories have lasted for centuries, right down to modern times. The Men-an-Tol, in particular, has a long tradition of possessing healing powers, which were said to be especially successful with children. Naked boys and girls were passed through the hole three times and each time they had to be pulled away towards the east. This, it was claimed, was an infallible cure for diseases such as rickets. We now know that rickets is a disease associated with poor diet, so how could dragging a naked child through a hole in a stone effect its cure? Did it, in fact, ever work at all? We simply do not know the answer to such questions. Rheumatism could also be cured, or so legend says, by the sufferer crawling nine times through the hole – again, it is said, in the direction of the rising sun. Sceptics might argue that any chronic rheumatic who could manage to crawl through the hole once, let alone nine times, was not so chronically ill as he supposed. Possibly so, yet the stories have lasted literally for millennia. The question that comes to mind is whether the stories are, in fact, derived from an experience of healing, or whether the stories of miracle cures have grown up to explain the otherwise inexplicable presence of such strange structures. Mystical experiences may or may not be real, but it is certainly true that sites which attract such stories tend to be concentrated in particular regions.

Take a look at the Ordnance Survey map for the tip of Cornwall and you will find, written in that splendid archaic script that the cartographers wisely reserved for pre-Roman antiquities, a whole series of intriguing names. Here are Chun Quoit and Lanyon Quoit, Men Screfys and the Nine Maidens, not to mention numerous logan stones. One would have to be a most incurious individual not to take time off to explore such a region, and those who do so will not be disappointed. Quoits, otherwise known as cromlechs or dolmens, are generally credited as being Neolithic or Bronze Age burial chambers. As they appear today, they consist of upright stones with huge flat stones, the cap-stones, resting on top of them. If they were indeed burial chambers they are remarkably airy, though theory has it that they were once covered with earth which has since eroded. This is no doubt all very reasonable and accurate, and similar structures can be found in many other parts of Britain. In Wales, for example, is what must be the finest example of all, Pentre Ifan. This is a huge cromlech, standing at the head of the Nevern Valley. Four tapering upright stones hold a cap-stone delicately balanced on their points. One uses the term 'delicately' because the overall impression is one of great lightness, yet the cap-stone itself is estimated to weigh around seventeen tons. Here archaeologists have found traces of a cairn, approximately 120ft long, so that the cromlech itself is only part of a much grander structure. It is a burial site, around which are grouped pits and courtyards used for religious rites. So, the mystery of the quoit is no mystery at all. It is just a part of an ancient graveyard. Yet the oddness and the strangeness never quite go away. Invariably, it seems, all kinds of supernatural phenomena are associated with such places. Perhaps, even probably, such stories are no more than an expression of that sense of awe which all of us feel when confronted with the inexplicable, and there is something undeniably strange about coming across a barren stretch of moorland to be confronted with massive stones placed there some 4,000 years ago. At least the quoits have a pretty credible and rational explanation for their presence. When one turns to stone lines and circles the mysteries multiply, and one finds that apparently rational explanations are at least as common-place as the apparently irrational.

For a start, let us look at the Nine Maidens. There they stand, not especially impressive, simply a group of stones set out in a circle. Yet things are not quite that simple. Nine more maidens can be found standing in another circle, also near Lands End, while another and even more impressive group, the Merry Maidens, can be found nearby at St Buryan. Here the maidens have increased their numbers to nineteen and stand around an 80ft circle. The stones, each standing around 4ft high, have clearly been positioned with great care and precision. But why are they there? What function did they perform? Legend has the almost inevitable answer. The maidens danced on the Sabbath, and were duly turned to stone for their wickedness. Two tall standing stones, a quarter of a mile away, have been incorporated into the story and named 'The Pipers'.

Other legends are no less exotic, and the more striking the setting, the stranger the legend. High on Bodmin Moor, not far from that odd natural phenomenon, the Cheesewring, stand the Hurlers, not one but three stone circles, their centres aligned on a north-east to south-west axis. The circles are each over 100ft in diameter and seem originally to have each held twenty-five to thirty stones, though the most that survive are the seventeen stones of the centre circle. They have all been carefully positioned and to ensure that they stayed put each was sunk several feet into the ground. It is not too difficult to guess what legend has to say about them. The first record dates from the sixteenth century: the historian William Camden wrote that the locals gave the stones their popular name 'being by devout and godly error perswaded that they had been men sometime transformed into stone for profaning the Lord's Day with hurling the ball'. It is a story which goes along with the various petrified maidens of other circles, but it is not the only legend associated with the Hurlers. It used to be claimed that no one could count the stones. The only way you could get an accurate count was to get a huge basket full of buns and count those. Then you had to go around the circles and place one bun on each of the stones. When every stone was topped by a bun, all you had to do was count the buns left in the basket, subtract that from the number you started with, and your calculation was complete. Just another old legend, you might suppose, but where did it originate? And, even more interestingly, why does the same tale crop up at other stone circles in other parts of the country, as at the Rollright Stones, which we shall be discussing later? At Rollright, the legend has a further elaboration in that even the bun-counting did not prove infallible, for as the would-be counters went round planting their buns, so the Devil would walk behind taking them off again. It is, to say the least, an odd little story, but it does have some very significant elements to it. Now, it soon becomes obvious to anyone who cares to try it, that the stones can be counted without investing all one's savings in bags of buns. If, however, you believe that legends are not the result of some pointless whim, but have survived down the centuries because they contain a core of truth, then the story cannot simply be dismissed. So here, on offer, is a personal interpretation which is based on quite unprovable theory.

One thing that many archaeologists are agreed upon is that many, if not all, stone circles have some sort of astronomical significance. Professor Alexander Thom has argued this case most convincingly, showing how the circles can be used for the calculation of seasonal changes and the like. The alignments are often connected with quite astonishingly accurate measurements. What this theory does not explain, however, is why such calculations were needed in the first place. True, an agricultural society needs to know when to plant and when to harvest, but scarcely with that sort of precision. No farmer lays down rigid rules that the corn must go in, say, at half past four next Wednesday afternoon or all will be lost. Accurate dating of phenomena such as the equinoxes and phases of the moon would, however, be required in a society that believed that the movement of the heavens had a practical importance in determining the course of their lives. If gods need to be propitiated by specific actions at specific times, then it might well be thought crucial that the timing should be accurate. Those who had the job of timing would be important members of society, and the time-keeping mechanism itself might also be considered of sufficient importance to merit a place in the temple structure. So here we have two elements. The stones are giant calculators, which only the priests would use: ordinary members of the society could not and must not meddle in the business of enumeration and calculation. Also, because the stones have religious significance, there would have been food offerings and sacrifices within the rings – and there is evidence of animal sacrifice at some ancient stone circles. Now all this was at least 3,000 years ago. We have long since lost the knowledge of how to use the stones, but is it not possible that these two elements have come down to us in the form of stories that combine the task of counting with the offering of food? That, at least, is one theory, but one of the great attractions of ancient sites lies in the fact that so many theories are possible. The circles are fascinating and mysterious, and we can all indulge in our own speculations. And there are still a lot more strange stories and legends to explain in this brief tour round the remains of the ancient past.

Maidens that are not petrified into circles are occasionally caught standing in a straight line. The Nine Maidens – the number nine occurs too often to be entirely coincidental – that are found near St Columb Major are, like the Hurlers, aligned on a north-east to south-west axis. They are spread out over 300yd and have even less obvious roles to play than the circles. This is, in fact, the only such alignment in Cornwall, but further east, on Dartmoor, the lines or rows are much more common. A very impressive example can be seen on the south-western edge of the moor at Merrivale. Here is a remarkably complex arrangement of stones, covering a wide arc. There are two double rows running east to west. The more northerly is 200yd long and ends in a single, large standing stone; the other is 70yd longer and also ends in a standing stone. Close by is a cairn, a third row and a circle. No one, it seems, knows for sure why they are there; or, to be more precise, no one can produce totally convincing evidence to support their own particular theory. Most agree, however, that these stones have a bearing on astronomical calculations. Many people also claim to detect strange forces at work on such sites.

In the summer of 1979, my wife and I were staying in a farmhouse at Sticklepath on the northern edge of Dartmoor. A few weeks before our visit, a dowser had been staying at the farm, and he had left behind his dowsing rods – nothing mysterious, simply a V-shaped device made from, of all things, plastic. Although I am by nature a somewhat sceptical individual, I am also a believer in putting things to the test. Walking around the lawns behind the farmhouse, holding the dowsing rods, I found to my considerable surprise that, at one particular point, the V suddenly pointed vertically downwards, without, as far as I could tell, any conscious movement on my part. What was even more surprising was the discovery that the experienced dowser had produced the same reaction at the same spot. The phenomenon was odd, but by no means a scientific test of dowsing in general or of my own particular sensitivity as a trainee dowser. The next day, we went for a walk across the moor and came across a set of stones, set in rows on the eastern side of Cawsand Hill. Memory stirred, and came up with a description of dowsing on such sites using a pendulum. Francis Hitching, in his book *Earth Magic*, describes how a pendulum, which is simply any heavy object suspended on a cord, will behave in an erratic manner at such sites. This memory on top of my recent experience of dowsing determined me to try another experiment. Using a pendulum improvised from a heavy compass and a long cord, I set it swinging along the line of the stone rows. Almost immediately, it began to change direction until, instead of swinging in a straight line, it was beginning to circle. Perhaps I was influencing it, wishing, as it were, for a spectacular result. That is certainly one explanation. Others would claim that the pendulum had been responding to some force which was known in the ancient world, but which we no longer recognise. I would not pretend to know the answer, but can offer a suggestion. Try the experiment. These sites, dating back 3,000 years and more, do exert a strange fascination and seem to hold mysteries which we can scarcely begin to penetrate. It may be that we shall never fully understand the significance of the stones, nor even explain the legends and stories that surround them. Some of course will deny that any true mystery exists at all and will dismiss all stories of 'strange forces' as so much nonsense, but here at least the individual can begin to make up his own mind and can attempt the simple tests for himself. The results may well be inconclusive, but then that is surely part of the fascination of such things. How dull life would be if every question came complete with an immediate and all too obvious answer.

So far, we have looked at what one might call the less well-known, less obvious survivors of the ancient world. It is not too surprising to find that when we come to look at the really major ancient monuments, the mysteries become ever deeper, and the explanations multiply. Some of the most spectacular, yet still relatively unknown, sites are to be found in Scotland. They are unknown to the general public simply because they are so remote, so far away from major centres. The supreme example is undoubtedly Callanish on Lewis in the Outer Hebrides. This is perhaps the most dramatic ancient site in the British Isles. The great stones stand on a promontory overlooking Loch Roag, on the west of the island, a bleak spot looking out across the flecked grey of the Atlantic. One might call it an inhospitable spot, but the term might be misconstrued and taken to refer to the inhabitants, and surely there are few more hospitable than those who live in the Western Isles. Indeed, if the lure of visiting Callanish is not sufficient in itself, then the charm of the people would make the visit worth while.

A bare description of the site can scarcely do it justice. For a start, there is a great circle of tall stones, thirteen in all with an average height of around 10ft. At their centre is a single stone, over 15ft high, 5ft wide and 1ft thick. Running away from the circle to the north is a double line of stones, 27ft wide and 270ft long, while shorter, single rows run off east, south and west. The circle thus stands at the centre of a cross, and within the circle itself, focal point of the whole pattern, is a cairn, which stands exactly half way between the central pillar and the circumference of the circle. The cairn appears to be older than the standing stone, and if that is so then it must have been important to the builders of Callanish. Its position could scarcely be considered the result of an accident.

The avenue of stones leading up to the great stone circle at Callanish *(Crown copyright, reproduced by permission of the Scottish Development Department)*

Inevitably, a whole cluster of stories has gathered round this strange and weirdly beautiful site. The most obvious fable tells of a group of giants who refused to accept Christianity and were promptly turned to stone. A much more interesting fable connected with the stones, though not this time with their origin, is that of the white cow. There was, so the story goes, a great famine in Lewis and a poor woman, desperate for want of food, went down to the sea with the idea of drowning herself, but once there she saw a white cow walking out of the waves. The cow spoke to her and told her to call all of the women of the island together and bring them to Callanish. There they were told that they could milk the cow, but no one could take more than a single pail of milk. There was, inevitably, one woman greedier than the rest who tried to collect two pailfuls, but without success. Angry at her failure, she decided to take her revenge. Next day she brought a sieve which could never be filled, and she milked the cow dry. The cow returned to the sea and was never seen again at Callanish. Similar stories are told of other stone circles, the best known being that of the White Cow of Mitchell's Fold. In this version, the greedy milker – a witch – is kicked by the cow and turned to stone, and can still be identified as the tallest stone in the circle.

How is it that such similar, almost identical, stories developed around stone circles as far apart as Callanish in Lewis and Mitchell's Fold in Shropshire with several other sites in between? There is one other legend attached to Callanish, and that tells how on midsummer morning, a shining creature walks along the avenue of stones. All the stories carry a fairly obvious symbolism: fecundity in the case of the cow, with a warning of the dangers of not behaving according to the rules; astronomy comes in again with the shining figure. It is interesting to note that it was at Callanish that Professor Thom's interest was first quickened with the idea that great stones could have astronomical significance. In 1934, at the end of a day's sailing, he anchored off Lewis, directly opposite Callanish and noticed what no one seemed to have recorded before – that the main elements were aligned on a north-south axis, leading to the pole star. Later investigation showed that at midsummer, if you looked down the avenue of stones, you would be looking straight at a full moon as it set behind Mount Clisham. Another shining white figure connected with the avenue must be more than mere coincidence. It seems to provide yet further evidence that the memory of the original use to which the stone circles were put has lingered on in fable and legend long after the practical details were lost.

The more one looks at these strange stones and their legends, the stranger they seem to become. In Caithness, near the village of Lybster, is what is accurately, if somewhat prosaically, known as the hill of many stones. There are around two hundred of them, set in rows, and it would appear that they are aligned with some precision. If the idea that stone rows have some sort of astronomical significance is correct then what we have here is an amazingly complex site. It might even be a sort of giant stone computer. There are few clues to help us even begin to establish what it could all mean. In the case of another well-known, if less complex, site, there is no shortage of hints, for the place is surrounded by a multitude of legends. The Rollright Stones in Oxfordshire consist of a stone circle known as the King's Men – a group of five stones huddled together, the Whispering Knights, and a large single stone – the King's Stone. The Knights were, in fact, a dolmen, or open burial chamber, the cap-stone having at some time fallen off the supporting stones. The groups are contemporary with each other, dating from around 2000–1800 BC. Many of the stories surrounding the stones have familiar themes – the King's Men cannot be counted, for example, without resorting to the old penny buns. Other tales concern movement – legend has it that at midnight the stones get up and dance, and on certain special nights they also wander off to a nearby stream for a drink, having worked up a thirst from the dancing, no doubt. Yet although the stones spend a good deal of time roaming and skipping about the countryside, they take a dim view of any mere human trying to shift them. It is said that a farmer decided that the cap-stone from the Whispering Knights was just the thing for bridging a stream that ran across his land – the same

The Rollright Stones look solid enough, but legend tells that at midnight the stones rise up and dance *(National Monuments Record)*

stream from which the stones were said to drink. Dragging the stone to the site proved an incredibly difficult job, the degree of difficulty depending on which version of the story you hear. In some a mere six horses were used, while in others fifty beasts were necessary, while a third variation has the horses dropping dead from the effort. And once the stone was in place, it refused to stay put. Every morning it had left the brook and was found lying in the grass. Eventually the farmer gave up the struggle and took the stone back, and for the return journey one horse moved it with ease.

With so many stories about the doings of these hyperactive stones, it is not too surprising to find that, in legend, they are given animal, and even human, origins. The best-known story of all concerns a king who was marching his army through the land, when he was stopped by a witch with these words:

> Seven long strides shalt thou take.
> If Long Compton thou canst see,
> King of England thou shalt be.

As Long Compton was close at hand, it seemed a reasonable offer, so the king duly strode forward with this reply:

> Stick, stock, stone,
> As King of England I shall be known.

When he had taken his seven strides, however, he found to his dismay that a large mound of earth – known as the Archdruid's Barrow, though it is neither a barrow nor anything to do with the Druids – blocked his view. He was not, it would seem, a man well versed in the ways of witches, who are generally recognised as unreliable in such matters. So it proved on this occasion, for she now added this incantation to her original offer:

> As Long Compton thou canst not see,
> King of England thou shalt not be.
> Rise up stick, and stand still stone,
> For King of England thou shalt be none.
> Thou and thy men hoar stones shall be
> And myself an eldern tree.

So the king was turned to stone, with his men standing in a circle and his knights huddled together in eternal conference.

So here we have mystery compounded: the previously familiar elements of astronomy and fertility seem to be of minor importance, while in their place we have all these stories of activity. If the theory that such stones have some relationship to old, forgotten beliefs, then what can all this signify? Many people have numerous different theories covering everything from spacemen arriving in flying saucers to set up the stones to the idea that the stones are some kind of battery, storing a special sort of power. The spacemen stories can be discounted for the present, not because they are obviously untrue but because there is no way of testing them – and anyway, if one decides that spacemen did indeed put up the stones we are still no nearer to an understanding of their purpose than we are if we decide they were put up by early man. But what of the idea of the stone circle as a place where some sort of force is concentrated? There are, after all, many forces which were unknown and unrecognised until quite modern times. We accept the notion of an invisible electromagnetic field because we can see its effect on, for example, a simple bar magnet. It has been suggested that just as there are forces which were unrecognised by the ancients, so too there were forces which they knew about but which we have subsequently lost from sight. A number of theorists have suggested ways in which the forces of the stones can be tested.

Being, as mentioned earlier, something of a sceptic, I am by no means eager to adopt such notions: being also trained as a scientist, I am a great believer in the experimental method. The pendulum test is easily carried out, and on one occasion I determined to try it at the Rollright Stones – and carried it one stage further in that I took along a tape recorder and recorded the whole exercise for the local radio station. As any pendulum should behave like any other pendulum, and as it was autumn, I took along with me a conker on the end of a piece of string. The listeners received the story as it happened, and could make of it what they would. My humble conker went berserk whenever it was brought near one of the King's Men in the circle, and if the listeners were surprised I was even more astonished. As with the Dartmoor experiment, I would not suggest that such a simple test proves anything, though since making it myself I have been less inclined to scoff at all theories that speak of the power of the stones.

Again, I would not suggest that anyone takes my word for it. Try it yourself: the worst that will happen is that you will probably feel intensely foolish. But it is certainly true that many visitors experience strange phenomena here. Try another simple test, which requires no equipment whatsoever. Simply rest your hands on one of the large stones and close your eyes. Many people find that the stone seems to rock, sometimes with considerable violence. This all no doubt sounds very odd, but then this is a book about oddities, so what else would you expect?

The strangest of all the sites of this type are the two best-known ones – Avebury and Stonehenge. The former does not have the immediate, dramatic impact of the latter, but this is largely due to the fact that Avebury is too large to be appreciated at a single glance. One look at Stonehenge and you know you are in the presence of one of the great monuments of the ancient world: at Avebury, you need to explore and the more you do so the more amazing it becomes. The whole site or 'henge' covers over twenty-eight acres and contains almost the entire village of Avebury within its boundaries – and extraordinary

Bank, ditch and stone ring at Avebury, a great monument at once astonishing and inexplicable *(British Tourist Authority)*

boundaries they are. The area is enclosed by a huge earthwork, a bank that originally stood as high as 50ft above a ditch 15ft in depth. There were four entrances into the ring, each one situated at one of the cardinal points of the compass. On the plateau formed inside the ditch stands the Great Circle of large stones, known as sarsens, some weighing as much as forty tons. These huge stones were brought here from Marlborough Downs and erected with what must have been a great deal of physical effort. Inside this main circle, which has a diameter of 1,400ft stand two smaller circles, each about 350ft in diameter, and there is a possibility that there was once a third circle. Even now we have not reached the end of the story. Leading away from the southern entrance is an avenue of stones, the Kennet Avenue. There are a hundred pairs of stones, set at 50ft intervals, and the avenue appears to terminate now, somewhat surprisingly, in a transport cafe on the A4. Here is a mystery indeed – but one which is easily solved. Originally there was another stone circle here, known as the Sanctuary, but it was destroyed in the nineteenth century. If that particular mystery has a solution, then the same cannot be said of the central problem. Why was Avebury ever built? We quite simply do not know, so anyone visiting the site can speculate to his heart's content. But it must be borne in mind that one is seeing only a fraction of a once greater original. Many of these stones were demolished by our zealous ancestors, and their demolition at least gives us a clue as to the significance of Avebury.

According to the Venerable Bede, when Pope Gregory sent Abbot Mellitus to Britain at the beginning of the seventh century he gave him these instructions: 'The temples of the idols in that country should on no account be destroyed.' The idols themselves were to be pulled down and the area depaganised by the sprinkling of holy water, after which the sites should be made over to Christian worship. 'We hope that the people, seeing that its temples are not destroyed, may abandon idolatry and resort to these places as before.' At Avebury, the parish church stands just a few yards outside the circle. It might seem incredible that such sites should still be places of worship as late as the seventh century, yet how much more amazing to find that Pope Gregory's advice was ignored, not during his own lifetime but a thousand years later when many of the stones were destroyed.

Christian zealots demolished them by using the technique known as fire setting – lighting fires against the stones, then when the stones were really hot dashing cold water against them to crack them. Stones were overturned by digging pits alongside and pushing the stones over. At least one of the demolition crew came to grief: later excavation revealed his crushed bones under a fallen stone. The process was, according to William Stukeley – an antiquarian who, writing in the eighteenth century, did more than anyone to draw attention to such sites – a 'barbarous massacre'. Sadness that so much has been destroyed has to be tempered with wonderment that, as late as the seventeenth and eighteenth centuries, the stones should still have been considered a source of moral danger.

We have not, even now, reached the end of the mysteries that surround this otherwise unremarkable and peaceful stretch of Wiltshire countryside. Less than a mile away from Avebury is the least explicable monument of them all, Silbury Hill. It is the largest man-made mound in Europe, standing over 130ft high and covering some five acres of ground. It must have been of immense importance, both literally and metaphorically, to the people who built it around 2500 BC, for the effort involved in its construction must have been prodigious. It might be called Britain's equivalent to the Pyramids. But we have some idea why the Pyramids were built; here all is bafflement. Its proximity to an early burial site, the West Kennet long barrow, has suggested that it too might be a great tomb. Yet excavations carried out in the late 1960s, in front of the television cameras, produced no evidence whatsoever to support this theory. We know no more than we did before, but the excavations did at least have the somewhat negative virtue of tending to disprove the theory that that there were vast burial chambers and important relics to be found under the hill. This makes it, in many ways, the most perfectly satisfying of mysteries. Where no evidence exists to support any rational theory, the way is open for a multitude of irrational ones. Theories proliferate, recent examples being the notion that Silbury Hill was a giant monument built in the shape of an upturned saucer to record the presence of a flying saucer all that time ago, or that it was an early astronomical observatory. There is no proof, but equally no disproof – so choose the likeliest explanation or manufacture your own.

Excavation and investigation have left the mystery of Silbury Hill intact — we still have no notion of why it was built *(British Tourist Authority)*

Finally, then, to the most famous stone circle of all: Stonehenge. It is so well known that it is easy to overlook its complexity and mystery altogether. For a start, there is not — strictly speaking — one Stonehenge at all, but a series of quite distinct Stonehenges. The first — Stonehenge I — was built around 2500 BC. It consisted of a circular bank and ditch nearly 400ft in diameter, with a ring of stones just inside the ditch. There was one break or entrance and by that stood the Heel Stone, a 15ft high sarsen.

Best known of all Britain's ancient monuments, Stonehenge *(British Tourist Authority)*

Stonehenge II followed two centuries later, in what was quite the most dramatic phase of the Stonehenge story. A double ring of stones was set up, each weighing around four tons, and an avenue was laid out stretching towards the River Avon. That may not in itself seem too extraordinary, but what is remarkable is that the stones were not brought from any local site, but from the Prescelly Mountains in Pembrokeshire. How were they moved? The most likely explanation is that they were brought around the coast and then floated up the Avon on rafts. After that they could have been moved on rollers for the short overland journey.

The next phase involved the demolition of Stonehenge II and preparation of the site to accommodate a new circle. Eighty sarsen blocks – this time from nearby Marlborough Downs, which had furnished the Avebury stones – were set up. They dwarfed the old blue stones from Wales, for these weighed up to thirty tons each. Five pairs of stones were set up, topped by equally massive lintels – which had to be placed with considerable accuracy since sockets on the lintels had to fit over projections on the uprights. Unlike the Avebury stones, these had been carefully dressed by masons so that they form smooth-sided oblongs. A trace of decoration has even been discovered on one of the great stones in the form of a small carved dagger.

Here is an excess of puzzles. How, given the state of primitive technology, were the stones erected? What is the significance of the dagger? Is it, as some have suggested, a link with the Mediterranean culture of Mycenae? And, if this is the case, is it just a casual graffito left by a passing Mycenaean tourist enjoying the sights of Britain or does it indicate some more important connection between the two cultures?

More stones were set up in the final phase, Stonehenge III. Stonehenge was now complete, leaving the biggest question of all for us to ponder over: what is it? Eighteenth-century antiquaries had no doubts – it was a Druids' temple, and when Stukeley sketched it, he included Druids in his drawing. Today, latter-day Druids gather at Stonehenge to celebrate the summer solstice and watch the sun rise over one isolated stone. This rite has become a tourist attraction, but has little other significance since the one thing we do know is that Stonehenge was there long before the first Druidic cult appeared in Britain. However, the idea that Stonehenge might have both religious and astronomical significance seems plausible, but no more than that. The mystery remains – the grandest mystery of them all.

All the monuments we have looked at so far have had one thing in common – an almost total lack of inscriptions. Stonehenge has its one little dagger, the rest nothing. Perhaps if we could find stones with markings on them, the story might become a little clearer. In fact there are many stones, particularly in the north of England, which have been covered with what are known as cup and ring markings. A very good example is a fine stone circle at Castlerigg in Cumbria, known as Long Meg and Her Daughters. The isolated stone, Long Meg, has a circular depression – the cup – inscribed on it and around this are the rings – concentric circles. Similar patterns can be found elsewhere, often in quite elaborate forms. Unfortunately, these do nothing whatsoever to clear up the mysteries, but only multiply the problems. But ancient man has left other marks on the land, and if we do not always know why he put them there, we do at least know what they represent.

A magnificent stone circle in a dramatic setting at Castlerigg in Cumbria *(British Tourist Authority)*

The Long Man of Wilmington in East Sussex is precisely what his name suggests – a long man, 231ft long to be precise. He is carved on the hillside of the downs, the white chalk showing through the turf to create the image. He stands there, arms outstretched, holding a tall staff in each hand. Seen from the air he is a very thin emaciated-looking character, but as no one was presumably expected to observe him from such a vantage point we should look at him from a distance on terra firma. He then appears in more conventional proportions. The giant is very old, we really do not have any idea of his exact age, and identification is not made any easier by the fact that he was restored in Victorian times, how accurately we have no means of knowing. Most archaeologists agree that he was originally given his hillside home not later than the seventh century and that he might well be considerably older. Having established even that much we are not a great deal wiser, for we still have no idea of why he was carved. Legend suggests that he is there to commemorate the death of an actual giant, but that might be no more than a very obvious explanation for a curiosity. However, we can get more clues elsewhere, for the Long Man has a cousin over at Cerne Abbas near Dorchester.

The Cerne Abbas giant stands 180ft high and in his right hand he holds a 120ft club. He is outlined in trenches, 1ft wide by 1ft deep, cut into the chalk. Unlike the Wilmington man a good many physical details have been added – eyes, mouth, ribs and a huge phallus. There seems little doubt that he was intended as a fertility symbol, and tradition supports the view. Further up the hill is a small enclosure, known locally as the Frying Pan, which is the centre for Mayday rites such as Maypole dancing. So, there is at least a continuity with old fertility rites. There are also fertility legends: women wishing to conceive would go to the giant, generally at night. This all makes sense, but still leaves unanswered the question as to who put him there in the first place.

The Long Man, over 200ft of him, looks down on Wilmington *(Crown copyright, reproduced by permission of the Department of the Environment)*

There are two main theories. The first comes from popular legend and associates the giant – unlikely though it may seem – with the local abbey. Quite what the pious monks were doing cutting giants out of hillsides, especially one so hugely endowed, is not clear. It was said to be a joke against the abbot – but at 180ft long it seems to be taking the joke a good deal too far. A more likely version attributes the giant to the Emperor Commodus (AD 180–93). Commodus developed a belief that he was the reincarnation of Hercules, and tried to persuade the citizens of the Roman Empire, including Britain, to worship him. Temples were set up to honour Hercules, and it seems reasonable to think that the Cerne Abbas giant was part of the cult. The 120ft long club is certainly Herculean. There is one other curiosity associated with the giant. Why, when apparently innocuous stones were being demolished over at Avebury, was this all-too-naked gentleman allowed to remain on his hillside? Here is yet another question wide open to speculation.

The strange and beautiful Uffington White Horse *(Crown copyright, reproduced by permission of the Department of the Environment)*

Westbury White Horse, with its odd, beak-like nose *(British Tourist Authority)*

The other popular hill figure is that of the horse. The finest example is the White Horse of Uffington, which gives its name to the Vale of the White Horse in the Berkshire Downs. Again it is a vast creature, nearly 400ft long, cut into the turf. Its date is uncertain, but the area was already known by the name White Horse at the time of the Norman Conquest. There is an Iron Age fort at the top of the hill, and as representations of horses were common in that period it seems reasonable to give the same sort of date to the White Horse. It is a very beautiful, sinuous creature, but again we have no real idea as to why it is there. Unlike henges, hill figures have to be regularly tended or they simply become overgrown and disappear. This horse is traditionally treated every seven years, and must have received similar care for some 2,000 years. It is tempting to think that perhaps it has no deep significance at all, but is simply a beautiful work of art that exists in its own right. It is an unlikely theory, but it is probably this aspect that ensures its survival – people like it and want to keep it. This is certainly true of a second well-known white horse, that at Westbury in Wiltshire. Here the horse was allowed to vanish almost completely from view and a new one was dug by a Mr Gee in 1778. In the process he changed the design – including turning the horse round to face the other way from the original. Although it has changed, it is still a popular and much admired beast.

Uffington and Westbury both date back to the Iron Age. When I was a schoolboy in Yorkshire, I used to be able to see a white horse on the distant hills – but it dated back no more than two centuries. In the eighteenth century, there was a great vogue for antiquities – but a limited supply of the real thing. What then could be more natural than to make imitations? The imitations were duly made and they were grouped together under one name – follies.

# 2
# Follies

There is a certain amount of doubt about the origin of the name 'folly'. The Oxford English Dictionary gives two alternatives. The common version is 'a name given to any costly structure said to have shown folly in the builder'. It then goes on somewhat tentatively to suggest a second definition, based on the French word 'folie', which indicates 'delight' or 'favourite abode'. Which then is the true meaning? Are we looking at absurd buildings put up by foolish men, or are we to see structures designed purely for delight? We can get some idea by looking at one, admittedly extreme, example.

Oban is a pleasant harbour and resort on the west coast of Scotland, looking out over the Firth of Lorn. It is an attractive spot, with a sprinkling of dour Victorian stone buildings – very much what one would expect to find. But stand by the harbour and turn your back to the sea and look up beyond the town to Battery Hill and you will see what at first glance appears to be the Colosseum of Rome, miraculously transported to the Scottish Highlands. This is McCaig's Folly. Here, you might suppose, is ample proof of the aptness of definition number one. Here is an obviously costly structure, serving no useful purpose whatsoever, and – even worse – the designer of the mock Colosseum has got it wrong. The building in Rome is oval, this one is circular. Where Roman architects invariably used semicircular arches, McCaig's are pointed and there is even a pointed arch for the entrance, topped by castellations. What could be more foolish than this shotgun wedding between the styles of ancient Rome and Scottish Baronial? Yet look into the history of the place and it begins to seem rather more sensible.

The builder was a local banker, John Stewart McCaig, who had one abiding passion in life: the art of ancient Greece and Rome. He gave lectures on the subject to the young men of Oban, and was always

The Colosseum apparently miraculously transposed to a hill above Oban: McCaig's Folly *(Laird Parker)*

lavish in his praise of the Colosseum in particular. Then, in the 1890s, circumstances arose that gave him the opportunity to express his great love in lasting form. Unemployment was high in the town, so he hit upon the idea of building a monument to his family, in the form of a museum for the town. It was a worthwhile project in many ways, not least in providing much needed work. He could never have had any doubts about what form the museum should take: it would have to be in the shape of his beloved Colosseum. It would stand on top of the hill, and become a prominent landmark. He must then have felt some twinge of dissatisfaction. If only a tower could be incorporated into the building, then it would supply magnificent views of the surrounding countryside and of the islands across the Firth. So he adapted his design and then realised that to have just the one anomaly would lead to charges of absurdity; he went on to make other changes. McCaig's museum was not, after all, to be a slavish copy of the great original, but an adaptation of an admired design to fit it to a new location and a new purpose. All kinds of refinements were planned, including statues of illustrious Obanites (especially illustrious McCaigs) in the arches. Five thousand pounds were spent, then McCaig died. No one else shared his enthusiasm for the project and it was left unfinished, much as we see it today.

Is McCaig's Folly foolish? One could argue that rebuilding the Colosseum in the Scottish Highlands is, by definition, silly. It certainly comes as a shock, but there are bigger surprises to be had elsewhere in the world. I remember my astonishment on looking out of my hotel window in Nashville, Tennessee to be confronted by a full-scale concrete replica of the Parthenon. At least McCaig could argue that the Romans did come to Britain, and did build structures in the same style as they had used in Italy. McCaig might also be called foolish for dreaming up such a grandiose monument to his own family, but then it was also intended as a boon to the town, and it was scarcely the fault of the originator that it was left incomplete. Also it derived in good measure from a charitable impulse, providing work where work was badly needed. The building may seem incongruous, yet it was built for the best of reasons – an expression of an individual's love and charity. It is, in short, more folie than folly – and this seems to be true of the vast majority of the structures we shall be looking at. The worst charge that can be laid against them is that they are idiosyncratic. And what is so wrong with that? Would to heaven we had a few more idiosyncratic buildings to replace the featureless slabs which deface so many of our towns and cities today. Let us celebrate the follies.

We have begun by looking at a latter-day imitation of an ancient site, and such constructions form an important part in the story of follies. Ilton is a village near Masham on the edge of the Yorkshire Dales. Nearby is a genuine henge, in the form of three great earthen circles at Thornborough. They date from the Bronze Age, are archaeologically important, but scarcely compare with Avebury or Stonehenge. Now, no Yorkshireman is going easily to accept the notion that any other county – especially one in the benighted south – can boast of having something bigger and better than his own home county. It was clearly an unfortunate oversight of ancient man, who failed to give Yorkshire the best: but what early man overlooked, modern man could put right. William Danby of Swinton Hall built his own henge – or 'Druid's

Circle' as it inevitably came to be known – early in the nineteenth century. He was an excellent faker, laying out his Stonehenge-like horseshoe of triliths in a moorland setting. There is just the right amount of disorder to suggest the decay of centuries; it is altogether a most convincing sham.

Here is, one might say, a case for crying out 'foolish extravagance'. There is no pretence that Danby's henge has any useful function to perform, unless, of course, you include in your definition of usefulness the supplying of pleasure and harmless amusement to generations of visitors. Unlike many another builder of follies, Mr Danby did make his monument accessible to everyone, rather than hiding it away in his private estate. This is in contrast to another 'Stonehenge' which is locked away in the gardens of Park Place at Henley-on-Thames. It can be briefly glimpsed by passing boats near Marsh Lock. It is quite an imposing structure, the largest stone rising to 10ft, and it comes complete with a dedication describing how it was originally used for human sacrifice. The inscription is in French, which is explained by the fact that when the henge was built the house was owned by General Conway, who was Governor of Jersey and brought the monument across from the island. It is not the only oddity in the garden, for he also built his very own Conway Bridge in miniature.

The great majority of sham ruins such as these date from the eighteenth and early nineteenth centuries. A new way of looking at landscape had arisen through the cult of the picturesque, which assessed landscape in terms of how it would look if framed to make a picture. Ideally it should look like the pictures of the French artists Gaspard Poussin and Claude. In their paintings, antiquities – preferably mouldering and ivy covered – formed essential elements. The new enthusiasts for the picturesque landscape looked for the same thing in their landscaped parks and gardens. One notable proponent of the new view was Richard Payne Knight, who published what he described as a didactic poem, *The Landscape*, in 1794. Here he describes the elements of the ideal landscape:

> Bless'd is the man, in whose sequester'd glade,
> Some ancient abbey's walls diffuse their shade
> With mould'ring windows pierc'd, and turrets crown'd
> And pinnacles with clinging ivy bound.

Bless'd too is he, who, 'midst his tufted trees
Some ruin'd castle's lofty towers sees;
Imbosom'd high upon the mountain's brow,
Or nodding o'er the stream that glides below.

Such was the ideal, but not everyone could boast a ruined abbey or decaying castle on their property. Landowners agreed that they were most desirable additions to the scene, so there was only one solution. Where the real thing was not available, the imitation would have to be supplied. If any one person could be said to have started the sham-ruin business then that man is Sanderson Miller, who inherited Radway Grange at Edgehill, Warwickshire at the age of twenty. In 1747 he built a mock castle, Radway Tower, which was set at a suitably martial site, said to be the exact spot at which Charles I rallied his forces for the Battle of Edgehill in 1642. As built, it was even more grandly romantic than it is today, for the tower originally boasted a drawbridge as well as battlements, and many notable guests came to admire the view, among them the poet Richard Jaye, who left this verse:

the broken arch
Or mould'ring wall, well taught to counterfeit
The waste of Time, to solemn thought excite
And crown with graceful pomp the shaggy hill.

The shaggy hill certainly helps to bring the ruin into prominence, and some of the best of such mock antiquities are those which stand on hill tops where they can be seen by everyone.

Mow Cop is certainly one of the best of the hill-top follies. It is ideally seen at a distance – usually, in the author's case, from a boat on the Macclesfield Canal. It then appears as a dramatic outline – a tall tower, with a high Gothic arch alongside and a jumble of ruined walls. It appears to be the perfect example of a medieval ruin, and it certainly satisfies the first rule for producing a convincing mock ruin as laid down by Thomas Whateley in his very influential work, *Observations on Modern Gardening* (1770): 'The mind must not be allowed to hesitate; it must be hurried away from examining into the reality, by the exactness and force of the resemblance.' Its arrangement, too, with the high tower balanced by crumbling walls, conforms with Whateley's ideals: 'There should be one large mass to raise the

The dramatic silhouette of the sham ruin of Mow Cop *(National Trust: photo Vernon D. Shaw)*

idea of greatness, to attract the others about it, and to be a common centre of union to all: the smaller pieces then mark the original of one extensive structure; and no longer appear to be the remains of several little buildings.' Mow Cop was built in 1750 by Randle Wilbraham, twenty years before Whateley's book appeared, and it must surely have influenced his thoughts.

Seen close to, the sham is at once revealed for what it is, but this is unimportant since the whole purpose was to provide a distant prospect. Mow Cop was, incidentally, to find fame in the nineteenth century as the home of Primitive Methodism, when a Stoke-on-Trent wheelwright, Hugh Bourne, organised a camp meeting on the hill top to discuss the proposition that Methodism should return to simpler forms of worship. Bourne's arguments found little favour among other Methodists, so he left to form his own Primitive religion. What a curious mixture this provides in this one spot: one man attempting to get back to a simple core of truth, in a place designed by another as a fraud, a monument to artificiality.

Medieval castles were very popular models for the builders of sham ruins. Another excellent example, by no means inappropriate to its surroundings, is Balcarres Crag or Craig to the north-west of the village of Colinsborough in Fife. The village itself was founded by and named after Colin, third Earl of Balcarres. He returned from the wars in the Low Countries at the beginning of the eighteenth century and the village was built to house his soldiers. So what could be more appropriate as decoration for such a martial village than a castle, replete with arrow slits and battlements? Another equally appropriate sham ruin is to be found at Reigate in Surrey. There was a real castle here, but it suffered the fate of so many of its contemporaries in being knocked down by Cromwell's men. In 1777, Richard Barnes used the original stone to build a ruined castle, complete with imposing gateway, guarded by two towers. One could argue that this is not so much construction as imaginative reconstruction. Perhaps so, but the emphasis should certainly be put on 'imaginative' rather than 'reconstruction', since it is highly unlikely that it bears any resemblance whatsoever to the original.

In discussing these often wholly convincing fakes, it would be pleasant if one could point to a single building and declare that there stood the very first of the breed. Alas, this is not possible. One of the earliest fakes must, however, be Alfred's Hall, near Cirencester. It is certainly one of the most romantic, its battlemented walls now overgrown with ivy. It was built by the first Earl of Bathurst, with the help of his great friend, the poet Alexander Pope, in 1721. Pope showed a taste for the exotic in his own garden at Twickenham (see p. 175), but here medievalism was to rule supreme. Yet this was something more than an attractive addition to the landscape, for behind the façade was a usable room, complete with handsome stained-glass windows. This is not quite the 'useless' structure that

The picturesque folly in the picturesque landscape: Balcarres Craig drawn by James Stewart *(BBC Hulton Picture Library)*

one thinks of when considering follies: it is simply a useful building, given an odd face, and later we shall come across a good many buildings that fall into that category. So one should perhaps look elsewhere for the sham that began the trend towards purely decorative fake buildings. For instance, at Weston-in-Gordano, to the north-east of Weston-super-Mare, you will find Walton Castle, one of the most convincing of imitations − walls crumbling and ivied in the best approved style. It also shows a rather cunning mixture of stylistic details, with Tudor-styled windows and chimney pots tacked on, as though the building had been adapted, as so many castles were adapted, before finally collapsing. Go inside the shell, however, and the fake is exposed, for there is not, and clearly never has been, the least trace of interior rooms. When it comes to documenting the folly, however, all is ignorance: we do not know who built it, when they built, nor why they built it. It might be the first successful example of the genre, or, equally, it might not: a most satisfactory condition of mystery reigns. If we cannot decide when the whole thing starts, then we are relieved of the responsibility of entering a tedious chronological exercise and can, with an easy conscience, simply continue to chronicle those shams which give delight and ignore those which do not.

Some builders felt that an entire castle was a little beyond their means, or at least beyond their inclinations, and they settled for a triumphal entrance. Brookman's Park arch was built at some time in the early eighteenth century, probably by Sir Jeremy Sandbrook, the owner of the estate at North Mimms in Hertfordshire. It, too, has its fair share of mystery. There was once a house here, and the estate was variously known as Gubbins', Gubyonn and Gobion's Park – then the house disappeared from view and the old estate was absorbed into Brookman's Park. But why build an arch, flanked with two castellated towers? There was once, it is true, an avenue of trees leading away from the arch, but as they led to nowhere at all, that is very little help. The arch is not stuck up on top of a hill, like Mow Cop and other eye-catching structures. One theory is that it was intended as a war memorial, since Sir Jeremy had already built one such memorial – to commemorate the Battle of Barnet. It has become known locally as Folly Arch, and one persistent rumour has it that the builder placed a farthing under each and every brick in the building. A rough estimate suggests that there is something in the region of twenty thousand bricks in the arch – say twenty pounds' worth of farthings, which in today's values would be equivalent to at least two thousand pounds. This must be either a very odd rumour or a remarkable case of costly eccentricity.

Another lovely arch – but minus farthings – can be seen at Renishaw in the north of Derbyshire, near Sheffield. It is not perhaps, strictly speaking, a sham ruin at all, but a building in the Gothic style, with pinnacles, castellations, pointed arches and tracery windows. It just about qualifies as a sham, in that the windows have always remained empty and unglazed and, even if it was not built as a ruin, it has certainly become one with the passing of the years. It was originally designed as an outsize garden ornament, intended to grace the grounds of the fine sixteenth-century house. It is a simple, quite

A grand gateway but an entrance to nowhere: the gatehouse folly at Brookmans Park
*(National Monuments Record)*

delicate structure, comparable to the Gothic chapel with traceried windows, built to do similar service for the grounds at Knebworth. Shams such as these are pleasant and delightful, but one's real admiration goes out to the full-blooded, rip-roaring, no-holds-barred fakes. Everyone has favourites, no doubt, but here are mine, given, as they say in beauty contests, in reverse order.

The third place winner takes the prize for the daring with which the builders used their skill not just to enhance a view but to produce a

The ornamental gateway at Renishaw Hall, being viewed in 1949 by Osbert Sitwell
*(BBC Hulton Picture Library)*

view that is itself one huge folly – Hawkstone Park Follies at Hodnet
in Shropshire. It might well have topped the list, but for the fact that
there is a natural advantage in the form of a genuine ruin. The basis
for the whole scheme is a high, sandstone bluff on which was once
perched a medieval castle of the same stone. The owners of
Hawkstone Park took this as a starting point for their fantasies. More
ruins were added to the genuine article, to enhance the scene. The
genuine castle ruins were 'improved' with extra fortifications and a

A suitably exotic home for a builder of follies: Hawkstone Citadel *(A. J. Rowen: supplied by National Monuments Record)*

ruined arch constructed at the top of the cliff. The builders then proceeded to lay out a series of complex cliff-side walks that wander bewilderingly through artificial caves and grottoes and provide sudden, startling views across the countryside. There was a time when all this was open to the public, with a guide to make sure no one tumbled over one of the surprise views. Sadly this is no longer so, and one can only hope to see the day when it will be back in all its glory.

Second place goes to a magnificent hodge-podge of styles – not only representing different centuries, but even different continents – Benington Lordship in Hertfordshire. Built in the 1830s by George Proctor of Benington, it is an extraordinary edifice, tacked on to the late-seventeenth-century house. It has a gateway with castellated towers and portcullis, but where other gateways lead nowhere this one leads to a courtyard, partially enclosed within convincingly ruined walls. And that is only the beginning. Here, too, is a moat and a ruined tower with pious stained glass and a no less pious, but perhaps more surprising, shrine to Buddha. There is also classical statuary in the form of a fragment of Trojan sculpture. It is not perhaps the most impressive of such monuments, but it is certainly the most unusual.

The winner of my choice is a very prominent and very well-known monument, Ralph Allen's Castle. It was built in 1762 by that most prolific and imaginative of folly builders, Sanderson Miller. He received the ultimate accolade of praise from the archpriest of the Gothic Revival, Horace Walpole of Strawberry Hill, who wrote of one of his works at Mount Edgcumbe: 'There is a ruined castle, built by Miller, that would get him his freedom even of Strawberry.' Ralph Allen himself was one of the leading citizens of Bath, who did a great deal to help make the city fashionable and prosperous, rewarding himself with a fine house, Prior Park, built in the classical style out of the lovely Bath stone. All it needed to achieve perfection was a suitable focal point for the view from the windows and this Miller provided.

The Hawkstone folly itself, part of the curious labyrinthine path through and round the cliffs *(A. J. Rowen: supplied by National Monuments Record)*

A magnificent folly, only a façade but wonderfully convincing: Ralph Allen's Castle, Bath *(Reece Winstone)*

He built a castle on the hill, with a high Gothic arch, flanked by round towers and castellated walls, ending in squat, square towers. It looked the model for the perfect medieval castle when viewed by Mr Allen. Close up the effect is somewhat different: the windows are blank, and so are the arrow slits; the rounded, rusticated stones of the facade appear from behind as dull, square blocks. But that was Miller's genius. He was like a brilliant set designer, creating a special effect for his audience. Ralph Allen and the other citizens of Bath could look up and enjoy their perfect castle.

Not all shams are castles, nor are all castles simply empty pieces of stage property. Several landowners came to the conclusion that if they were going to be put to all the trouble and expense of manufacturing mock medieval buildings, they might just as well put them to use. The prize for enthusiasm and ingenuity must surely belong to the eleventh

Duke of Norfolk. He was a man of strong political feelings, a Whig, and a passionate advocate of the American cause in the War of Independence. Their victories, he decided, deserved to be commemorated. Sir John Vanbrugh had already built a castle-like farmhouse for the Howard family at Castle Howard. The eleventh Duke decided to improve on that beginning. At Greystoke in Cumbria he built two fortified farms and named them after American victories. Bunker's Hill is an attractive farmhouse, partially castellated and having Gothic windows. It is no more than a mild exaggeration of the popular Gothic style. Fort Putnam, however, is fort-like indeed. It could well pass as some military stronghold, were it not for the huge pointed windows that look as though they might have been borrowed from the local church. Here the outbuildings have also been brought into the design, and the farm's cows reside in what must be one of the world's most handsome cowsheds, decorated by a colonnade joined by blind arches. There is also a Jefferson Farm, but that can boast nothing more extraordinary than its name. The Duke did not, however, limit his

Not a castle but a farmhouse with delusions of grandeur in Sledmere Park *(National Monuments Record)*

building activities to American celebrations. Spire House gets its name from its most prominent feature – a lead-clad spire that stands on a short tower, which in turn rests on another castellated building. The result is, to say the least, strange but by no means unpleasing. It certainly adds a fitting conclusion to the Duke's collection of farmyard oddities.

Another fine farmhouse in the same tradition can be seen at Sledmere in Humberside. The grounds at Sledmere Park were laid out by Capability Brown for the owner, Sir Christopher Sykes, who put in hand a good deal of extra building work. He enlarged the house, adding one oddity in the process in the shape of a room filled with Turkish tiles, and he then set about improving the estate. Here, it appeared, was a happy conjunction of circumstances. A dower house was considered to be a necessity, while at the same time the park lacked a centre of interest. So a house was built in the very best castellated style. The entrance is through a huge Gothic arch, flanked by towers and set within high walls which quite engulf the little conventional house itself. The dowagers were unamused by this building, and for a time it was used as an estate office before finding a permanent use as a farmhouse.

Any large estate contains an accumulation of buildings, and no self-respecting estate would be complete without at least one lodge. Often these were built in a style which was intended to match the main house or the grounds. At Middleton Stoney in Oxfordshire, for example, there are the remains of a Norman motte and bailey castle within the grounds, so it seems perfectly reasonable for the owners to order castellations for the lodge. Logic, however, does not seem to have ruled the day at Rendlesham Hall in Suffolk, which could boast no fewer than five lodges, two of which can quite reasonably be placed in the 'folly' category, in that they are splendid examples of quirky individuality. The first of the odd buildings was perhaps only slightly strange in conception. An arch strides across the driveway, and the lodge appears as a tower on top of the arch. The other is absolutely extraordinary. It can best be described as a cathedral in miniature,

*(opposite)* The gatehouse at Rendlesham must be the most extravagant example anywhere in the country *(A. Rumsey: supplied by National Monuments Record)*

The Old Gaol in Buckingham *(British Tourist Authority)*

only no cathedral was ever built to quite such an exotic plan. It is hexagonal, with flying buttresses and pinnacles and a structure in the middle very like a belfry. The details are as carefully considered as the outline, with tracery windows and castellations. Perhaps the strangest part of the story of the Rendlesham lodge is that it has survived at all. The Old Hall was pulled down in the 1870s, but the lodge was preserved; the New Hall was then, in its turn, demolished and still the lodge survived. It looks out over parkland no longer, but stands guard instead over the flat acres of an airfield. What good fortune that it is still with us, for it is doubtful if we shall see its like again. One can imagine a planning officer's response to a hexagonal building in which the chimneys were to be disguised as flying buttresses!

Sham castles could be used for other things besides homes. There are two examples in Buckinghamshire which could scarcely provide a greater contrast in use. In the county town of Buckingham there is a very castle-ish building, which in fact dates from 1758, though there are a few nineteenth-century additions. It was in fact the gaol, so its grim appearance is not altogether inappropriate. The second sham is Dinton Castle, which stands beside the Thame—Aylesbury road. It was actually built to house Sir John Vanhatten's fossil collection, but now it simply crumbles quietly away, so that with every year it more and more resembles a genuine medieval ruin.

Castles were definitely the most favoured form for builders of sham ruins, but there are other examples. The Deer-house at Bishop Auckland was built by Bishop Trevor under the castle walls. It is in its way a very practical building, providing shelter and visual cover from which to watch the deer, yet in style it seems to belong much more to the religious than to the secular world. It closely resembles a fine, old cloister, and it is almost too sensible and practical to feature in these pages at all. The same cannot be said, however, for the Hoad Hill monument at Ulverston, though even here there is a certain logic at work. The monument was built to commemorate the life and work of Sir John Barrow, explorer, writer, Secretary to the Admiralty and father of the Royal Geographical Society. His name is perpetuated in the Barrow Straits in Arctic Canada. It might seem wholly appropriate to choose a lighthouse as a monument to a great seafarer, but it is nevertheless slightly odd to build a lighthouse several miles from the

Dinton Castle, built to house a fossil collection *(National Monuments Record)*

sea — and with no light. The lighthouse is as sturdy and strong as any to be found around the British coast, but this one serves no useful purpose whatsoever. One cannot help feeling that Sir John might have preferred a memorial that would actually have helped later generations of seamen, even if it could not be set down near his birthplace.

What should follow a lighthouse with no lights? Perhaps a house with no rooms. Leinster Gardens is a typical West London terrace, built early in the nineteenth century. Now the essential characteristic of such a terrace is its unity, and this was threatened in the 1860s when the Metropolitan Railway wanted to drive their line straight through the middle. This would have left a nasty, empty space between numbers 22 and 25. A solution was found that allowed the railway through, yet preserved the essential unity of the buildings. Numbers 23 and 24 were preserved as a façade, complete with balconies, pedimented windows, cornices — all just as before. But the façade is all that is left, like the street fronts on a Hollywood back lot. There is a sad postscript to this story, which would otherwise be a splendid tale of the triumph of good sense and good taste. The

Metropolitan Railway preserved the façade at a good deal of expense: modern developers and architects have not. Close to the false houses, the old classical detailing has gone, and in its place is a blank facade with dull, unadorned windows. No doubt they are more efficient, but are we really less ingenious than the men of the Metropolitan Railway? Could we not keep the old and still introduce modern comforts? Or do we simply not care any more?

Without exception, the sham castles, churches and ruins we have looked at so far have dated from the eighteenth and nineteenth centuries, but the greatest sham of them all was built in the twentieth century. It is not too difficult to conceive of some fantastic structure to complement a landscape, but it requires imagination touched with genius to visualise a section of the Welsh coast as a piece of Italy. Clough Williams-Ellis came to Wales in the 1920s and set about building a reincarnation of the Italian village of Portofino. This was no direct copy, but an attempt to capture the ambience of the place. Williams-Ellis's village, Portmeirion, was designed not to reproduce a particular architectural style so much as to capture a particular atmosphere, to re-create a place of lightness and beauty, a spot given over more to frivolous pleasure than sententious scholarship. The miracle is that he succeeded. Portmeirion is a fairyland. It has been compared with Disneyland, but the comparison is unjust. Disneyland is a place of economic exploitation in the name of family fun, a way of cashing in on a proven success. Portmeirion is a bold enterprise, begun out of love rather than any certainty of profit. It seems, at first glance, as colourful and insubstantial as a confection at a banquet, yet the Italianate buildings are not simply showpieces. They are substantial buildings: they are homes. Serious architectural critics have complained about the diversity of styles and the air of unreality. Yet for others it is wholly convincing in the way that the best surrealist paintings are wholly convincing. One accepts the world of Magritte, say, as having its own reality, indeed as having its own inevitability. So it is with Portmeirion. Noel Coward, it is said, wrote *Blithe Spirit* here during a week's stay, and attitudes towards Portmeirion are very similar to those towards Coward's play. They are, depending on one's point of view, either wholly successful artifices or an irredeemably shallow gloss on reality. Everyone must decide for themselves, though no one could surely deny that it is 'folly', if not folly taken to its ultimate development.

The factor that has drawn all the structures in this class of folly together is their resemblance to, or imitation of, older buildings. Yet there is another whole class which seems to owe little or nothing to anything outside the originators' vivid imaginings. These are objects and structures scattered around the countryside which seem to proclaim at once that they are expressions of personal whims. Reverting again to canal travel, those who take their boats along the Macclesfield Canal have scarcely got used to the sham ruin of Mow Cop before they are presented at Bollington with another hill-top structure, which seems to have no useful function nor to relate to anything else in the surrounding country. Dazzlingly white, it resembles a bell or a sugar loaf, depending on your fancy, but stands some 13ft high and has a stone table and benches under its cover. No one seems altogether clear as to why it is there. One theory has it that it acted as a boundary marker for the local landowner, Colonel Gaskell; another, that it was put up to celebrate the British victory at Waterloo. The latter suggestion seems to accord with the triumphal bell shape. There is a third, and very satisfactory, explanation. It was built for the very excellent reason that it seemed like good fun to build something that would please many and harm none.

There were always some who erected strange structures for no better reason than the wish to be remembered. Having done nothing else in their lives to merit remembrance, they determined to leave a physical presence that would command attention. John Knill was mayor of St Ives in Cornwall at the end of the nineteenth century, a very respectable and honourable position for any man to hold – but Mr Knill wished to be distinguished from all other mayors of St Ives. In his will he made provision for the building of what he considered a suitable memorial. It is a stone pyramid and stands just to the south of the town, and just in case the monument itself did not attract sufficient attention, Knill left money in his will to pay for a special ceremony to be performed at five-yearly intervals. Ten virgins and a respectable matron – the latter to keep an eye on the former – were required to dance around the pyramid, while singing the hundredth psalm, 'Make a joyful noise unto the Lord, all ye lands'. It all suggests a somewhat

Variations on the number 3, the triangular tower at Rushton *(British Tourist Authority)*

inflated ego and, truth to tell, his pyramid does little to improve the landscape. At least the builders of shams enhanced the land to a greater extent than was achieved here — in spite of the virgin psalmists.

Another pious monument can be found at Rushton in Northants, but here at least the piety is directed towards something beyond the builder. Sir Thomas Tresham was brought up as the son of a Catholic family during the Reformation. Open practice of the religion would have been dangerous, if not suicidal, so the boy was given the outward show of Protestantism, while being secretly educated in the Catholic faith. The life of secrecy and intrigue seems to have left its mark. He became obsessed with the more obtuse branches of theology, and with such arcane subjects as numbers and the power of numbers. It was a dangerous world, where witchcraft and orthodox Christianity were close neighbours. It was a world which expressed itself in ciphers. Tresham gave such ideas solid reality in his triangular lodge.

Everything about the lodge relates to the number three, and that in turn relates to the idea of the Trinity. The building is three-sided and three-storeyed. The rooms are triangular or hexagonal. It is decorated with trefoils and triangles, which themselves come in groups of three. Even the date on which it was begun is significant and is recorded on the façade by the numbers 93, short for 1593, but also serving as a plain hint to the building's numerary significance. There are Latin inscriptions, with thirty-three letters to each phrase, three gables to the roof − and so it goes on. Wherever you look, the same number dominates all. It is a building of quite astonishing complexity, for when you think you have explored every conceivable variation of the number three, you find that there are still more to be discovered. If ever there was a monument to a single − or triple − obsession, then this is it.

A monument of a very different nature can be seen at Alnwick in Northumberland. It would seem to provide a demonstration of the fact that while an obsessive can do what he likes with his own monument, it is not always wise to try and do it for him. Pandering to what you take to be another's vanity may not always have the desired effect. Much of the land around Alnwick belongs to the Percy family, the Dukes of Northumberland. During the Napoleonic Wars, prices of agricultural produce, especially fodder, were subject to violent fluctuations. When prices rose, the Duke decided that with their increased profits the tenant farmers could afford higher rents. Then followed the inevitable slump and where most landlords kept rents high, the Duke brought his down again. The tenants were astonished and delighted and, as things began to improve, they decided to show their appreciation. They raised a subscription to pay for a vast and impressive monument to the Duke, in the shape of an 80ft fluted column, topped by a lion. It was now the Duke's turn to show his delight, which he duly did − and his astonishment. He declared himself amazed that the tenants he had previously thought so poor could raise funds for such a memorial – and accordingly put their rents up again. This is one of the few follies from the great age of follies that comes complete with a moral – never rely on flattery.

Another moral that might be drawn from the last story might be that the best follies are those which were never intended to serve any useful purpose. Morality should have nothing to do with folly building, though there is one group of follies which might at best be described as amoral, but might equally well be described as immoral. They are certainly associated in popular legend with downright immoral, not to say infamous, activities. That, of course, only serves to make them all the more interesting. The rake has ever been a more intriguing character than the saint, and they do not come any more rakish than Francis Dashwood of West Wycombe. If he had not existed, Georgette Heyer would have had to invent him. His outward respectability as a government minister masked a very different life-style, for Dashwood was the founder of the notorious Hell-Fire Club. Just how wicked Dashwood and his Apostles were in reality is difficult to determine: one suspects they were considerably less evil, and consequently a good deal duller, than popular history would have us believe. A truly secret society devoted to the Black Arts would surely never have become that well known. Still there are quite enough stories of dark deeds, orgies and Black Masses to give an air of dangerous romance to an interesting set of follies. Whether they would be quite as interesting without the lurid tales is quite another matter.

The Dashwood folly hunt begins properly at Medmenham Abbey on the bank of the Thames. In essence this is an Elizabethan manor built on the ruins of an abbey of the late twelfth or early thirteenth century. In true eighteenth-century style, the ruin was, as it were, brought back into prominence by the addition of a sham ruined tower. The Hell-Fire Club held their 'secret' meetings here, which, it seems, everyone for miles around knew about. The walls of the old abbey were covered in sexy paintings, though whether the infamy ever extended beyond turning a respectable house into a passable imitation of a modern Soho bookshop is uncertain. It certainly attracted a good deal of attention, and Dashwood and his compatriots, growing tired of the inquisitive gaze of the hoi-polloi retired to an even more romantic setting at West Wycombe. Here they constructed a new home for their revels in the Hell-Fire Caves, where they could take their whores and drink themselves stupid without the fear of interference. They now seem rather sad creatures, desperately looking for titillation to reawaken long-sated appetites, but one has to confess that they strode off along the road to perdition with a certain style, and they displayed that style in West Wycombe Park. It could be said, however, that the principal way in which they showed that style was in having the good sense to hand over the whole design to one of the leading landscape gardeners of the day, Humphrey Repton. Though whether the work is actually Repton's own or that of one of his disciples is a question open to discussion.

A number of pagan temples in the grounds, dedicated to gods not necessarily associated with the virtues – Bacchus, for example, was exceptionally well housed – have been taken as further evidence of wickedness and debauchery. These were, however, no different from other classical fragments set down in English parklands. Here, though, is one truly original concept. West Wycombe church is a pleasant building in which irregular flint walls contrast with smooth brick dressing, but which boasts one striking feature which makes the church a landmark for miles around. On top of the bell tower is balanced a great golden ball. From a distance it looks no more than a very odd form of decoration, but when seen close at hand it appears to be remarkably large. Even closer inspection reveals it to be hollow. It is in fact, large enough to hold ten people, and it was here that Dashwood and his friends would meet to make their plans and gaze at the world around them through squints in the globe. They could, at least, be certain of not being overheard, and they could look down on the tiny figures scuttling around beneath them. As G. K. Chesterton pointed out in one of the Father Brown stories, *The Hammer of God*, even the righteous can get strange thoughts if they spend too long looking down on the rest of humanity. One can so easily end up looking down in a figurative as well as a literal sense. 'Humility is the mother of giants. One sees great things from the valley; only small things from the peak.' It is doubtful if there was much humility present amongst the inhabitants of the golden ball above West Wycombe church.

West Wycombe church — the golden ball above the tower is hollow and was used by Francis Dashwood and the Hell Fire Club *(National Trust: photo John Bethell)*

One can overestimate the wickedness and the importance of the Hell-Fire Club, so before leaving West Wycombe let us look at one entirely harmless conceit which had very little to do with the aristocratic hooligans. There is a monument at the end of the road to High Wycombe, a stumpy column topped by what appears to be a stone Christmas pudding and it records the information that you are now thirty miles from 'The City'. It was put there by the road builders themselves to commemorate their labours, and it cost them £27 7s 8d. It is a pleasant thing to come across — not really a folly at all for it is quite a useful milepost — and it is refreshing to find a note of honest pride among so many emblems of dishonesty.

West Wycombe is one of the very few places where one can find a whole group of follies, but the finest collection must surely be at Wentworth Woodhouse near Rotherham. The famous Yorkshire steel town might seem an unlikely spot to find a single folly, let alone a collection, yet here they are – three fine follies, built over a period of some fifty years. The earliest of these is a 100ft pyramid, known as Hoober Stand. There is no mystery here for the builder has left an inscription, telling precisely why it was built:

> 1748. This Pyramidal Building was Erected by his Majesty's most Dutiful Subject, Thomas, Marquess of Rockingham in Grateful Respect to the Preserver of our Religion, Laws and Libertys, King George the Second, Who by the Blessing of God having Subdued a most Unnatural Rebellion in Britain, Anno 1746 Maintains the Balance of Power, and Settles A Just, and Honourable Peace in Europe. 1748.

The column then is no more than a memorial to the victors of the '45 rebellion. It seems, however, to have given the Marquis a taste for monument construction. In 1778, he built a more conventional column, in the Doric style, which stands 50ft higher than Hoober Stand. This was built not to celebrate a victory but a defeat – that of Admiral Keppel at the Battle of Ushant. After the battle, the Admiral was court-martialled, but was able to demonstrate that much of the fault for the defeat lay in the wretched state of the fleet, which had been starved of funds for essential repairs. The blame was, for once, fixed where it belonged – on Lord Sandwich, who had pocketed the funds. So one might say that the column celebrates a victory after all – a victory for justice.

The two monuments are easily explained, but the third – the Needle's Eye – is a very different proposition. Here is a genuine curiosity indeed. It is a stone pyramid, with a somewhat precarious-looking urn balanced on the point. The pyramid itself is pierced by an ogee arch. What does that commemorate? The answer is nothing at all, unless one counts the winning of a rather foolish wager as an event worthy of permanent commemoration. We are not quite certain which of the owners of the estate had the curious structure built somewhere around 1780, but whoever it was had succumbed to what appears to have been a common failing among Georgian gentlemen – he had made an idle boast. In this case, he had boasted that he was such a fine

*(opposite)* 'Jack the Treacle Eater', one of the Messiter follies. Who Jack was or why he ate treacle is uncertain. *(Reece Winstone)*

Another of George Messiter's follies in Barwick Park, a tower built for no other reason than that Messiter wanted a tower – and to provide work for the unemployed. *(Reece Winstone)*

driver that he could take his horse and carriage through the eye of a needle. Someone had then got up and demanded that he should put his money where his mouth was, or whatever the eighteenth-century equivalent might be. The wager was on, and the boaster then had to build himself a Needle's Eye and drive through it. The wager was won, but whether it was worth the expense is not recorded. A similar story crops up among our next group of follies.

If folly building is thought of as an expression of exuberance, a zest for the unusual for its own sake, then the king of folly builders must be Mad Jack Fuller of Brightling Park, Dallington in East Sussex. Fuller was literally and metaphorically a larger-than-life character, weighing in at over twenty stone. All his follies have a certain perverse logic about them. Take the sugar loaf, a cone built of stone and concrete which stands on top of a neighbouring hill. It appears to have no function at all, to be the result of no more than a mad whim – yet, if

One of Mad Jack Fuller's follies at Dallington, said to have been built to win him a bet
(*Reece Winstone*)

old stories are to be believed, there is an entertaining explanation for its presence.

Mad Jack was dining out with friends, during which he boasted of the fine view of Dallington church spire to be had from his dining-room window. The statement was challenged by fellow diners, convinced that no view, fine or otherwise, was to be had from that vantage point. Bets were laid. Mad Jack hurried home, where he saw to his horror that the hill did indeed block the view, but he was not a man to accept defeat easily. He called his workmen together and sent them off at top speed to re-create the top of the spire on the hill. Seen from a distance it was a convincing spire — more convincing, perhaps, than this old tale. Still, the story has it that Fuller's friend, who had enough local knowledge to dispute the spire's visibility, did not have enough common sense to spot the sugar loaf. Fuller won his bet.

That is only one of Mad Jack's follies. On top of the hill to the west of the church there is an obelisk, and for once there is no story to explain its presence. It might be significant to note that in 1820, when Fuller's folly-making was in full spate, Cleopatra's Needle was presented to Britain to mark the coronation of George IV — though it was to remain in the desert for another half century before it was to reach its present home on the Thames embankment. It seems quite reasonable that the Brightling Needle, as it is known, was built to show that anything the Egyptians could do, could be done just as well by a Sussex squire.

Fuller had a small temple built by Robert Smirke in the form of a rotunda and observatory. This, it is said, was not built for observation of the stars but for observation of Fuller himself. His servants were expected to stay there during their master's absence at Westminster where he was a Member of Parliament, to keep an eye open for the first appearance of the carriage bringing him home. Then they were to dash from the observatory to the house to get everything ready for his arrival — slippers warmed, hot meal ready, glass filled. This might seem a somewhat extravagant way of managing a household, but the nineteenth-century landlord was a powerful man, and men such as Fuller had the means to indulge their whims. One could look for other examples and, if the reader will forgive a short diversion, there is a particularly charming example in Wales.

Flagpole halt on the Bala Lake Railway *(Pete Briddon)*

The Bala Lake Railway is now one of the few preserved narrow-gauge railways where steam trains still run. It was formerly part of the mighty empire of the Great Western Railway. The line runs down one shore of the lake, while on the opposite shore stands a grand house which once belonged to a director of the company. A small halt was built opposite the house and this was manned by a look-out, who when a flag was hoisted outside the house would halt the train, which would then have to wait for the director to chug across the water in his steam launch.

If one can keep a man on permanent duty and hold up a train on scheduled service, then manning an observatory seems a comparatively minor matter. Fuller himself even came close to having one of his follies permanently occupied. He decided that what his grounds needed was a hermitage, so he built a remote tower but was unable to persuade anyone to occupy it. In this he fared less well than some of his contemporaries who also tried to bring back a touch of the Middle Ages.

William Beckford installed a hermit in a fully furnished cave above the lake at Fonthill in Wiltshire, while at Burley House, Burley-on-the-Hill, Leicestershire, the Earl of Nottingham built quite a cosy little circular hermitage with a thatched roof. He had no difficulty in finding an occupant, though it is not clear just what the hermit was expected to do, apart from sitting around looking thoughtful.

Mad Jack Fuller saved his finest folly for the last, and here again the building is the subject of a good tale. As local squire, Fuller owned much of the property in the village, including the village local, the Fuller's Arms. Now this particular pub stood along the way from the village to the parish church, and the vicar complained that too many parishioners were stopping off for a quick pint on their way to the service – and some never made it to the church at all. Fuller was approached and he agreed that there had to be a change. He would arrange for the pub to be moved, but only on condition that he, Jack Fuller, should be allowed to design his own tomb to stand in the churchyard. The vicar agreed, though if he knew Fuller at all he must have had doubts. Fuller kept his word. The old pub was closed down, and an empty cottage converted into a new inn at a suitably safe distance from the church.

Fuller now insisted on his side of the bargain. The tomb was duly built – and the vicar's doubts were shown to be well founded. He built a huge stone pyramid, which quite dominated the churchyard. It was kept open to await Jack Fuller's demise, and when he eventually died in 1834 at the age of seventy-seven, it was here that he was duly interred. Local legend could not allow that such a colourful character was buried in any conventional manner. He was, it is said, sat in his favourite chair, and a table was laid before him. One would love to believe the story, for what more fitting end could one imagine for the greatest of the folly builders.

There can only be one possible competitor to stand up to Mad Jack Fuller and that is George Messiter of Barwick Park. He built four follies in the park in about the year 1820, including an obelisk with a distinct bend at the top. But the one monument which raises him into the ranks of the great is an almost perfect folly. It manages to be both architecturally incongruous and inexplicable. It consists of a rough stone arch, topped by a round tower, on top of which stands a winged Mercury. What it is or why it is there are questions that remain unanswered, and its splendid name only adds confusion rather than clarification – Jack the Treacle Eater.

The art of folly building might seem to have all but died quite early in the last century – partly because tastes changed and partly because the number of landowners who could afford such frivolities has been steadily dwindling. Those in charge of the modern large estates can afford little if anything that does not show a profit if the estates are to survive. The modern rash of safari parks and fun fairs are not follies but necessities, though one suspects that Jack Fuller and his like would have been vastly amused at having their parkland stocked with lions. There is still, however, room for the modest folly lover. At Scarrington in Nottinghamshire, a local man began to build an obelisk in 1946. It is constructed entirely of horseshoes, stands over 15ft high and contains around 35,000 horse shoes – a figure which I have not attempted to check. It is absolutely steady, and is topped off with three shoes forming a sort of crown. So the art of folly making is not quite dead after all, for this is surely a perfect, classic folly, serving no purpose other than to please the eye of the beholder – and, of course, Mr Flinders who built it. Long may it remain.

# 3
# Every Prospect Pleases

It might seem to us a very natural human trait to want to get up to a high place to view the surrounding scenery, yet it is really a comparatively modern phenomenon. It is only in the past 250 years or so that man has begun to appreciate scenery in the sense that we understand the phrase today. Daniel Defoe travelling through the hills of the Pennines and the Lake District in the 1720s would have been astonished by the suggestion that he might wish to climb any of them to admire the view. To him the hills had 'a kind of an unhospitable terror in them'; all was 'barren and wild, of no use or advantage either to man or beast'. It was with an obvious feeling of relief that he left Westmorland, 'a country eminent only for being the wildest, most barren and frightful of any I have passed over in England' and returned to the lower ground and the delights of 'some very pleasant, populous and manufacturing towns'. But with the growth of the picturesque and the later Romantic movements, the gentry began to discover the delights of surveying the land from on high. Those fortunate enough to have natural hills close at hand could walk to their summits: others deprived of this advantage had to find other means of enjoying the sensations described by James Thomson, the fashionable poet of the eighteenth century:

> Heavn's, what a goodly prospect spreads around,
> Of hills, and dales, and woods, and lawns, and spires!
> And glittering towns, and gilded streams, till all
> The stretching landskip into smoke decays.

The age of the belvedere and the prospect tower had arrived.

The two terms 'belvedere' and 'prospect tower' often seem interchangeable, but strictly speaking a belvedere is a turret room or lantern room, part of the main structure of the house, while the prospect tower is a quite separate structure. Belvederes can be, indeed frequently are, charming structures, but there is seldom anything very strange about them. With the prospect tower, however, the builders could let their imaginations go. In essence, the only thing that was absolutely required was that the structure should be high enough to enable the would-be viewer to see the required view: something as plain and functional as the wooden watch towers which are a feature of present-day forestry land would suffice. Happily for posterity, most designers of prospect towers had the common sense to realise that the owner would be likely to spend more time looking up at his tower than he would spend looking down from it. There was every reason, therefore, to make the tower itself interesting. Those that survive offer splendid proof of how well the designers succeeded.

There is a certain amount of dispute over which is the oldest prospect tower in the country. The honour is usually claimed for Freston Tower, which stands to the south of the River Orwell in Suffolk. It is certainly old, having been built by the Latimer family in 1549, but is it a prospect tower? It certainly offers a prospect that improves as you climb up through its six storeys, and the view is further improved by the fact that the windows get larger as you ascend, a reversal of normal building techniques. Alternative versions of why the handsome tower was built include the somewhat unlikely suggestion that it was once part of a larger house, of which all trace has vanished. Another, much more interesting story, has it that it was built as a sort of vertical study.

Lord Freston had a beautiful daughter, Ellen de Freston, and he was determined that wisdom should be added to beauty. Her week was divided up to include six days of study in the tower. Monday saw her busy with embroidery on the ground floor, up a floor she went for music on Tuesday, up again for languages on Wednesday, English literature occupied Thursday, and Friday was spent in painting. By Saturday she had reached a sufficient elevation for the study of astronomy and astrology. She was then, presumably, allowed down for Sunday and was ready to start the ascent again the next day. It seems a somewhat bizarre way to organise a course of study, and a very expensive method of providing a school for one pupil. The tower itself is attractive but somewhat plain in comparison with its successors, but the mysteries surrounding its original use make it a fit companion for the exotic company we shall be visiting.

If the story of Freston Tower is true, or if it was indeed part of a grand house, then it might be termed a belvedere. The true prospect tower should keep its role unpolluted by anything like usefulness. But what name would you apply to a prospect tower which no longer has a prospect? One such curiosity began its life as part of the old home of the Dukes of Sutherland at Trentham in the Potteries. This was a fine belvedere in the form of a tower, the top of which was a viewing platform surrounded by stone arches and topped with a balustrade. The house was pulled down in 1905, but Lord Harrowby took a liking to the belvedere and bought it for a modest hundred pounds. It was carefully taken down, every stone numbered, and re-erected at Sandon Hall, just north of Stafford. It now presents an odd aspect, for it no longer stands on top of a tower but sits rather forlornly on a low brick base in the grounds – a belvedere with no view.

Haldon Belvedere at Doddiscombsleigh between the Haldon Hills and Dartmoor is not so much a belvedere attached to a house as a prospect tower expanded to become a house. It was built in 1788 by Sir Robert Palk, in memory of his friend Major General Stringer Lawrence. It has two quite distinct personae, for the inside is in a quite different style from the exterior. Outside it is very much the fashionable Gothic. The plan is triangular with battlemented turrets at the corners, and windows with pointed arches and intersected tracery. It seems a fitting building for a moorland setting. Inside, however, one is at once transported from the English Middle Ages to a land a long way to the east. There are two stairways, built out of beautiful Indian marble, presented by the Nizam of Hyderabad, while the ballroom has a magnificent floor of mahogany from the East Indies. The delicate plasterwork decoration of the rooms could scarcely be more different from the rough, stern exterior.

The great attraction of prospect towers lies in their variety and there is something especially attractive to the collector of curiosities about these towers whose only true function is to act as ornate step-ladders.

*(opposite)* Britain's oldest prospect tower, Freston Tower built in the sixteenth century *(National Monuments Record)*

Haldon Belvedere (in the distance), from which the owners of Haldon House could look down on their estate *(BBC Hulton Picture Library)*

Some can be quite small and rather charming. Kimmeridge Tower, overlooking Kimmeridge Bay in Dorset, is just that, though now sadly ruinous. It consists of a simple round tower with a quatrefoil parapet at the top and a Doric colonnade at the bottom. To purists, the mixture of classical and Gothic styles might be offensive, but it is so well proportioned and has such a marvellous situation on the cliff top, that one can only envy those who came here to laze away a sunny summer afternoon.

For a complete contrast, travel north in the same county of Dorset to Horton, where you will find Sturt's Folly. This is a quite early tower, built in the 1720s on a massive scale. Again it has a triangular plan as at Haldon, with three circular turrets joined together by three pedimented walls. A great hexagonal tower rises up in the centre. It looks as though it would be capable of withstanding a siege, but it was built for no warlike purpose. Inevitably, with such a grand structure, there are a number of stories suggesting various uses for which it was intended: a common version has it that it was originally intended as an

Horton Tower, or Sturt's Folly, a massive structure built not to withstand a twelve-month siege but to provide a viewpoint from which to watch deer on Cranborne Chase *(National Monuments Record)*

astronomical observatory, but the builder either went bankrupt or
became bored with star-gazing before completion. In fact the builder,
Humphrey Sturt, used it for watching the deer in Outer Cranborne
Chase, though such a simple purpose could surely have been served
without the expense of building a seven-storey fortress.

The first great age of tower construction began in the middle of the
eighteenth century, when some of the most exciting and bizarre
structures were begun. Naturally, the combination of sham castle and
prospect tower was irresistible to many. Blaise Castle at Henbury to
the north of Bristol is a fine example. It follows the familiar triangular
pattern, but here the designer, who is reputed to have been the great
folly man Sanderson Miller, kept a cylindrical motif throughout as
well. The gap between three circular towers is filled by a third squat,
circular tower, rising above them. All four towers have their full
complement of defensive details, from crenellations to arrow slits. It
was built in the grounds of Blaise Castle in 1766 for a local merchant,
Thomas Farr, and from his lofty towers he could enjoy splendid views
across both the Avon and the Severn valleys. The same area was to be
blessed by even more bizarre buildings − a whole hamlet of them −
half a century later (see Chapter Five).

One becomes used, after a while, to seeing these fine towers rising
above the surrounding countryside, and when one sees that
countryside it is easy to understand why anyone would be happy to
spend hours in its contemplation. The attractions of the moorland at
Haldon or the coast at Kimmeridge are obvious. It still comes as
something of a surprise, however, to find a tower which gives a view
over Birmingham. True, Birmingham has no shortage of tall
buildings, but these are modern and plainly businesslike, the plainness
being the dominant theme. But why, one wonders, should anyone
build a prospect tower in Edgbaston, unless of course they were
hoping for a free seat to view the cricket. But the tower was built as
early as 1758 by John Perrott of Rotton Park, in the days when Rotton
Park was still a country estate, and before cricket came to Edgbaston.
Then came the Industrial Revolution and Birmingham began to grow,
and gradually the terraces crept up to the foot of Perrott's Folly until it
was surrounded. Yet the encroachment has not detracted from the
gracefulness of the tower: if anything it has added to it, by acting as a

foil. The tower, in turn, has added this touch of grace and individuality to a city sadly in need of both commodities. It stands seven storeys high, is decorated with Gothic windows and a castellated parapet – and as with so many such towers, comes complete with a variety of stories, each of which claims to be the true explanation of its existence. Here are three to choose between.

Firstly, it was built by John Perrott in his old age to enable him to follow his favouite sport of hare coursing. In this splendidly unlikely version, we have an old gentleman so infirm that he cannot get to the carriage that would take him to the coursing, so he climbs seven flights of stairs instead. In the second story, we have Mr Perrott as a widower who built the tower so that he could see his wife's grave ten miles away. In the third account, Perrott is an amateur astronomer who viewed the stars and planets through a telescope mounted at the top of the tower. There is an actual connection with the third version in that the tower was used for a time as a observatory, but for viewing the weather not the stars. No one, it seems, has put forward a fourth version – that John Perrott built his tower because he thought it might be rather fun to have a tower on the estate.

Prospect towers might seem to non-aficionados to be rather boringly similar to each other, but closer acquaintance reveals a great richness of architectural styles and an even greater richness of stories attached to them. Some of these stories seem to put the towers well within the folly category, in the sense of being exceedingly foolish conceptions. This applies in particular to those towers which were built to provide the owner with a quite specific view – which they then singularly failed to provide. Take, for example, Admiral Stratten's observatory at Little Berkhamsted in Hertfordshire. Outwardly, it is a pleasant, if not very dramatic, tower. The virtues of the building are very much those one associates with its period, the late eighteenth century: its proportions are exemplary, its aspect dignified. It is a classic piece of Georgian design. Look at the windows in the main, circular tower, which are held within the unifying enclosure of a tall arch. At the bottom is a square window, at the top a round one, while in between is an oblong window topped by a semicircular arch: a lovely exercise in symmetry. Yet this eminently rational piece of design topples over, if only metaphorically, into absurdity if the popular story of its

A charming tower built by Temple Simon Luttrell at Eaglehurst to enable him to watch the passing ships in the Solent *(Landmark Trust)*

construction is true. It is said that the Admiral sorely missed his life at sea and he built his tower so that he could sit at the top with his telescope and watch ships on the Thames. But even with the best telescope, there was never any chance of seeing even a topmast from this tower, so all his efforts were wasted.

Nineteenth-century tower builders failed, it seems, to learn from this and similar examples. The Bishop of Llandaff built an 80ft tower at Offwell in Devon, so that he could see into his diocese without the tedious effort of actually going there. He must have been an optimistic gentleman to have expected to see as far as Wales, even if the Quantocks had not been inconveniently in the way. These are really rather sad stories, for one would not like to think that the Admiral having commissioned such an attractive work ended up by being disappointed in the result, though one feels a good deal less sympathy for the idle cleric. Here, by contrast, is a thoroughly romantic story of another aspect of seafaring life.

Luttrell's Tower at Eaglehurst near Southampton was built by Temple Simon Luttrell in about 1780, and was probably designed by James Wyatt. Whoever was responsible, it is certainly a fine piece of work. It has a castellated base, with many fine features including an oriel window, and from this base the circular tower itself rises. Here there is no question about the view of passing ships – the vista is there all right and is quite superb. A watcher from the top of the tower has a perfect view right across the Solent and all the busy traffic to and from Southampton. That, however, represents only the commonplace part of the story, for tradition has it that the tower was built for a much more sinister purpose than the idle watching of ships. Under the tower are exceptionally large cellars and from these an underground passage ran down to the beach. Luttrell's Tower was said to be the headquarters of the local smugglers. Why else, so the argument goes, should a simple prospect tower require such a huge cellar? There is an answer to that. Luttrell was a good friend of the Prince of Wales and entertained him at the tower. Anyone who expected to entertain Prinny on a regular basis would certainly have needed a large cellar!

Although so many stories cluster around the construction of prospect towers, there are few which go on accumulating stories after they are built. Luttrell's Tower is, however, one of those few. It has a curious monument, for example, in the shape of a pair of black granite feet mounted on a plinth. They were actually brought here by Lord Cavan, Luttrell's son-in-law, who became the tower's second owner. He had commanded the British forces in Egypt from 1801, and the feet are said to belong to a statue of Rameses II. Quite why he should want Rameses' feet is not known − nor is it known if there were any more bits of Rameses lying around for the taking, though it would seem logical to suppose that the feet were the sole remains (no pun intended). The tower passed out of the hands of the Luttrell family and at one time was nearly purchased by Queen Victoria when she considered buying Eaglehurst House, but eventually settled for Osborne instead. Marconi used the tower for radio experiments at the beginning of this century, and he laid a cable for mains electricity which is still in use today. Clough Williams-Ellis, of Portmeirion fame, came here and built a pair of magnificent monumental gates at the top of a staircase from the tower to the beach. It is good to know that the future of this particular tower seems assured, for it has been acquired by the Landmark Trust, an organisation devoted to taking over and restoring buildings of character, which they then let out as holiday homes. The fortunate visitors can enjoy the same view as that which pleased the Prince of Wales. Little has changed at the tower − though that cellar, alas, is now empty.

A tower whose associations with thieves, highwaymen and the like are all too well documented is Hull's Tower at Leith Hill in Surrey. In general outline it is not dissimilar to Luttrell's, but the effect is much more forbidding. Where the Hampshire tower gives the effect of a Georgian house grown unexpectedly tall, with a touch of Gothic sprinkled around for effect, Hull's Tower actually could pass as a medieval fortress. It has a beautiful hill-top site, but it was not built simply to furnish the owner with a better view than unaided Nature provided. The hill stands at a height of 965ft above sea level, and Hull was irritated by the fact that his local hill did not quite reach the 1,000ft mark. A hill under a 1,000ft is a mere pimple on the land, whereas one that overtops the magic figure can properly qualify for the title of hill. So he built his tower, artificially extending the summit to reach that altitude. By the end of the century, however, the tower was being used as a hiding place by local criminals, who became such a

Hull's Tower at Leith Hill, presiding over a snowy prospect *(BBC Hulton Picture Library)*

menace that eventually the drastic decision was taken to fill up the tower with rubble, thus closing it to everyone for all time. Later, a Victorian owner had a change of heart and built an exterior staircase, so that he could again enjoy the view from the top of his tower.

One of the last, if not the last, towers to be built in the eighteenth century was Broadway Tower which stands on the western edge of the Cotswold escarpment, looking out over the Vale of Evesham. It is very much in the fashionable Gothic style, hexagonal in plan with the familiar castellated towers, though it does also have some rather

Impressive Broadway Tower from which it is said one could see thirteen counties —
but that was before the recent meddling with ancient boundaries *(Antony Miles Ltd)*

incongruous balconies. It promises and provides an excellent prospect
with, it is said, a view of thirteen counties. It may well be so, though
how it is possible to tell what counties one is looking at is a mystery; in
any case, one seems to be able to see just about as much from the hill,
without bothering to climb the extra 60ft of the tower's staircase.
However, if the story of its construction is not mere fantasy, then it
was built to be looked at rather than to be looked from. The moving
force behind its building was the young wife of the sixth Earl of

Coventry, a vain young lady with a well-developed sense of self-importance. Before work began, she ordered the tenants to build a beacon on the hill top, so that she could be certain that the tower would be visible from her home fifteen miles away. She then spent the rest of the night driving around the other important houses of the neighbourhood to make certain that they could look up and see her tower. She was well satisfied with the night's work, and the tower was completed in 1797.

If there is a certain sameness about eighteenth-century towers, then that criticism could never be levelled against their nineteenth-century successors, especially the Victorians. If, however, one begins with the early years of the century, then there is no sudden break with the past, rather a straightforward continuation of styles. Paxton's Tower near Llanarthney in Dyfed is on the old triangular plan with a battlemented tower rising from the centre. Yet it is one of the grandest of all such structures – as it needs to be for it has to compete with the genuine medieval fortress nearby. Dryslwyn Castle is famous as the seat of the turncoat Lord of Dryslwyn, Rhys ap Maredudd, who in 1282 supported Edward I against the Welsh, and then in 1287 revolted against the English king. He suffered the penalty of the unsuccessful rebel, being executed in 1291. Sir William Paxton, the builder of the tower, had a somewhat less dramatic history and met a happier end. Nevertheless, there is one story that features in his life which typifies an aspect of life in Georgian Britain, just as the story of Dryslwyn typifies one of the more violent aspects of life in the Middle Ages. That story concerns the building of the tower.

Sir William Paxton was a Whig politician, who was determined to beat the local Tory at the county elections of 1802. No expense was spared in an effort to woo the electorate. He treated them to 11,070 breakfasts, 684 suppers and 36,000 dinners, during which they got through 8,879 bottles of porter, not to mention similar quantities of other goodies. The grand total for this exercise in mass bribery came to £15,690 4s 2d – and in spite of all that largesse, the ungrateful voters elected the opposition. One hundred and seven of them drank his porter, ate his food and went out and voted Tory! What has all this to do with the tower? Well, rumour spread throughout the district that all this extravagance had bankrupted Paxton, so he determined to give

Paxton's Tower, built in memory of Nelson, as it was in the days of its grandeur *(National Trust)* and *(opposite)* as it is today *(National Trust: photo Derek Powell)*

his critics visible and irrefutable proof that he still had money to spend. He built the tower, completed in 1805, to demonstrate to the entire neighbourhood that Sir William Paxton might have lost the election but he had not lost his wealth. It has to be admitted that there is another version of the origin of the tower: that it was erected to honour Lord Nelson. Yet the election story is undeniably true: the money was spent, the rumours did circulate, and really there seems no reason why the two stories should not be combined. Perhaps Paxton built his tower both to honour Britian's most famous admiral and to prove his own wealth.

At almost the same time as Paxton was building his architecturally conventional tower in Wales, over in Kent a splendidly eccentric gentleman by the name of John Powell was constructing his own quite astonishing edifice. Quex Park lies near the village of Birchington in Kent. The tower itself is unremarkable, yet another Gothic pile, but as you look up to the top of the building, you see a second, quite different structure, looming over the battlements. This is an open-work spire of

A miniature Eiffel Tower arising from a gothic structure, at Quex Park *(Powell Cotton Museum)*

cast iron, rising up on four legs like a Kentish Eiffel Tower. The spire and the tower that supports it make an incongruous pair, but there is a logic at work here. Powell was an enthusiastic campanologist, and the tower contains a peal of twelve bells – and peals of bells are traditionally associated with churches, and churches are associated with spires. Powell himself was buried in a mausoleum within the tower, where he can rest contented, for the bells are still in use.

Now for two towers which show the extremes of Victorian taste. The popular spa town of Matlock in Derbyshire is surrounded by some of the most beautiful countryside in Britain. It therefore seems only reasonable to build a tower which will provide the best possible view over it. So, just such a tower was duly built on the Heights of Abraham, and the builders took a severely practical attitude towards their task. The tower was there for viewing the countryside, so there was no need for any embellishment. It was reduced to the ultimate in plainness, with just a hint of extravagance in the battlements at the very top: otherwise it is a plain cylinder, sheer from ground to top.

Whatever one might say about the tower known as May's Folly at Hadlow in Kent, one could never accuse it of plainness. It is a Gothic extravaganza, a cross between a castle and a cathedral, a total denial of architectural logic and stylistic unity, a deplorable example of Victorian excess and lack of refinement. It is also wholly delightful. It was built as an addition to Squire Walter Barton May's sham castle of a house – and the additions leave everything else in the shade, literally, for the tower rises to a height of 170ft. Arches and tracery, pinnacles and towers pile up one on top of the other in this splendidly mad caprice of a building. Why was such an amazing stucture ever built in the first place? As one would expect, there is a multitude of explanations, including the almost standard one that May wanted to see the sea, built his tower, and only then noticed the Downs which stood in the way. Two other versions have rather more originality. In one, May's wife ran away with a local farmer, and the squire built the tower so that wherever she travelled in the neighbourhood she would be reminded of her abandoned husband. The other story is as splendidly bizarre as the tower itself. There was, it is said, a mysterious prophecy that foretold that when Walter May was buried beneath the earth, his family would lose the estates. Rather than perch his coffin in a mausoleum a mere few inches from the ground, May determined that his body should be raised as far above the earth as possible. The tower was to be his mausoleum – and his body was to perch at the very top of it.

Here now are three final examples of Victorian towers – the first is included because it has the best situation of all, the second because it has the best story of all, and the third because it is the biggest of all.

This splendid wedding cake of a tower is Hadlow Castle or May's Folly *(A. Rumsey: supplied by National Monuments Record)*

A delightful tower in a delightful setting at Portquin in Cornwall *(National Trust)*

The first of the trio is one of the smallest of all prospect towers, a simple two-storey building in restrained Gothic, built around 1830 and known as Doyden Castle. It has no need of any great height, for it stands on Doyden Point, on the cliffs overlooking Portquin Bay, one of the wildest and least populated stretches of the lovely north Cornish coast. Locals say it was built by a man who wanted to drink himself to death in solitude, but one needs no fanciful story to explain away Doyden Castle. Who would not welcome quiet and solitude when surrounded by scenery such as this?

A prospect tower in concrete at Sway *(National Monuments Record)*

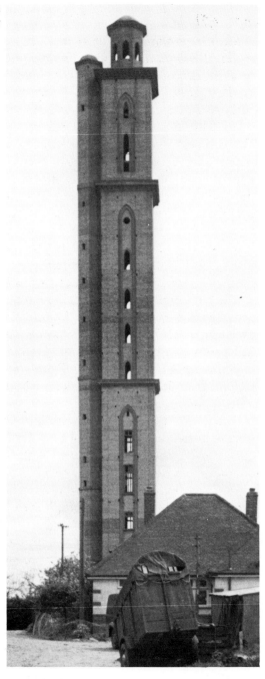

The next example is perhaps more of a monument than a prospect tower. It is Ammerdown Park Column at Hemington in Somerset. It is, as its name suggests, a circular column, but as with the Monument in the City of London, there is a staircase inside which leads to a curious lantern, shaped like an old-fashioned parrot's cage. It was built in 1853 by Lord Hylton to the memory of Colonel Thomas Joliffe, a kindly thought since it is unlikely that he would otherwise have been remembered at all. Lord Hylton, at any rate, seems to have been delighted with the monument, and encouraged his friends to climb to the top to look out over the surrounding countryside and the neighbours' lands. One of these neighbours, Mr Turner, took a dim view of being perpetually overlooked and decided it was time that he had a turn at the overlooking. He then proceeded to build his own tower, 30ft higher than Lord Hylton's. As the visitors had once looked down on Turner, so Turner could now look down on the visitors, and it was Lord Hylton's turn to get annoyed. Then John Turner died, and when the estate was put up for sale, there was never much doubt over who would buy Taylor's Tower — Lord Hylton. As soon as he had possession, he announced that he was desperately short of good building stone, and Turner's Tower was demolished. The Park Column had its old pre-eminence back again, the tallest tower for miles around.

Fortunately, the village of Sway in the New Forest is a long way from Somerset and the estates of Lord Hylton, so there was never any danger of Peterson's Tower being bought out and demolished. It is a quite extraordinary structure in many ways, built by a retired judge from Calcutta, A. T. T. Peterson. Its structure represents a pioneer use of a new building material, for it is entirely composed of concrete blocks. There are eleven rooms in the great tower, all reached by a spiral staircase, and the top of the structure stands 250ft above the ground. Yet the whole edifice was completed without the use of scaffolding, which says a good deal for the calm nerves of the building workers. No one would put it forward for a prize as the most elegant prospect tower, though its slender height might be thought to have something of the minaret about it. The concrete, however, does little to enhance the general effect, suffering as concrete almost invariably does from ugly weather stains. It proved, in any case, to be slightly unsafe and had to be reinforced later. One might well wonder why the judge should have used such a material in the first place. There is a legend that he was visited by the ghost of Christopher Wren, who told him that he must inaugurate a great new age of building, The Concrete Age. The ghost must have temporarily lost the traditional spectral ability of seeing into the future. Wren would surely never have espoused the use of the material which would, in the twentieth century, surround and almost obliterate his own great masterpiece, St Paul's Cathedral.

The slightly oriental appearance either explains the origin of the other story which describes the tower's construction − or the tower was indeed built to satisfy Indian rituals. The judge, having spent several years in India, was said to have become obsessed with Hindu

One of the twentieth-century architectural follies — in the older sense of the word: Lord Berner's Folly at Faringdon *(Reece Winstone)*

ideas and Hindu religion. The tower was built, according to this theory, to hold his own body and that of his wife: himself at the top of the tower, his wife in an inferior position at the bottom.

There are many other nineteenth-century towers, but none which displays any particularly outstanding features nor which has anything to offer which we have not already met. That, one might imagine, closes the subject. Not so: there is one last tower to note. It stands alone among a little clump of trees on the edge of Faringdon in Oxfordshire. It is remarkable because of its date, 1935 – not a date when officialdom was casting a notably favourable eye on folly builders. Lord Berner, whose brainchild it was, must have been a man of remarkable perseverance. One can imagine the acres of forms to be filled in, the endless bureaucratic arguments.

'What is the purpose of this building?'

'I want to stand on top of it and look around me.'

Where would that fit into the system? Inevitably, there was an army of objectors, who claimed that a 140ft tower would be a permanent blot on the landscape. They could scarcely object on the grounds of style, for in comparison with its predecessors it is a model of restraint. The tower itself is plain with small rounded arched windows, the whole being topped off with a little pinnacled octagon. There were, however, numerous complaints from those who did not wish to see any tower at all. A retired admiral appeared for the opposition, claiming that the tower would obstruct the view from his house. When the lawyers for Lord Berner attempted to parry his arguments by pointing out that the admiral could only see the tower at all if he looked through a telescope, the admiral expressed himself astonished by the defence argument. Of course, he declared, it was only visible through a telescope, but how else would they expect an admiral to view scenery? The final arbiters were, in those days, the Department of Health, though why they should be involved at all is not clear. They, however, over-ruled the local council who had turned the planning application down, and the tower was built. It has long since been accepted, and there would probably be protests now if anyone tried to pull it down. Prospect towers were, like all follies, generally built out of love – and in time they have won the affections of us all.

# 4

# Not What It Seems

One of the distinctive features of prospect towers is that they frequently appear under disguise – as castles, church spires or the like. There is no special reason why their true function should be hidden in this way, other than the whim of the builder. In other cases, however, the element of disguise had a genuine camouflaging job to perform. The building in question had to be 'dressed up' to make it respectable, to help it to fit into its surroundings. The building was designed, quite deliberately, to look like something other than what it actually was. Many of such buildings were, in fact, part of the workaday world of industry which began to make its presence felt in the land in a major way during the course of the eighteenth century. Some builders said to themselves that they were going to build a factory, an engine house or whatever so why should it not look precisely what it was. Others hoped to ease acceptance of the brash newcomer by dressing it out in the clothes and fashions of its older and more respectable neighbours. Some of these dressed up industrial structures were so convincing that they could well have found a place in one of the previous two chapters.

One of the most prominent landmarks in Halifax, Yorkshire is Wainhouse's Tower, 270ft high, topped off by a colonnade, a balcony and a cupola – instantly recognisable, one might suppose, as a typical nineteenth-century prospect tower. Nineteenth century it certainly is, built in the 1870s. Prospect tower it briefly was – but that is not why it was built. John E. Wainhouse was owner of a local dyeworks, and being more public spirited than many of his neighbours he was determined that he, at least, was not going to add to the level of pollution in the district. He would build the tallest factory chimney for miles around to keep the smoke clear of the town, and so the chimney was duly built and named Wainhouse's Tower. He was not content to

It started life as a factory chimney, has been a prospect tower and now just stands there: Wainhouse's Tower, Halifax *(Metropolitan Borough of Calderdale)*

leave it at that – keeping smoke off the Monday washing. After all, a 270ft factory chimney was going to be a dominant feature in the landscape and might even be less popular than a lower, smokier version, condemned as an eyesore on the fair face of Halifax. So Wainhouse combined the notion of the chimney with that of a prospect tower. The chimney proper was to be built of plain brick, and then the tower was to be built of stone around it. As with so many of the best folly stories, everything went wrong. The chimney was supposed to be connected to the works by an underground flue, but before this was begun the works themselves were sold and the new owner declared that he had no qualms whatsoever about pouring soot over his neighbours' smalls. He declined to include Wainhouse's Tower in the purchase. Wainhouse was left with little option but to continue with the prospect tower plan, and this was duly completed. At least he could now trudge up the steps to view the world at large. Alas, Wainhouse was no giant, and when he got to the top he discovered that the architect had overestimated his employer's stature – the unhappy mill owner was too short to see over the parapet. He now owned a chimney that would never smoke and a prospect tower with no prospect. At least he was able to do something about the latter, for he simply refused to pay the building costs until he was provided with a parapet that he could look over. The tower still stands, arguably the most ornate and certainly the least-used factory chimney in the land.

One can see a certain logic in disguising a factory chimney as a watchtower, and it fits in with our notions about Victorian taste. There is, however, a much more extreme and elaborate form of disguise over in Suffolk which belongs to the twentieth century. In 1910, work was begun on an extraordinary holiday village on a rather bleak and desolate section of the Suffolk coast. Cottages were built around the focal centre of a clubhouse and the whole notion was to make a holiday resort that would appeal to the comparatively well off. It was described in early brochures as the 'Home of Peter Pan' and the islands in the local lake were given the names of Barry characters. The aim was to combine a certain amount of whimsy with modern, practical comfort which, of course, included an adequate supply of running water. A decent head of water to supply the taps was easily

(above) Said to be the smallest pub in Britain – the Smith's Arms, Godmanstone (British Tourist Authority); (right) the iron fountain at Coalbrookdale in Shropshire, built for the Great Exhibition (Anthony Burton)

(overleaf) the Chinese house in the grounds at Shugborough in Staffordshire (National Trust: photo Jeremy Whitaker)

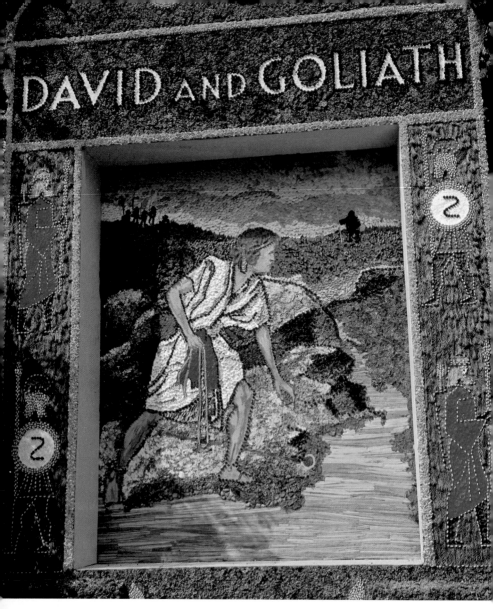

One of the colourfully dressed wells of Derbyshire *(British Tourist Authority)*

provided by the construction of two large water tanks, raised to a suitable height, but here was a problem. How do you fit large iron tanks, raised high on metal frames, into the 'Home of Peter Pan'? The answer was found – in disguise. One water tank was simply hidden away from view by enclosing it within a stone tower which looks like a cross between a church tower and a Norman keep. The second received far more imaginative treatment. The supporting iron frame of the tank was covered by weather boarding, which was then pierced by windows and doors to make a five-storeyed tower. The tank on top overhung this main structure; it was also covered by weather boarding into which windows were let and the whole covered by a pitched roof. The whole thing finished up looking like a giant fungus and was given the name 'House in the Clouds'. And house it was, at least in part, for the lower part was and is habitable; the upper part surrounding the tank remains a fraud, complete with false windows at which can be seen false curtains. It is a genuine curiosity, but then the whole of Thorpeness, as the 'Home of Peter Pan' is more prosaically known, is a happy hunting ground for the curiosity seeker. The boating lake was provided with a sham fort complete with sham guns, not to mention sham concrete crocodiles lurking in the shallows. There is a pleasant conceit at the golf clubhouse, where the four towers are topped by giant tees. Thorpeness can also boast a handsome windmill which the architects restored, arguing quite rightly that a windmill makes a suitably picturesque addition to any scene. Indeed, windmills are now so popular and so widely admired that the notion that they need to be dressed up to be enjoyed strikes us as slightly absurd. It was not always so.

Chesterton Green is a small village in Warwickshire which can boast the country's oddest windmill. Technically, there is nothing odd about it all – it is of the very common type known as a tower mill. This is one in which, as the name suggests, the milling machinery is contained in a stone or brick tower, while the sails are mounted on a cap at the top of the building, which can be rotated to bring the sails into the wind. Chesterton fits that description in all particulars, but what sets it apart from its fellows is the tower. Where other towers sit solidly on the ground, this one is raised on a series of arches. It stands in its hilltop field, sparklingly white on sunny days and visible for miles

Elegance and utility combined: Chesterton windmill — working parts by an unknown millwright, building design by Inigo Jones *(National Monuments Record)*

around. And that explains why it was built to such an ornate design, for it acted both as working mill and eye catcher. It was built as early as 1632 to the design of no less a personage than the great Inigo Jones.

Few, if any, industrial buildings can boast the touch of quite such an eminent architect: most are as anonymous in origin as they are in style. Sometimes, however, the builders have tried to produce a mill or factory that attempts to turn a different face to the world. The easiest way to achieve this is to build a perfectly conventional factory, and then stick on a false front. This was once a comparatively common practice, but not many examples have survived the passage of time and the bulldozer. One that has is the Anglo-Scotian Mill in Beeston, near Nottingham. The mill was devoted to the traditional Nottingham trade of lacemaking, and in this particular case the façade is a good example of nineteenth-century Gothic with lancet windows and castellated towers and parapets. It is not, truth to tell, a particularly convincing performance. It looks well enough when seen absolutely straight on, but viewed at any sort of oblique angle and the false front is seen exactly for what it is.

Bolder mill builders tackled the whole building, sometimes producing something quite exceptional in the process. One of the very finest examples is to be seen just to the west of Chipping Norton in Oxfordshire. Bliss tweed mill was established in the middle of the eighteenth century, but the present amazing building dates from the time when water power was replaced by steam power. The main mill building is really no more than a standard, squared-off block with embellishments. It has four storeys with towers at either end, and the main decoration is a balustrade and cornice at the top of the walls. It looks as if it might be a second-rate country mansion, and if that was all there was to it, then it would scarcely rank as very extraordinary. The mill, however, is more than a building to hold machines, it is also a building to hold a steam engine. Steam engines require boilers and boilers require tall chimneys, both to provide a draught to the furnace and to carry away the smoke. Mill chimneys are a commonplace, and one often sees them rising up at the end of the main building. Here, however, it rises from a dome in the very centre of the building. One can see what the builder had in mind. The mill looks like a country house, country houses often have domes, and if you put the chimney in the dome it does not look quite so tall. Perhaps the whole thing will still look like a country house. The builders were trying a game of pretend with passers by – pretending the thing was not a mill at all. The result does not look especially like a mill, but then it looks even less like a country house. If it does have any associations, then it is rather reminiscent of a giant pepper pot. As a piece of disguise, however, it is a dismal failure, since its curious design – far from aiding it to find a comfortably, anonymous place in the countryside – has produced an object for which the old cliché about sticking out like a sore thumb is all too apposite.

A far more successful piece of disguise can be seen at Coventry, though here disguise was not the objective. The introduction of the power loom, the removal of weaving from the cottage to the factory, aroused violent opposition in the nineteenth century. The hand-loom weavers rioted and their outbursts of machine-breaking recurred throughout the first half of the nineteenth century. One industrialist, Joseph Cash, felt that he understood the problem thoroughly. It was not, he felt, that the workers disliked the factories as such, nor was it the change from being able to work to times of their own setting to working hours dictated by the factory owners that upset them. The problem, Mr Cash decided, lay in their dislike of having to walk from house to factory in the morning, and then back again from factory to house at night. You can see his solution to that problem in Cash's Top Shops, built in 1857. At first, one sees what appears to be a perfectly conventional terrace of Victorian houses, except that they are three stories high and very markedly top heavy. The windows on the top floor are several sizes larger than the rest. In fact, the first two floors do represent a perfectly conventional terrace of houses – but the third floor is Mr Cash's factory. The houses surround a courtyard in which one can still see the ornate mill chimney, but the main work went on at the top of the houses. No need here for weavers to be unhappy about the walk to work. When the whistle blew they simply opened the trapdoors in their ceilings and popped up to the factory – without even getting their boots dirty. What life must have been like in those houses with the machinery thundering overhead one can only guess, but in one sense at least the scheme was a success – Cash's are still at work. The factory above the houses is now only storage space, but down in the courtyard they turn out the Cash's name tapes which identify a million items of school clothing every year.

There is an alternative method of disguising your factory. Instead of turning it into a facsimile of a country house or medieval castle, treat it in such an exotic manner that no one could have the faintest idea what it might be. How about, for example, turning your factory into an ancient Egyptian temple? Early in the nineteenth century, John Marshall established a flax mill in Leeds in which flax was broken up into fibres for manufacturing linen – a mundane enough process. Marshall, however, was a man of vision – and his vision was of the glories of the Nile. So the mill was built in the style to be seen in temples such as that at Tanis, with the façade of massive palm columns. In its working days it must have been an even more extraordinary sight. The building has a flat roof which was covered with soil for insulation, to ensure a constant temperature for the flax processing. Having got the soil up there, it seemed to Marshall to be rather a waste simply to leave it, so he sowed it with grass. Having got the grass there, it seemed equally wasteful simply to let it grow, so he put a flock of sheep up there to graze. The sheep, alas, are gone as is the flax business, but the Egyptian temple remains in the heart of Leeds. A century later, another 'Egyptian' factory appeared, this time in north London – the Carreras cigarette factory. Egyptian cigarettes were in vogue, the company employed a cat motif – a very Egyptian symbol – so what could be more appropriate than an Egyptian-styled factory in Mornington Crescent? It is not as wholehearted in its Egyptianness as is Marshall's mill, but it is pleasant to discover that the same individuality and quirkiness have extended into the modern age.

The great age of the exotic factory undoubtedly came in the nineteenth century, and no factory could be more exotic than the former West Street Cotton Company works, now Templeton Carpet Factory, on Glasgow Green, Glasgow. It can perhaps be most accurately described as a riot in no known style – though the dominant theme might be described as Arabian Nights Fantastic. To describe the building as highly decorated would be a gross understatement. Anything that can be decorated is decorated – in colour. It is such an amalgam of bits and pieces that you would need a short book just to give a description of the façade, but just look, for example, at the staircase tower in one corner. It has simply been turned into a minaret, and one would not be too surprised to hear that the workforce was summoned in the morning not by bells and whistles but by incantations. There is colour everywhere, and not just the multi-coloured bricks popular with the Victorian designers. Tiles are inlaid to simulate mosaics, in brilliant reds and blues. There is an equally colourful mixture of styles – a medieval oriel window stands above a very Arabic arch. The circular tower at one corner is balanced – if that is the right word – by an octagonal tower at the next with a bartizan, a form of turret, in between. It is all remarkably grandiose, and it succeeds magnificently in not looking like a cotton mill. It

Mock Tudor tool-shed in London's Soho Square *(British Tourist Authority)*

succeeds equally well in not looking like any other known building either.

Disguise need not be grandiose to be effective. One very successful example, in a minor key, is the little mock-Tudor building in the middle of Soho Square, London. It is quite charming, adds a pleasant touch to an already pleasant scene yet is nothing grander than a tool shed. It has to be admitted though that the real attention-grabbers are those of the nineteenth century, many of which are very grand indeed. Perhaps the grandest of all such Victorian buildings, taken as a group, are the structures designed to hold the mighty pumping engines of the new water or sewage works. Waterworks can easily be conceived as suitable candidates for civic dignification, but sewage works are not exactly high on every sightseeing list. We tend to think of them as being best kept out of sight − and downwind. This was not the Victorian view. Proper treatment of sewage was a great public good and was to be recognised as such, so they saw nothing in the least incongruous in building their sewage pumping stations to look like cathedrals. Take, for example, Crossness pumping station on the Thames. It was officially opened in 1865 by the Prince of Wales. He might well have mused over the fact that the building with its ornate iron columns and elaborate decoration was considerably grander than many a royal residence. The great steam engines that did the work have long gone from Crossness, though the building itself still stands.

To see the sewage pumping station in its true splendour, one should go to Leicester. Abbey Mills Pumping Station is typical of the pride shown by the Victorians in their civic achievements. From the outside it could, at a pinch, be mistaken for the town hall, though the tall chimney is something of a give-away. This seems reasonable enough – putting on a bold, outward-looking face to impress the ratepayers, but the Victorians did not stop there. The interior is equally, if not even more, elaborate. The main structural supports consist of vast iron columns, with fluted decoration to both base and capital. The walls are brightly tiled and the engines themselves are a delight; gleaming brass everywhere with highly polished wood surrounding the cylinders. but who was there to see all this grandeur? Who was there to impress? Perhaps the most delightful feature of the building is that this whole interior was kept in immaculate condition, yet was only seen by the very few who worked here. There was no practical necessity for such elaboration, but what a satisfaction to the designers to know it was there – no dirty neck beneath the clean collar. The pumping station is preserved as part of the Leicester Industrial Museum, and in the boiler house is a collection which includes a vehicle which might seem to have very little to do with the rest of the building. It is a hearse. Yet there is a very real connection between this and the building which houses it. We tend to be rather ashamed and embarrassed by some topics today. We talk openly about sex, but only snigger over something as useful as sewage disposal and prefer not to mention death at all. Sewage works and funerals are no longer suitable subjects for conversation. The Victorians treated both with pomp and, it must be admitted, on occasions pomposity.

Abbey Mills, however, is comparatively plain when set against some of the magnificent water pumping stations. Here are two: the first is chosen for its amazing exterior, the second for its even more astonishing interior. Exterior first: Ryhope pumping station was built by the Sunderland and South Shields Water Company to house two vast beam engines built by Hawthorn's of Newcastle in 1868. The station comes in three parts: chimney, boiler house and engine house. The tall chimney stands on its own, rising from a square base, and could easily be mistaken for a memorial. Indeed, if the rest of the buildings were knocked down − which heaven forbid − it would no doubt be generally assumed to be just that. Next to the stack is the boiler house, and here the essential style of Ryhope appears. The dominating features are the shaped gables, ending in little pinnacles, giving the building a distinctly Jacobean flavour. The mood is reinforced in the main structure, the engine house, which really could pass itself off as a Jacobean house, and one of considerable character at that. Where somewhere like the Templeton Carpet Factory impresses by its idiosyncrasies, here there is an overall and convincing unity of style. What makes it nevertheless seem slightly odd is the fact that the style has so little to do with the contents. Why should nineteenth-century pumping engines be given a pseudo-seventeenth-century setting? That is what they have and that is what they will continue to have, for Ryhope and its engines are being preserved.

Papplewick pumping station, near Nottingham, has an exterior which almost rivals that at Ryhope − and an interior which far surpasses it. Archaeologists coming upon the site in the year 3000 might well decide that nineteenth-century man worshipped the machine, and they could be right. Certainly Papplewick has an aura of devotion around it, a temple dedicated to the gods of steam. The great supporting pillars which both help to hold up the building and provide a frame for the engines are the first things to catch the visitors' attention as they push open the huge wooden doors of the engine house. Looking up to the capitals, one sees magnificent gilded ibises and a relief of water lilies. The columns too are richly decorated with figures depicting suitably watery themes: lacquered brass plants entwine their way upwards, while an assortment of fishes swim in amongst them. Waterfalls, rushes and reeds all appear and the same motif is continued in the windows. These have stained-glass insets, each one different and showing some water plant or creature. Until recently, when it was opened to the public, the lovely engine house must have had few visitors. All this splendour, so lovingly cared for, was seen by no more than a handful of water board employees. It represents a splendid example of Victorian self-confidence. The builders were quite certain that they were building for posterity, and so they gave of their very best.

The desire to embellish the practical, to declare to the world that you were producing something of lasting importance, was very strong amongst those who worked to improve transport in the eighteenth and nineteenth centuries. It is a very human, and on the whole rather commendable, characteristic – and has often resulted in purely functional structures having a charm they might otherwise lack. It has also, it must be admitted, sometimes led to otherwise honest, straight-forward structures being deluged with badly applied decoration. We shall try and keep away from the latter, and look at the more pleasing and successful examples. Take for example such a simple building as the toll house or toll booth. From the late seventeenth century onwards, road improvement was paid for by travellers paying tolls, and each road had a number of little houses where the money was collected. All that strict practicality required was that the collector should have shelter and accommodation, and an office for his business. Many road builders argued, however, that as such buildings were an essential part of the whole project, they should reflect the project's importance. So we find different road authorities vying with each other in the production of suitably dignified or exotic toll houses.

The first essential for a toll house is that the collector inside it should have a good view of the travellers outside it: he should have a fly-like ability to look in all directions simultaneously, or at least get as close to that ideal as possible. Toll houses usually stand at or near junctions, so the collector had to peer down every avenue to make sure nobody slipped past with dues unpaid. To ease his task, the builders of toll houses produced a splendid variety of multi-angled buildings, with windows facing in all directions. They therefore start out as buildings on a somewhat unorthodox plan, often hexagonal, sometimes circular. They often have apparently illogical details, such as a blank window above the main door. It is actually not a window space, but the spot where the notice board was placed, informing travellers of the different charges they could expect to pay. The toll house at the end of

Castellated toll-house near Devizes, photographed when tolls were still being collected, circa 1860 *(Reece Winstone)*

the famous iron bridge from which the town in Shropshire gets its name, records the slightly bizarre information that if you travel in a horse-drawn carriage it will cost you the same money whether you are alive or dead: travel for a live body in a chaise being two shillings, as is that for a dead body in a hearse. Livelier individuals able to cross on their own feet went a good deal cheaper. Such toll houses are common enough, but only a few have that extra ingredient of oddity that might turn the head of the passing motorist.

An excellent example can be seen on the outskirts of Devizes, at the junction of the Chippenham and Trowbridge roads. It may have been built merely for toll collection, but it seems ready to withstand siege from an army of highwaymen and footpads. It is a massive stone structure with heavy battlements on top. It came to be known locally as Shane's Castle, though no one any longer remembers who Shane was.

Occasionally, the case for castellating everything in sight can seem obvious. When Thomas Telford came to build the Conwy suspension bridge, its close proximity to Conwy Castle made it virtually certain that the supporting towers should have their full complement of

A style to match the situation: Telford's suspension bridge at Conwy *(British Tourist Authority)*

battlements and arrow slits and that the accompanying toll house should be in the same military vein. Telford had a strong liking for the Gothic and for the application of medieval defences to the most modern structures of the day. He was particularly fond of applying such styles in Scotland, where he felt they were especially appropriate. It certainly fits well with the stone bridges, such as the one across the Dee at Tongland, but when you get a thoroughly modern iron bridge across the Spey at Craigellachie in Grampian, it does begin to look a little odd. The stone towers with arrow slits might convince us that they were put there to defend a stone bridge against attack. At Tongland one can just about accept the notion of armed knights galloping across in full armour – but over an iron bridge? There the effort becomes too much, and in any case the illusion is quite destroyed by a prominent cast-iron plaque set on one of the towers and carrying the message 'Cast at Plas Kynaston, Ruabon, Denbighshire, 1814'. One can scarcely get more prosaic than that.

This habit of castellation spread from the roads to the transport newcomers of the eighteenth century – the canals – though it was never widely popular. There is a pleasant little lock cottage at Camden Town on the Regent's Canal in London but, as with the roads, it was Telford who produced the most extravagant piece of Gothicry. The Engine Arm Aqueduct carries a short arm of the Birmingham Canal across the main line; it was quite an oddity in its own right in the early days of canal building when the very idea of one boat sailing over another boat seemed quite extraordinary. In the case of the Engine Arm Aqueduct, however, the novelty had worn off, for aqueducts were common by the time it was built. It is its style that earns it a special place in the catalogue of strangeness. It was built of cast iron, then the most modern building material available, yet the style looks back hundreds of years. The arch is built up of an elaborate tracery of smaller, pointed arches, giving the whole a distinctly ecclesiastical look.

The world of the canals is not much given to extravagant gestures: plainness and simplicity were more the key notes. Nevertheless some quite remarkable features did appear, of which quite the most remarkable in appearance is the Anderton lift. The very idea of such a device is in itself extraordinary. Boats float into large water-filled

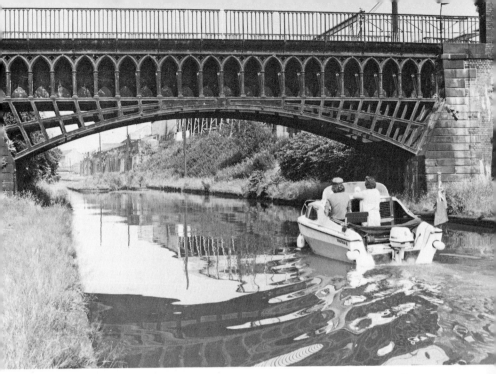

Gothic arches and an iron aqueduct make a strange combination on the Birmingham Canal *(Derek Pratt)*

tanks, which can be raised and lowered, the idea being to join the Trent and Mersey Canal at the top of the hill at Anderton with the River Weaver down below. To lift this huge tank of water, complete with boat, would be very hard work indeed unless the whole thing was counterbalanced as in an ordinary lift in a tall building. As the tank goes up, so a weight goes down and vice versa. But in this case, one weight was insufficient, so a whole series of heavy weights were hung all round the frame of the lift, giving it a decidedly Heath Robinson air.

Tunnels are not, one would imagine, either very odd or very exciting things, but the canal system can boast one splendid exception in Dudley Tunnel. Where most tunnels are no more than holes going in one side of a hill and coming out the other, Dudley is a labyrinth, for it connected up a series of underground workings where limestone was quarried. The tiny main tunnel opens out into great basins and there are underground watery crossroads, of which the most spectacular has a vaulted roof, known very appropriately as Cathedral

Not a construction site but a finished lock. Modern boaters wisely prefer the old lock to the vast steel locks at Thurlwood *(Derek Pratt)*; *(opposite)* the Heath-Robinson-like boat-lift at Anderton *(Derek Pratt)*

Arch. And at one of these wide sections — not unlike one of those grottoes manufactured by eighteenth-century gardeners — one can, on special days, go in by boat to watch a theatre performance. A disused limestone working under Dudley Hill, with the only access by canal boat, must surely rank as the country's oddest theatre.

The twentieth century has produced its own strange transformations on the canal scene. At Thurlwood on the Trent and Mersey Canal, two locks sit side by side. Subsidence from mining caused fears that the lock sides would fall in, so engineers decided to build a lock that would not collapse — and there it sits, a hugely elephantine grey box of steel, closed off at either end by steel gates that drop like guillotine blades. The irony is that the steel box was so big and strong, it stabilised the lock walls of the traditional lock next to it

Spaghetti Junction becomes a concrete forest when seen from the old canal *(Derek Pratt)*

– and the new wonder of modern technology never gets used at all. It just sits there, not so much the grey elephant as the white elephant of the waterways.

Other modern developments that have changed the appearance of canals have usually not come from inside the canal world at all, yet some of these developments have had the effect of transforming what was a perfectly plain, conventional little canal into something altogether strange. Take, for example, the Gravelly Hill interchange on the M6 motorway, better known as Spaghetti Junction. In itself it is a remarkable piece of civil engineering, and can be quite bewildering for anyone trying to thread a way through it. In a car, however, you can never quite catch the whole complexity of the structure. This becomes immediately apparent if you see it from the air – or from the canal, for the old canal runs right through the junction. The concrete pillars stand on either side and even in the middle of the canal, while the roadways swoop in giant curves overhead. What one of the boatmen who first used the canal two centuries ago would think of this concrete maze if he could see it one cannot imagine.

An even more remarkable transformation has been effected in Manchester. Here the Rochdale Canal plunges through the heart of the city and was, in its day, one of the major transport routes to serve the growing industries of Lancashire. That role has long since ended, and now the canal is usually thought of as a nuisance to planners who have to fit in their new building schemes. What do you do if you have a prime site for a new office block just off Piccadilly, but there right in the middle is this wretched little canal and one of those inconvenient locks? The answer is – build over it. Few people up in the busy streets are aware of the canal's existence, but those who travel by water are very aware of the presence of the office block, for they are presented with the daunting sight of their canal disappearing underneath it. There, in among the foundations, is the lock, and the boat crews must fumble around in the dark while typewriters clatter somewhere over their heads.

If the canal engineers and architects had, on the whole, opted for simplicity of style, then the same could not be said of their successors on the railways. When it came to building a new station for city, town or village every architectural style known to man was investigated, and most tried. We have stations like castles and stations that are doing their best to pass themselves off as stately homes; there are stations like cottages and stations like cathedrals. In the ranks of the mock medievals, few carry the style through more convincingly than the little station at Battle in East Sussex. Outside, there are the predictable trappings, such as thin lancet windows, but what is more surprising is the interior, with a waiting room like a baronial hall boasting a beamed roof and hooded fireplace. A train of knights might as easily appear beside the platform as the 3.15 from Tunbridge Wells. Stoke-on-Trent on the other hand preferred its hurrying passengers to believe that they were going to a Jacobean house party – though today's travellers, once they get behind the ornate façade, will find the station itself transformed into just another set of British Rail tearooms and echoing platforms. Façades such as Stoke's are all too commonly fronts disguising a duller reality – duller nowadays than the original builders intended. The hand of conformity has fallen heavily on the glorious individualism that characterised the earlier buildings.

Old station buildings had a message to convey to travellers, 'an image' in modern jargon. They might be homely cottages, such as that at Fenny Stratford in Buckinghamshire with its elaborate half-timbering, where the message for the would-be traveller was: 'Don't be frightened by these new fangled engines – Look here where you start off in a nice, comfy little house, just like your own home.' Alternatively, a station such as Monkwearmouth, Tyne and Wear, in the Greek revival style with porticoed entrance, wants you to know that you are in the presence of something gentlemanly and imposing. Different styles, different messages, but both are buildings of character. It is sad to see the indignities that even the finest of such structures have suffered in recent times. Look, for example, at the splendid mock medieval of Temple Meads station in Bristol. Its old train shed has a wonderful roof that might have graced a grand hall or an Oxbridge college library: today the hammer beams preside over ranks of parked cars. It is ending its days as a car park.

We all probably have our favourite examples of quirky railway architecture, but if popularity was to be decided by vote then there is little doubt what would come out on top – St Pancras. Most passers-by tend to think of the pinnacled and towered building, with its spires and shaped gables, as the main station building. It is, in fact, the Midland Grand Station Hotel, designed by George Gilbert Scott. The popular story has it that Scott originally intended the design to be used for the new Houses of Parliament, and when that idea came to nothing he simply shifted the design down the road to St Pancras. It is a charming notion that Parliament and a station hotel are in some ways interchangeable, but alas there is no truth in the tale.

All over Britain you will find these strange quirks in station build-ings, and other bits of railways came in for similar treatment. The engineers often followed the example of the road engineers when it

*(opposite)* An exception to prove the rule that canal bridges are always purely functional: a footbridge across the Birmingham and Fazeley Canal *(Derek Pratt)*

St Pancras, the ultimate in Victorian railway Gothic *(British Tourist Authority)*

came to elaborating on bridges. When Robert Stephenson came to build his railway bridge next to Telford's road bridge at Conwy, he too opted for a suitably castle-like entrance to the bridge − though the bridge itself with the rails carried within vast hollow tubes is as far in feeling from the medieval as it is possible to get. Other sites with castles in the vicinity led to a profusion of mock-medieval detailing being stuck on to otherwise conventional viaducts. One of the best-known, and most attractive, examples has graced a thousand calendars − the viaduct across the Nidd at Knaresborough in Yorkshire. It is actually the second Nidd viaduct, the first having fallen down, blocking the river so that locals were picking up fish on their front doorsteps for days.

The same love for the grandiose effect was to be seen in tunnel entrances. Two notable examples of castellated entrances are at the north end of Clayton tunnel on the London to Brighton line, and at the northern end of Bramhope tunnel outside Leeds. At one side of the latter is a three-storeyed circular tower. This was no mere embellishment; it was the tunnel-keeper's house. Here, in this lonely spot, he guarded the entrance, controlling traffic through the tunnel in the days before efficient signalling systems made his job superfluous. His was not only a lonely life, but must also have been hopelessly inconvenient in the narrow, circular house, built not with the occupant's convenience in mind but with a view to making an imposing effect in the landscape. In the one structure, Bramhope tunnel manages to combine the pleasing incongruity of the medieval-style railway tunnel with one of the country's odder houses. We have not yet reached the end of the list of oddities concerned with Bramhope tunnel, but the last oddity must wait for a later chapter.

The industrial world of today produces few curiosities to compare with those of a century or more ago. Factories tend to look just like factories, and no one has suggested a mock Tudor airport terminal. But if we step back from the industrial scene, we can find another group of old buildings which are not so much disguised to look like something else but rather designed to look like nothing else at all. They are indeed so peculiar in appearance that if one did not know the answer in advance, one would be hard put to it to work out what possible function they could serve. In the village of Wheatley in Oxfordshire there is a small stone pyramid by the roadside. It might be a minute folly, but folly builders seldom favoured the small scale. It might be a monument, but there is no sign of plaque or inscription. There is, however, a small door, so obviously it was designed to hold someone or something. But what or whom? The answer can perhaps be deduced from the name of the adjoining road – Pound Way – for this uncomfortable, dark little building was the village pound or lockup. Here the local drunk was deposited on Saturday night to sober up for Sunday morning, and here the poacher, unlucky enough to be caught with an illegally obtained rabbit, awaited his interview with the

(above) Not a folly but a grimly practical building – the Wheatley lockup provided the night's resting place for the local drunks *(Reece Winstone)*; *(opposite)* Shenley lockup, beside the village ducking-pond *(BBC Hulton Picture Library)*

An unwelcome sight to drunken sailors: Barmouth lockup *(Reece Winstone)*

magistrate. There are similar lockups all over the country, and all have similar characteristics. They are dark, airless, uncomfortable places, but they are often built in rather curious shapes.

At Shenley in Hertfordshire, the lockup is unusual in that it actually contains windows, though they are small enough in all conscience and heavily barred. Its shape is rather like a beehive, and admission is through a doorway with a pointed arch. The prisoner, brooding either over the heinous nature of his crimes or his misfortune in being caught, has suitable inscriptions to consider on every hand. 'Do well' and 'Fear not' they exhort, while others entreat the reader to 'Be Sober' and 'Be Vigilant'. Such inscriptions clearly come too late for the prisoner, but as they are on the outside of the building anyway they were presumably intended to keep the rest of the population out of the lockup rather than reform those already inside.

A combination lockup and beacon at Walsingham *(BBC Hulton Picture Library)*

The majority of lockups are what one would now describe as unisex, in that all offenders were simply shoved inside the single cell. Not so that at Barmouth in Gwynedd. The round lockup by the harbour had its busiest time when sailors returned from their voyages and celebrated in style and preferably in company. The company, it seems, frequently finished up as drunk and unruly as the sailors, so the lockup has a division inside and two separate doors, though it says something for the behaviour of the women in that their portion is smaller than that set aside for the men.

One authority decided that it was a waste of a perfectly good building merely to use it as a lockup. At Walsingham in Norfolk, the lockup also housed a conduit and a stone pillar rises up from the roof, which was topped with a basket and served as the village beacon.

One of the oddest lockups is perched on the bridge across the river at Bradford-on-Avon. The bridge itself dates back to the fourteenth

The old lockup on the bridge at Bradford on Avon *(British Tourist Authority)*

century and the little building was originally used as a chapel at which travellers could pray for a safe journey. By the seventeenth century it was generally agreed that roads were then safe enough for men to move around the country without divine protection – or alternatively, they might have decided that safety was more effectively provided by locking up known malefactors. So the chapel became the lockup.

The lockups were known by a variety of different names – cage, lockup, pound, round house and so on, but they were without exception exceedingly uncomfortable places in which to stay. Now that they are no longer in use, however, the grim aspect has been forgotten and we are left with an array of pyramids and cones and other funny little buildings whose stones have mellowed with time. Today these miniature prisons seem decidedly strange, yet they are no stranger than many of the houses built by honest men as their own homes.

# 5

# A Home of Distinction

The phrase 'a home of distinction' has become a commonplace in the jargon of estate agents, who use it to try and indicate that a suburban villa falls only marginally short of classification as a stately home. If, however, one thinks of the word 'distinction' as indicating the possession of a distinctive character rather than membership of a distinguished élite, then it must be said that Britain is full of distinguished homes. Nowhere can you find such a rich variety of styles, nor such a mixture of building materials, as one can in the comparatively small compass of the British Isles. We are not talking about the grand and the stately but of the vernacular architecture of the country. It is only quite recently that such buildings have received very much attention at all and indeed the very word 'architecture' was limited to those buildings designed by an architect or master builder. Vernacular architecture was therefore not only unregarded but, within these terms of reference, an impossibility. Vernacular buildings were, at best, quaint, a picturesque element within a picturesque landscape. As we shall see later, some architects set out to produce their own version of vernacular in order to create just such a picturesque effect. The country cottage, the farmhouse, the workers' home: each category conjured up a particular image – a thatched roof glimpsed over a garden of hollyhocks, a low stone building surrounding a yard full of cows, long dreary terraces. Yet to think in such stereotypes is to close your mind and your eyes to one of Britain's greatest glories – the astonishing richness and variety of just such apparently ordinary buildings. It is this complexity that is itself astonishing.

The diversity is no longer quite what it was. The Industrial Revolution used cheap transport to bring materials such as brick and slate to all parts of the country, so that there has been a gradual blurring of regional differences. This has perhaps been most marked in towns and cities: in the country the differences can more readily be seen. And these differences extend to every aspect of building. What greater contrast could there be than that between the slate roof of North Wales and the reed thatch of Suffolk or the stone walls of the Pennines and the tile-hung walls of Kent. And the differences extend beyond building materials to the basic patterns of building. Travel through Scotland and you are at once struck by the great numbers of single-storeyed buildings, extended occasionally to two floors by attics and dormer windows in the roofs. They are as distinctive in their way as the long terraces marching up the hillsides around the collieries of South Wales. Perhaps we natives tend to take all this diversity for granted, but visitors to these islands are invariably astonished by it and often wonder how it comes about that such a small country can display such diversity.

The answer is to be found in the underlying geology of the land. In the days when transport was both difficult and inordinately expensive, builders had to make do with what was near at hand. If you lived in stone country, then you used the local stone – whether the grey granite of eastern Scotland or the honey-coloured Bath stone of south-west England. Other areas turned to timber or brick burned from local clays, to flint or cobble. Different materials demanded different building techniques and so each locale developed its own peculiarities, as distinctive as the local accent. Against this background of astonishing variety, to find any house at all that could be called odd or strange might seem unlikely. Yet there have always been those who were not content even with this varied scene. They wanted something quite different from their neighbours, and they often went to considerable lengths to get it. There were, and are, individualists.

My own childhood was spent in Yorkshire, and each day I travelled three miles to school in Knaresborough. The school devised an annual torture for its male pupils in the form of a compulsory cross-country run which involved running, stepping, staggering or walking, depending on personal fitness and inclination, up the steps that led from the path by the River Nidd to the top of the cliffs that dominate the northern bank. The less energetic among us had a chance to ponder the work of one Thomas Hill, who some two centuries before had expended even more energy on those same cliffs than had we, the unwilling schoolboy athletes. Thomas Hill decided to make himself a house not on the cliff, but in it. In 1770 he began the long task of carving his dwelling out of the rock face. This was no troglodyte cave, but a proper home, multi-storeyed and many-roomed. It took Hill sixteen years to complete, during which time he continued to earn his living as a weaver. His extraordinary house soon attracted a good deal of attention and a great many visitors, including the Duchess of Buccleuch, in whose honour he renamed the house Fort Montagu. The locals tended, as is the nature of Yorkshire folk, to mock such pretensions and took to referring to the owner as Sir Thomas Hill. But Hill himself was not to be that easily put down, and went one better by adopting the title 'Governor of Fort Montagu'. He even issued his own currency in the form of a tuppence ha'penny note, suspiciously similar in design to a conventional fiver. In the fulness of time, Hill died. His banknotes vanished, but the house he had hacked from the rock has survived to fascinate generations of visitors to the quiet market town on the Nidd. It might, of course, simply have crumbled away, but Knaresborough became established as a tourist attraction as a result of two other local curiosities – both well worth a diversion.

The best-known inhabitant of the town, apart from Guy Fawkes who spent some time there plotting ways to circumvent the current electoral system by producing his own version of the dissolution of Parliament, was Mother Shipton. That lady also lived in a cliff dwelling, though neither as comfortable nor as elaborate as that of Thomas Hill. It was a cave, and a well-worn rock is shown to visitors as the Mother Shipton bed. In this case, however, it is not the home that is so interesting as the lady who inhabited it. During her lifetime she made several prophecies, many of which later proved accurate – man would sail in iron ships, fly in the air and so forth. More alarmingly, she also predicted the end of the world, and if her prognostications prove as accurate in this as in other fields, then the calamity is due any day now.

The second curiosity once seemed as magical as Mother Shipton's prophecies. The Dropping Well is a petrifying well. Objects suspended in the water appear to turn to stone. In fact, they are coated with a calcite deposit which solidifies around objects hung in the

This house in Conwy is said to be the smallest in Britain, and certainly looks a likely candidate *(Reece Winstone)*

Another tiny house built into the cliffs at Porthcurno *(Reece Winstone)*

The unique Minack Theatre, hewn out of the cliffs at Porthcurno *(British Tourist Authority)*

drips. Visitors come along and leave a remarkable collection of things at the well, which eventually form into stone gloves, hats, teddy bears and the like.

Perhaps it was the existence of Mother Shipton's cave in the rocks and the nearby petrifying well that set Hill on to thinking of similar stony themes and decided him to carve his home in the cliff. Equally it might have been just one more example of what was a general tendency for some people to find the most laborious and quirky method possible for house construction. Another example of a house in a cliff can be seen in the Rock Cottage at Wolverley in Worcestershire, which also claims to be one of the smallest houses in the country. The claim of being the smallest might be disputed for there is a strong contender in the restricted shape of 10 Lower Street, Conwy. The house has a total frontage of a mere 6ft, is 8ft 4in high and just over 10ft deep. It has two rooms, one above the other, and was lived in until 1900, though there is something of a mystery as to how its last inhabitant survived his tenure, for he was 6ft 3in tall. Another contender for both titles of smallest and most unusual rock dwelling can be seen carved out of the cliffs at Porthcurno in Cornwall.

Cornwall is a very happy hunting ground for the searcher-out of oddities and curiosities. Porthcurno itself boasts another oddity, for it possesses what appears to be an ancient Greek theatre. It is set half way down the cliffs and is built in the traditional Greek pattern, with tiers of seats rising up in a half-circle from the stage, which itself has been created in a natural dip in the cliffs. The stage area is flat with a spectacular backdrop – literally in this case – for there is a steep fall down to the sea which beats a regular accompaniment at the bottom of the cliffs to whatever is being played up above. It is a magical theatre, but quite modern, largely the work of Miss Rowena Cade whose brainchild the theatre was. As anyone who has played at the Minack Theatre can testify, it combines the unique atmosphere of an open-air theatre with superb acoustics.

However, to return to the theme of this chapter, Cornwall is also an area rich in odd houses. Think of Cornwall and you probably think first of the sea and the little fishing villages and then of the mining industry which has left the landscape littered with the ruins of

House on props, Polperro
*(Reece Winstone)*

hundreds of engine houses. These buildings, soundly constructed to withstand the pounding of the great steam engines they once housed, have often appealed to enterprising individuals looking for a home with a difference. One of the best examples can be seen on the other side of the county from Porthcurno, at the north coast village of Porthtowan. In fact, the effect is not dissimilar from that created by the former's house in the rocks, for the engine house stands on the beach, hard against the cliff wall. One can see the attractions of converting it into a seaside retreat, but the man must have been something of a recluse who chose to convert the engine house of the South Phoenix mine high up on Bodmin Moor, between the village of Minions and the Cheesewring.

The Duchy can boast other strange houses. At Polperro, there is the so-called 'House on Props'. It is just that − a house built out on supports above the waters of the River Pol. It may look strange, but the props do have a function − they raise the house above the flood levels.

There is no such obvious factor that governs the buildings at Veryan, a little further to the west. Here is not just one odd building, but a whole collection of them: the Round Houses of Veryan. The village of Veryan would attract attention without the round houses, for it is one of those pleasing little places, full of narrow undulating streets that are such a feature of the south-west. The houses are, however, unique. They are not all strictly round: some are hexagonal, though the corners are rounded to give an impression of circularity, an impression heightened by the conical roofs. Taken individually, they are curious buildings, with oddly shaped windows and doors, the shape often picked out in pebbles and shells; in each case the conical roof is topped with a cross. They become even odder when seen as a group, each one slightly different from its neighbour yet all fitting into the same general pattern. They are spread out around the edges of the village, and no one knows exactly why or when they were built. There is, however, agreement on one point: they were intended to thwart the Devil in his evil designs on the good citizens of Veryan.

The strange round houses at Veryan, designed to keep the Devil at bay *(British Tourist Authority)*

There are two main theories as to how these odd little houses would thwart diabolical schemings. The first rests on the well-established view that the Devil, ever on the look-out for souls to pull down to the nether regions, spends a good deal of his time lurking in dark corners. It follows then that a house with no corners of any description, dark or light, would provide no suitable lodging place. Surround the village with such houses, and Old Nick would soon become discouraged and slope off to look for more congenial surroundings. In version two, the Devil comes to the village and is confronted with a house topped by a cross, which keeps him away. He then moves off to be faced by more of the same, all identical, which causes a great deal of confusion in the Satanic mind. Discouraged by all this, he again gives up and goes away to find a less well-protected village. The citizens of Veryan could sleep easy in their beds, untroubled either by the Devil or the thought of what evils he might be perpetrating down the road.

Quite the most bizarre house in Cornwall is to be found in Penzance. Like Marshall's flax mill in Leeds it was built in the Egyptian style which enjoyed a brief flourish of popularity after Napoleon's Egyptian campaign at the very end of the eighteenth century. It could easily have turned up in a different section of this book, for it was not originally intended as a dwelling. It was to be a museum and geological storehouse, for the beaches of the area were and are full of fascinating pebbles, stones and crystals. The style certainly gives no idea of the possible use, for it is Egyptian at its most flamboyant − not to say absurd. The doorway is flanked by lotus columns and above are two sphinx-like ladies, staring out at the world. Above them is a rather more domestic motif in the shape of the lion and the unicorn. Apart from this oddly British note, the rest of the façade is extravagantly Egyptian and colourfully so at that, for it has been restored to its full polychrome glory by an organisation that specialises in such work, the Landmark Trust. They not only renovated the building, but they put it to use as a holiday home, so that now, at least, one can say that the Egyptian House is indeed a home of distinction.

(opposite) The Egyptian House, Penzance (Landmark Trust: photo T. A. Dulake)

*(left)* Once an engine-house, now a holiday home: Danescombe Mine in the Tamar Valley *(W. Proctor: supplied by Landmark Trust)*; *(right)* a place to play out your fantasies: Fort Clonque on Alderney is now a holiday home *(Landmark Trust)*

The Landmark Trust are, in fact, responsible for a number of Britain's most remarkable houses. For example, they have converted a Cornish engine house in the Tamar valley, and made a magnificent job of it as well. That is just the beginning. Holidaymakers can live out their fantasies in some fascinating surroundings. Would you care to defend Britain against the French and other benighted foreigners? Then you can stay in the massive fortification built on Alderney in 1842, Fort Clonque, or − more modestly − in a martello tower near Aldeburgh in Suffolk. This is just one of the chain of towers built to help keep Napoleon at bay, and the Landmark Trust are by no means the first to hit on the notion of transforming them into homes. The best-known converted tower is the one just outside Dublin, which was briefly occupied by James Joyce and which he used as the setting for

the beginning of *Ulysses*. If you prefer playing trains to playing stations, then there is Alton Station in Staffordshire, though this is also something of a curiosity in its own right. It was built for the much-loved 'Knotty' railway, the North Staffordshire, but unlike their other stations – which tended to be Jacobean or Tudor in style – Alton is a rather grand Italianate. Perhaps its somewhat exotic appearance was intended to help it fit in with the even more exotic architecture of nearby Alton Towers. The great thing about such conversions is that people clearly love the idea of staying in forts, stations and the like, and many others have found that similar buildings make splendidly characterful, permanent homes. Railway stations are particularly popular, and a few deserve special mention for the owners' ingenuity in finding an appropriate name. In Yorkshire, you will find Booking Hall, while in Devon, a conversion has been named (no doubt with feeling) Beeching's Folly, in honour of the doctor of that ilk whose axe lopped off so many railway branches in the 1960s.

(above) Alton Station was designed in the style of an Italian Renaissance house, and now actually is a house (Landmark Trust); (below) another castle as house, but this time merely a fine façade to an otherwise conventional building: Clytha Castle near Abergavenny (John Evetts: supplied by Landmark Trust); (opposite) exotic fruit making an exotic house: the Pineapple at Dunmore Park (British Tourist Authority)

The Landmark Trust, in their role as keepers and preservers of buildings of historic interest, also take on buildings which are themselves particularly strange. They own a splendid mock castle – Clytha Castle, near Abergavenny – but the strangest of their collection is to be found at Dunmore in Central (Scotland). It was not originally a house as such, but rather a two-storey summer house: it is remarkable because its form is that of a giant pineapple. At ground-floor level it is conventional enough, built in the Gothic revival style, with tracery windows topped with ogee arches. Above that, however, the style is pure pineapple, a succulent fruit realised in beautifully carved stone. It was built for the Earl of Dunmore in 1761, a time when the pineapple was an exotic novelty. The craftsmanship is superb, and were it not for the size one could easily imagine having it for lunch.

Not all conversions are conversions into houses. At Chipping Norton in Oxfordshire, the old Salvation Army Citadel fell into disuse and was taken over and transformed into the little theatre. 'Little' is certainly the operative word, for it has a little auditorium and a tiny stage. Nevertheless the author has seen a performance of *Don Giovanni* here, and very successful it was – even with an orchestra of one. The original inhabitants might just about have tolerated Mozart – the opera is after all highly moral, with the wicked Don disappearing down into flames at the end – but what would they have thought of the bar and the sale of liquor? No doubt they would do as their successors do – smile bravely and march in to sell *The Warcry*.

One way to ensure that you have a home of distinction is to disguise it as something else. At Tattingstone in Suffolk there stands a building which has every appearance of being the parish church. It has a tower, lancet windows and – final and most convincing touch – a rose window. Yet all this is no more than a façade, behind which lurks a humble cottage. This is no conversion, but a deliberate attempt to disguise a cottage as a church. Vicarages often, and not surprisingly, have an almost equally strong ecclesiastical flavour, but their builders seldom go to the lengths of the designer of the Harrington vicarage in Northamptonshire. Not content with the conventional chimney that tops the conventional house, he designed one that looks exactly like a miniature church steeple. The smoke does not come out at the top, but

Disguise revealed: a plain farmhouse hides behind the fake church tower at Tattingstone (*A. Rumsey: supplied by National Monuments Record*)

escapes through holes concealed in the side of the 'steeple'. It is not always clear why people should want to hide their cottages behind churchish façades or go in for other elaborate disguises, but in the case of some apparently strange buildings there is an explanation readily available.

Throughout Britain, one can find villages which are, in effect, part of the estate of the great house. In such cases, the landowners considered it quite proper to mould the villages and design the houses in whatever style and pattern seemed appropriate. Often this produced no more than dull, regimented rows of cottages, standing guard on either side of the main road. Occasionally, however, the landowner had decidedly quirky notions about how such a new village should appear. The villagers had, at best, only a slight say in the matter, and had to make do with what they were given, no matter how bizarre.

Marford in Clwyd was a typical village of little cottages, scattered around the main road from Chester to Wrexham. Then, in 1805, George Boscawen set about modelling the whole village to suit his taste, and eleven years later the work was complete. Gone were the low-walled, thatched cottages scattered higgledy-piggledy; in their place came the new, on a neat and formal plan. Neatness and formality, however, begin and end with the overall plan, for the houses themselves are disorderly in the extreme. No two cottages are alike, and each is more than a little strange. They conform to no known style, though they could be classified as rural picturesque with Gothic overtones. Roofs are tile instead of thatch, but have been given built-in instant ageing by the architect, who designed them with curving ridges to imitate the sagging roofs of older buildings. Walls also curve, in regular undulation. Windows come in all shapes and sizes – rounds, ovals, extravagant ogees, lancet – everything it seems except the common rectangle. Add to this bits of Gothic detailing stuck on almost randomly and you have the Marford cottage. And all this seems to be not merely the brainchild of Boscawen the landowner but actually to be the work of Boscawen, amateur architect extraordinary.

Some village planners only showed their idiosyncrasy in the odd building rather than the whole village. A fine example can be seen in the village of Ripley in North Yorkshire, alongside Ripley Castle, the seat of the Ingilby family. William Ingilby was Lord of the Manor during the early years of the nineteenth century and in the 1820s he set about rebuilding Ripley as a model village. Houses were arranged in neat terraces and built of the dark, local stone which gives such a distinctive character to this part of the country. They have the almost compulsory hint of Gothic, but are otherwise pleasantly unremarkable. Ingilby, however, was an ardent admirer of things continental. The family home had been plain Ripley Castle since the middle of the fourteenth century, but to this member of the family it was 'The Schloss'. He dreamed of bringing European style and grandeur to little Ripley, and decided that what the village most needed was a Hall – not a village hall nor a town hall, but a Hotel de Ville in the French manner. What the villagers would do with a Hotel de Ville was clearly of little interest and of less importance. A Hotel de Ville they would have, and in the grand manner at that. And there it stands in mock medieval splendour, with turrets and battlements, mullioned windows and all the trimmings, lording it over the terraces of stone cottages.

The most famous of all planned villages is Blaise Hamlet, the village near Blaise Castle just outside Bristol. We have already seen how

Blaise Hamlet's cottages are specially designed for their picturesque effect *(National Trust: photo P. D. Barkshire)*

stately home owners in their enthusiasm for all things picturesque had set about transforming their parks and gardens with imitation ruins designed to suit the style. One aspect of this construction movement was the cottage ornée, a kind of idealised country cottage, irregularly shaped, preferably thatched and representing a very romanticised pastoral ideal. Such cottages had about as much to do with the genuine cottages of farm labourers as pastoral poetry did with the actuality of working life in the country. The cottages were, however, undeniably attractive additions to the big estates. John Scandrett Harford, a local banker, took the whole concept one stage further. Where others had been content with one cottage ornée, he was determined to build a village full of them. Unlike other landlords, such as the builder of the over-ordinary village of Nuneham Courtenay near Oxford, he did not have to destroy existing cottages and transfer existing tenants, willing and unwilling alike, to their new homes. Blaise Hamlet was an entirely new construction. Harford called in one of the most distinguished architects of the day, John Nash who − with his associate George Repton − set out to construct an idealised English village. The cottages were individually designed and grouped round a green. There are only nine of them, but between them they cover every conceivable pastoral style. There are thatched roofs and tiled roofs, though no cottage is allowed a single, unadorned roof: each has a multiplicity of levels. There are verandahs and porches; leaded windows and plain. There are Tudor chimney pots, and one cottage has little holes cut in the boarded façade in imitation of a dovecote − though heaven help the elderly residents for whom the cottages were intended if pigeons ever decided to use them. Blaise Hamlet is an artifice, a conceit, an exercise in nostalgia, and the forerunner of thousand upon thousand of countrified houses that make up twentieth-century suburbia.

The idea of the model village has never died away − it can be seen in the New Towns of today, but it probably only achieves idiosyncrasy when it is the work of a single-minded individual. Some might see the ultimate achievement of the movement in the garden city, but a good place to look for a curious character is in the industrial village conceived and built by an industrial concern − Port Sunlight and Bourneville are examples. They are often slightly odd, in that one does not expect industry to produce such un-industrial offspring. The most remarkable, however, is certainly the town built on the banks of the Aire by Sir Titus Salt and called, somewhat unimaginatively, Saltaire.

Sir Titus Salt was a manufacturer of alpaca cloth and in 1849 he became mayor of the great woollen city of Bradford. He was horrified by the conditions he found in the industrial slums and determined to set an example to his fellow manufacturers. He built a mill beside the Aire and across the Leeds and Liverpool Canal and next to the mill he built his town. The style of the mill is Italianate and the same style was carried over to the houses and other buildings. It is not an exceptionally exaggerated style, but it seems remarkable in context. It is not what one expects in a mill town. The houses are somehow rather florid and, in contrast to the mean terraces that were the norm for industrial housing at this period, large and comfortable. But it was in the public buildings that Salt's builders produced the true exotic flourish – in the church, the almshouses and the library. Saltaire was to have everything the community needed – with one exception. Sir Titus was a lifelong teetotaller and he decreed that there should never be alcohol on sale in his town, so no pub was ever built. He did however produce the fine houses, and hoped that others would follow his lead. He had a 50–50 success rate. There is still no pub, but Bradford industrialists declined to build their own Saltaires.

Elsewhere in industrial Yorkshire, there were some strange and ingenious solutions to the problem of finding homes for the workers in the textile industry. The familiar solution comes in the form of rows of back-to-backs clustering round the mills. But what do you do when the mill is not surrounded by convenient, flat ground but by steep hillsides? The answer at Hebden Bridge was to convert back-to-back into top-to-bottom. Look at the houses from the top of the hillside and you see conventional rows of two-storey houses; look from the bottom of the hill and you see unconventional four-storey rows. What you are seeing are two rows of houses stacked one on top of the other. The upper house has one frontage on the street, but at the back faces out into space. The house underneath has its back up against the hillside and its front on the lower road. Like the tenements of Scotland, they are the forerunners of the modern block of flats. The planners have all been trying to solve the same problem – how to cram as many people as possible into as little space as possible.

The Coffin House at Brixham, before it became Ye Olde *(BBC Hulton Picture Library)*

It is comparatively rare that oddity in houses comes about because of some grand, overall plan. Far more often it is the result of an individual wishing to express his individuality; and quite often there is a bonus in the shape of a suitably romantic tale to explain the curiosity. The Old Coffin House – or as it is now somewhat irritatingly known – Ye Olde Coffin House – at Brixham in Devon has just such a tale attached to its construction. It owes its name to the fact that, in plan, the house is coffin-shaped, not the shape that one would think of as first choice for a jolly family home. The prosaic-minded might note that it fits very well into an awkward plot of land on a hillside site: others might prefer the following explanation. A ship's chandler had a daughter, and being a man of some importance in the little fishing village, he took care to ensure that she made a suitable match. She, however, had other notions, for she fell in love with a most unsuitable young man. 'I would rather see you in a coffin than married to that man', declared father. The suitor took him at his word, and the 'coffin' was built to accommodate the lady. The father, impressed either by the show of affection or the architecture, relented and the couple were duly wed. Truth to tell, the story is rather more remarkable than the building, but there are other cases where odd stories are matched by equally odd buildings.

The Pack o' Cards Inn at Combe Martin in Devon looks very much what you would expect from its name. Why build a house to look like stacked-up playing cards? And why carry the card motif even further, by building it with four floors to correspond to the four suits, and then make sure everyone gets the point by putting in fifty-two windows? The builder, George Ley, made his fortune at the gaming tables in the late seventeenth century and this seemed an obvious way for him to commemorate his good fortune. But why did someone build a cottage in Lyme Regis to look like an umbrella? Did they make a fortune on a wet day? The answer is sadly dull: no one built it to look like an umbrella at all, for the cottage was built long before the first British umbrella was unfurled. It is a cottage which has been changed and added to over the years, the additions including the hemispherical thatched roof that overhangs the walls by over 2ft. The shape of the roof is entirely appropriate for a house built on a hexagonal plan, and the shape of the building itself is equally appropriate for the cottage's original function as a toll house, so all the oddity derives from the shape and the shape is an answer to a practical problem.

The shape of the house known as 'A La Ronde' in Exmouth serves no practical end, and to add to the confusion it is not round at all. It is in fact octagonal, built to the same plan as the famous Church of San Vitale at Ravenna. It has, at its centre, an octagonal hall, and all the rooms radiate out from this. The idea for the house came from two sisters, Mary and Jane Parminter, who visited Ravenna in the 1790s. The house would, by its design, qualify for any list of strange buildings, but the passing years have greatly added to its character. Inside it has become rather like a grotto with, it seems, every inch of surface decorated with shells. This reaches its culmination in the shell gallery, where abstract design and pictorial representation mix happily together. Other house owners, fascinated by the decorative possibilities of sea shells, have preferred to decorate the outside rather than the inside of their homes. You can find shell houses as far apart as Polperro in Cornwall and Anstruther in Fife.

How one chooses to ornament one's home is largely a matter of personal taste, but some decoration is so strange that one feels there must be a story behind it. In the case of the Cat House at Henfield in West Sussex there is. It is soon obvious where it got its name, for under the eaves of this little thatched cottage marches a platoon of cats in black silhouette against the whitewashed walls. Each cat holds in an uplifted paw a small, unhappy bird. The tale is a simple but sad one. An old lady who lived here had a much loved canary; the vicar had an equally adored black cat. The two pets met with predictable consequences. The old lady hung a cat in effigy at her door as a constant reminder of the immorality of the cat and as a reproof to the man of the cloth who tolerated such a wicked companion. Subsequent owners were not inclined to continue the somewhat gruesome practice of hanging cats, even in effigy, but by then the whole story had become part of village lore. So the effigy went and the frieze appeared instead.

Other 'decoration' can seem quite nonsensical until the story is known. Take the case of the lock cottage at the great staircase of locks on the Leeds and Liverpool Canal at Bingley. Those who look closely will see large painted letters, much faded, spread all around the

Exuberant shell decoration in the house known as A La Ronde, in Exmouth *(British Tourist Authority)*

PLEASE DO N
TOUCH THESE
WALLPAPER BLOC

building. The letters, though, often seem incomplete, while some are upside down and others turned sideways. None seem to make sense. Crossword addicts, accustomed to solving anagrams, might actually work out that the house was built out of stone blocks, rather like a child's alphabet blocks, and that rearrangement would produce the words 'Leeds and Liverpool Canal Company'. This was not deliberate mystification on the company's part. The stones originally belonged to a small warehouse at Liverpool, which was demolished at much the same time as a new lock cottage was required at Bingley. The old stone was used for the new cottage, and no one worried about the letters at all.

An even more bizarre decorative effect can be seen at Harpsden, near Henley-on-Thames in Oxfordshire, though not on a house, but on two barns near the church. These are panelled with highly decorative blocks of wood, covered in elaborate patterns, some floral, others geometrical. Originally, the blocks were used for printing patterns on material, or on wallpaper, and when they were discarded they were bought up and used to panel a shooting lodge on the Harpsden estate. When the lodge was in turn demolished, the blocks were removed and re-employed, ensuring that the village of Harpsden can confidently boast of owning the country's most exotic barns.

Interest always seems to attach to things which are the extreme example of something or other – if not the most exotic, then the oldest, the largest, the smallest and so on. This is as true of houses as it is of anything else. The title of the oldest standing house is usually claimed for Aaron the Jew's House in Lincoln, which was built around 1100. It owes its name to its occupancy by one Aaron, a highly successful moneylender, whose clients included the ever impecunious King John. The city can also boast one of the most romantic – one cannot be more precise, romanticism not being measurable – groups of buildings in the land. They date from the sixteenth century and span the River Witham in what is known to travellers on land as High Bridge and to those who go by water as the Glory Hole. They would be splendid examples of the period wherever they were set, but being

*(opposite)* Old wallpaper blocks built into a barn at Harpsden *(Reece Winstone)*

The Jew's House in Lincoln dates back to the twelfth century and can claim to be the oldest in Britain *(Reece Winstone); (opposite)* High Bridge in Lincoln, popularly known as the Glory Hole *(Reece Winstone)*

built out across the water they have gained that little bit extra over their rival claimants for romantic honours.

Another bridge house has a claim to romantic fame, if only for its very romantic setting of Ambleside in the Lake District. It also lays claim to another title – smallest house in Britain. It spans water – not a wide, navigable river like the Witham but Stock Beck, which at this point is a mere 10ft wide. There is some question as to whether it was ever used as a dwelling at all. The National Trust, who own the property, say that it was probably a garden house in the eighteenth century. A further argument against it ever having been lived in is the external staircase, but with a house as small as this it is difficult to see how it would have been possible to fit a staircase inside the building. In any case it is so attractive that it needs no claims to justify its

The tiny but attractive house on the bridge at Ambleside *(British Tourist Authority)*

inclusion in anyone's list of outstanding odd buildings. Which is just as well, since it would probably lose the title of 'smallest' to the Conwy house (see p. 137).

At least there is no argument over which is the smallest pub in Britain. The Smith's Arms at Godmanstone in Dorset was originally, as the name suggests, a smithy. The story goes that Charles II stopped off to have his horse shod and demanded a beer while he was waiting. The smith explained that he had no licence to sell ale, at which point the king demonstrated one of the advantages of royalty by promptly granting the licence and getting his ale.

Having looked at claimants for being the oldest and the smallest house, then smallest pub, what can one say about oldest pub? Very little if one does not want to get into an endless argument, for this is a field with a great many rivals and as many problems. For a start does one mean the oldest building which is now a pub, or the building that has been a pub the longest? How does one deal with the pub that has been changed so much over the centuries that little if anything of the original remains? There has been a Fighting Cock at St Albans since the eighth century, but you will not find much of the eighth-century building left. The Trip to Jerusalem in Nottingham on the other hand is a relative upstart from the twelfth century, but a good deal of the original building does remain, including the cellars carved out of the rock on which the castle stands. There are three good reasons for paying it a visit: it is very old, it has a good deal of its old character left, and it sells decent ale. So what better place could one select to end a tour of some of Britain's stranger houses?

# 6

# A Garden Is a Curious Thing, God Wot

One's house may be eccentric, but probably is not. For most of us it is simply a building that provides warmth, protection from the elements and space in which we can go on with the everyday business of living. The garden can also be thought of as purely utilitarian, a place which should be devoted entirely to growing vegetables for food. In this view, the garden is only as good as it is productive: no space here for sentimentality. It is a view of gardens that goes back a very long way. As long ago as the sixteenth century, the very aptly named Richard Gardiner wrote his *Profitable Instructions for the Manuring, Sowing and Planting of Kitchen Gardens*, a title which would not lead the reader to expect any very wild flights of romantic fancy: and, indeed, Mr Gardiner has none of that in his work. He reserves his highest praise for the humblest vegetables. 'Sowe Carrots in your Gardens', he admonishes his readers, 'and humbly praise God for them, as for a singular and great blessing.'

Yet the paradise inhabited by Adam and Eve was a garden, so perhaps simple delight in the beauty of growing things could be said to predate a concern with its usefulness. To Francis Bacon, writing at much the same time as Richard Gardiner, the garden represented 'the purest of human pleasures'. It is all a matter of viewpoint: to the medieval labourer, the patch of ground where he could grow his crops could quite literally mean the difference between survival and starvation; for the wealthy lord, the garden was a place where fancy could be given full play. As our concern here is more with whimsy than subsistence, we shall be meeting more wealthy men than paupers, but that should not be taken as evidence that the wealthy had or have a monopoly on imagination, but merely that they had the cash to pay the poor to turn their dreams into reality. Gardens, for all the innocent pleasures they can provide, are not produced without hard work, as Kipling wrote in his poem 'The Glory of the Garden':

> Our England is a garden, and such gardens are not made
> By singing – 'Oh, how beautiful!' and sitting in the shade,
> While better men than we go out and start their working lives
> At grubbing weeds from gravel paths with broken dinner-knives.

As all who have ever felt the pains of an aching back can testify, it is all too true that gardens do not make themselves, yet the miracle is that the well-tended garden looks as though it had arrived ready made. Elaborations of flowers come as if ordered full grown and self planting, while shrubs appear to have trimmed themselves into the right shape. The hard work has to be put in, but it should never show. The garden is capable of taking a myriad different forms – and whimsicality and mild eccentricity are by no means absent in many of them.

The British have not, until quite recently, been great innovators in the world of gardening. Bacon, in a famous essay, 'Of Gardens', wrote of the 'great beauty' that can be obtained by adding a fountain to a garden – though he was absolutely opposed to still ponds, which 'make the Garden unwholesome, and full of Flies, and Frogs'. The fountain was, however, popular in Europe – especially in France – long before it received the endorsement of Sir Francis Bacon. We have become so accustomed to seeing fountains that their oddness is scarcely noticed, yet they are pleasingly perverse devices. The nature of water is, after all, to fall down, not to shoot up in the air. For a long time, sheer altitude was the main criterion by which any self-respecting fountain designer might expect his work to be judged. This view of fountain building was enthusiastically shared by the sixth Duke of Devonshire and the man who was appointed as head gardener at Chatsworth in 1826, Joseph Paxton. Together they planned for a great fountain, and to get a sufficient head of water, a reservoir was created covering some twenty acres of ground. The fountain was to be known as the Emperor Fountain, for it was first to play when Tsar Nicholas came on a visit. The reservoir was dug, the plumbing laid and then in the best tradition of all such basically irrational ventures,

The great fountain at Chatsworth, in its day the highest in the world *(British Tourist Authority)*

the visit was cancelled. It is doubtful whether Paxton and the Duke minded very much, for they still had their fountain. It was then the highest fountain in the world, sending a jet of water some 300ft into the Derbyshire air. In any case, there is some evidence that they were blessed with a sense of humour, a great advantage when dealing with tsars. They repaired the willow tree fountain, first built at Chatsworth at the end of the seventeenth century. The tree is made of metal, and when the visitor goes for a closer inspection of the iron foliage it proves itself to be a genuine weeping willow by showering water on the unfortunate person. It is, in fact, a lone survivor of what was once a popular piece for the garden − the joke fountain. It also provides an interesting comment on the durability of old jokes. Seeing people get wet clearly sent the Dukes of Devonshire into paroxysms of mirth 300 years ago and when, in modern times, the inventors of cinematography first brought comedy to the screen, the first known cinema comedy shows a gardener getting wet. But such garden jokes are comparatively rare, and most fountains provide nothing more than the innocent pleasure of seeing water rising and falling.

A whole garden full of oddities can be seen at Alton Towers in Staffordshire, which is now open to the public as an amusement park. In among the swings and roundabouts is one rather splendidly odd fountain known as the corkscrew fountain, for it has a curiously twisted body down which the water runs in attractive patterns. The garden was furnished with a fine collection of follies by the Earl of Shrewsbury, so that you could turn quite happily from the contemplation of a Chinese pagoda to the study of a phoney Stonehenge, a huge pile of carefully arranged rocks known as the Devil's Sideboard. Happily, the magic of Alton still survives, and one could quite certainly say that the addition of modern amusements is very much in keeping with the already anarchic spirit of the place. Some might argue that stately homes have a dignity that should be preserved, but is there really any less dignity in today's dodgems than there is in yesterday's joke fountains?

The Victorians took fountains to their hearts. No decent civic park was complete without one, and the middle classes could buy them off the peg as it were from the manufacturers of ornamental cast-iron work. Among the leaders in this field were the famous Darby works at Coalbrookdale in Shropshire, and in their museum they have a quite magnificent example which was specially made for the Great Exhibition of 1851. Designed by John Bell is consists of a trough mounted on a pedestal in the centre of which is a figure which purports to depict Cupid and a swan. There is certainly a large if not especially swan-like bird, which has its wings spread out and is spouting water from its beak. It has a somewhat distressed look about it, which is not too surprising seeing that the gilded Cupid is sitting on its back and appears to be doing his best to throttle the unfortunate creature. No doubt other cast-iron boys squeezed water from cast-iron birds in numerous British gardens, but the day of such rather grotesque statuary is really over. That does not mean that there is any shortage of individuals who spend their time filling their gardens with equally strange beasts.

The most popular of modern garden ornaments is undoubtedly the gnome, a cheerful little fellow who has two main occupations – standing with his hands on his hips and fishing. Occasionally he has a frog for company. Mr John Fairnington of Branxton in Northumberland has gnomes in his garden, 232 of them at the last count. He also has animals, not moulded in plaster but built out of durable concrete. There are around 150 of those, and Mr Fairnington has not limited himself to frogs. There are tigers and polar bears, lions and monkeys, stags and unicorns. There is even a Loch Ness monster. Humans are not forgotten. A concrete Robert Burns looks out benignly on the menagerie that surrounds him, though his interest might well be centred on a concrete fisher girl nearby. The most extraordinary thing about Mr Fairnington's garden is that he did not begin work on it until he retired from his job at the age of eighty. His is

The famous maze at Hampton Court *(BBC Hulton Picture Library)*

perhaps the most extraordinary of modern gardens, though he has stiff competition from another artist in concrete Mr Bill Talbot of Measham in Leicestershire. His speciality is not zoological but ecclesiastical. He builds model cathedrals to decorate his garden. These two men, working with their own hands, have produced gardens as curious and strange as any to be found among the homes of the great.

One type of garden ornament is not only mysterious, in a quite literal sense, but also looks back to even older mysteries: the maze. These became popular as early as the sixteenth century, though the best known of British mazes dates from the end of the seventeenth century. Hampton Court's is the type known as a hedge maze, which means that once inside the visitor cannot see the overall plan. In spite of its fame, it is comparatively small, but its pathways are so convoluted, doubling back on themselves so frequently, that the total length of pathways extends for half a mile. It appears, at first, to be a simple enough business to win through the maze to the centre and out again. Readers of Jerome K. Jerome's classic story of a trip up the Thames, *Three Men in a Boat*, will remember Harris's valiant but doomed attempt to lead a party through. Eventually in despair, they called for a keeper, who attempted to direct their progress from the top of a ladder. When that, too, failed he went in to collect them:

> He was a young keeper, as luck would have it, and new to the business; and when he got in, he couldn't get to them, and then *he* got lost. They caught sight of him, every now and then, rushing about the other side of the hedge, and he would see them, and rush to get to them, and they would wait for about five minutes, and then he would reappear again in exactly the same spot and ask them where they had been.
>
> They had to wait until one of the old keepers came back from his dinner before they got out.
>
> Harris said he thought it was a very fine maze . . .

One can quite see why mazes became popular. A device that will amuse and, if necessary, lose one's guests has a good deal to be said for it. For the thousands of visitors who still go to visit Hampton Court, it is all good entertainment and good fun. Yet if one looks back over the history of the maze, one finds something that was not intended for fun at all. Something of the special nature of the older mazes and labyrinths is preserved at one of the newest, the maze at the rectory at Wyck Rissington in Gloucestershire. It is, like Hampton Court, a hedge maze which was begun by the rector in 1944 as the result of a dream. It was finally completed and fully planted in 1950 and every year the local children are brought to wend their way through the maze. It is still good fun, but the maze represents something more than that. It also acts as a symbol for the journey through life, starting with birth at the entrance and, if you follow the right path, ending in Paradise at the centre. Each wrong turn represents a sin that leads away from the goal, and as you penetrate deeper in, travel further along the path, so the maze becomes more complex, mirroring the increasing complexity of life as one gets older. This symbolic journey has much more in common with the earliest mazes than with the fun and games of Hampton Court.

Early mazes and labyrinths undoubtedly had a very real significance for the communities that built them. That significance was probably religious, though exact meanings are far from clear. Certainly, mazes were well known in the ancient world, quite the most famous being the labyrinth through which Theseus made his way to kill the half man–half bull creature, the Minotaur. This association with the great legend of Troy is often acknowledged in the most ancient of British mazes – the turf mazes. 'The City of Troy' is the name given to such a maze near the tiny village of Brandsby in North Yorkshire, while there is an even stronger connection with a maze at Somerton, a village in Oxfordshire. It is in the grounds of Troy Farm and is known as 'Troy Town'. The turf mazes are not only different in purpose from what one might call the fun mazes, they are also quite different in design. The maze walkers can see the maze as a whole spread out in front of them, cut into the turf. Furthermore, in most of these mazes, there is no element of puzzlement, no decisions to be taken as to which route to follow. You step along the path of raised turf and it leads you to the centre, and though the route itself is convoluted and complex it is also quite symmetrical. In fact, if one goes from turf maze to turf maze, what is striking is the similarity between, say, the maze at Wing in Leicestershire and that at Hilton in Cambridgeshire. The latter has a pillar in the centre, which carries an inscription informing the reader that it was constructed in 1660 by one William Sparrow. Seventeenth century or far, far older, the differences between mazes are far less striking than the similarities, for many follow a pattern that can be seen all over Europe and dates back to at least Neolithic times. The turf mazes are, then, in every sense of the word, mysteries, and it is very hard to avoid the conclusion that they must once have had ritual significance. Those possessed of vivid imaginations can conjure up pictures of our forebears holding hands and treading the maze in a long, sinuous line. It is a large step from that solemn invocation of a now forgotten god to the more familiar mazes designed for harmless amusement, but quite clearly the former provided the inspiration for the latter.

Many people love puzzles, hence the fascination with mazes – and the more difficult the maze is to penetrate, then the more successful it should be considered. Yet there is really rather more to it than that. The best mazes show a sense of design as well as offering a challenge to the visitor. One of the largest and best designed is also one of the most recent, and this particular maze can be found in the unlikely setting of the municipal park – Hazelhead Park in Aberdeen. The

The turf maze at Wing *(Reece Winstone)*

Lord Provost in the early 1930s was Sir Henry Alexander who rather than follow hallowed tradition by presenting the city with a dull statue or duller portrait, gave it this delightful and cunningly devised maze. It covers the best part of an acre and the path to the centre – marked by an infuriatingly visible but seemingly unapproachable flagpole – is over a quarter of a mile long. He is a clever visitor who reaches the centre without walking a good deal further than that.

The Aberdeen maze is based on a very popular oblong format, which fits in well with the kind of formal, geometric garden that reached Britain via France. An outstanding early example of such a garden is that of Hatfield House. Here the maze is neat and precise with lovely yew hedges to divide the pathways. But formality need not be restricted to a regimen of straight lines. The maze at Somerleyton House in Suffolk is as pleasing in its symmetry as that at Hatfield but entirely based on curves. There is an incentive to reach the middle in the form of a little pagoda, the roof of which can be glimpsed tantalisingly over the yew. The pattern is not especially complex, but it is a full 400yd from the entrance to the centre. If, however, you seek maximum complexity combined with maximum charm, then there is no doubt which is the outstanding maze of Britain. In the lovely gardens of Glendurgan House near Falmouth in Cornwall is an equally lovely maze. Its laurel hedges are as tightly curled around one another as a nest of snakes, and it is a fiendishly difficult route to find, with a multiplicity of dead ends. A large part of its appeal derives from its apparent naturalness, so that one might just believe that Nature had conceived the problem unaided. With its surroundings of trees, it is as great a delight to the eye as it is a puzzle to the mind.

Hedges and shrubs are splendidly versatile additions to any garden. They can be laid out in formal, symmetrical patterns à Le Nôtre; they can be the makings of labyrinths or mazes or they can be transformed into quite remarkable shapes by the art of the topiarist. One of the great delights of a walk through the suburbs is to pass row upon row of polite privet and then suddenly to find among the regulated rows, a hedge turned into animal or bird, ship or locomotive. Topiary began in somewhat statelier surroundings than this, long before suburbia existed at all. It all started in the days when platoons of gardeners could be employed to clip and tend until the shrub which Nature

A complex maze in the beautiful setting of the gardens at Glendurgan *(National Trust)*

intended should take one shape had been dragooned into some other, quite different form.

Topiary came to Britain through France and Holland, though the urge to clip evergreens seems to be common to all gardeners. The French could be said to have developed this clipping into topiary proper, when they started producing those pyramids and orbs of evergreen which are such a familiar feature of every château garden. The habit seems to have spread to the Dutch, who preferred slightly less geometrically exact shapes, and from there it came to Britain during the years of the House of Orange. It was not immediately popular with the British who, apart from their inbuilt distrust of all things foreign, did not always take kindly to the over-precise trimmings of the continentals, as the essayist Addison wrote:

We see the marks of the Scissars upon every Plant and Bush. I do not know whether I am singular in my Opinion, but, for my own part, I would rather look upon a Tree in all its Luxuriancy and Diffusion of Boughs and Branches, then when it is thus cut and trimmed into a Mathematical Figure.

There is a lot to be said for this argument, nevertheless the contrast between natural tree and shaped bush can be very effective, as can be seen in many formal gardens such as those at Lanhydrock House in Cornwall. It is also in such surroundings that one can see the big, dramatic effects. Take, for example, one of the loveliest of the great houses of Britain, Compton Wynyates in Warwickshire. It was built at the end of the fifteenth century, when the country had finally achieved peace under the Tudors after the long, bloody years of the Wars of the Roses. At last the rich felt that they could put comfort first and defence and safety second. The fine Tudor house is matched by equally fine grounds, and the two make a splendidly coherent whole. The topiary garden is particularly magnificent, yet it was not planted until the end of the nineteenth century. For a long time, it has been considered quite normal to consider the Victorians as a band of latter-day Goths and Vandals, heedlessly wrecking the country's heritage. Certainly some of the so-called restorations of parish churches seem to have been designed not so much to restore what was there before as to provide what would have been there if only the builders had been blessed by a proper sense of what constitutes good taste. Yet here we have a piece of Victoriana which manages at the same time to be strikingly original and yet in complete harmony with its surroundings. The centre piece is the chess set, rows of evergreen chessmen waiting for a game that can never be played − and would not now be seen, for the gardens are closed. The surroundings are a delight, yet the chessmen are slightly unnerving. A chessman only exists so that he can be moved about a board, but these are forever rooted to one spot. Yet that is part of the appeal of topiary: it is a paradox, a statue that lives, yet never moves. The character − bird, animal or human − is set solid, yet is only kept in its shape by a good deal of hard work. There is even something faintly ridiculous about the whole business, as the satirist Alexander Pope pointed out in an essay in *The Guardian* in 1713. He described how he had found 'A virtuoso Gardener who has a Turn to Sculpture', and then proceeded to list the wares he could produce:

> Adam and Eve in Yew: Adam a little shatter'd by the fall of the Tree of Knowledge in the great storm; Eve and the Serpent very flourishing. The Tower of Babel not yet finished.

St George in Box; his Arm scarce long enough, but will be in a condition to stick the Dragon by next April.

A green dragon of the same, with a Tail of Ground-Ivy for the present. N.B. These two not to be Sold separately.

.    .    .

A Quick-set Hog shot up into a Porcupine, by its being forgot a Week in rainy Weather.
A Lavender Pig with Sage growing in his Belly.
Noah's Ark in Holly, standing on the Mount; the Ribs a little damaged for want of Water.
A pair of Maidenheads in Firr, in great forwardness.

It is in a way a fair indictment of the pomposities that can prevail when gardens are discussed, and of the slight air of silliness that can attend on topiary. Often topiary turns out to be quaint, with little effort of imagination on the part of the designer: the privet peacock is intended to give the all too solid and stolid redbrick villa the

A pair of evergreen squirrels stand guard over a garden entrance at Great Dixter in Sussex *(British Tourist Authority)*

atmosphere of a country mansion. But at its best, topiary can produce some lovely results. The garden at Ascott House in Buckinghamshire has a topiary sundial which is most attractive, and what is more you can actually use it to tell the time – though deciphering the Roman numerals can be a bit of a problem if the gardener has got behind with his trimming.

Gardens such as Ascott and Compton Wynyates have superb examples of the gardeners' skills and designers' fantasies, but this is one area where the ordinary gardener in the ordinary house can compete as an equal. Here you can find expressions of individual passions which are generally the work of a solitary gardener. On the Shropshire–Hereford border you can see a splendid locomotive steaming along a quiet hedgerow, though it will never reach its destination. In Somerset, an evergreen cruiser that will never see the

A topiary menagerie in permanent pursuit at Knightshayes Court in Devon *(British Tourist Authority)*

Alexander Pope's house at Twickenham, famous for its garden grotto *(Victoria County History: supplied by National Monuments Record)*

sea stands as a reminder of the house owner's days in the Royal Navy. These are the real delights of the topiary world, and it would be unfair to the owners to list them too exactly. In any case, examples can be found all over the country, and anyone who travels with his or her eyes open will find a rich variety of objects and animals, even if, on occasion, time and lack of care have combined to turn the pig into a porcupine.

Though Pope might scoff at the pretensions of others, he was by no means guiltless himself of possessing a taste for the bizarre and the extravagant. In fact he was as responsible as anyone for beginning a fashion for what is perhaps the oddest form of garden decoration – the grotto. He bought a house in Twickenham, the garden of which was divided by a main road. He decided to unite the two halves by means of a tunnel and, in the words of Samuel Johnson, who did not greatly approve of such frivolities: 'he extracted an ornament from an inconvenience, and variety produced a grotto where necessity enforced a passage'. Pope himself left a far more poetic description:

I found there a spring of the clearest water, which falls in a perpetual rill, that echoes through the cavern night and day. From the river Thames you see through an ivy arch, up a walk of the wilderness, to a kind of temple wholly composed of shells in the rustic manner; and from the distance, under the temple, you look down through a sloping arcade of trees, and see the sails on the river passing suddenly and vanishing, as through a perspective glass. When you shut the door of this grotto, it becomes in the instant, from a luminous room, a camera obscura, on the walls of which all the objects of the river, hills, woods, and boats, are forming a moving picture, in their visible radiations: and when you have a mind to light it less, it affords you a very different scene. It is finished with shells, interspersed with looking glass in regular forms, and in the ceiling is a star of the same material, at which when a lamp of an obicular figure of thin alabaster is hung in the middle, a thousand pointed rays glitter, and are reflected over the place. There are connected to this grotto, by a narrow passage, two porches; one towards the river of smooth stones, full of light and open, the other towards the garden, shadowed with trees, rough with shells, flints, and iron ore.

The bottom is paved with simple pebbles, as is also the adjoining walk up the wilderness to the temple, in the natural taste, agreeing not ill with the little dipping murmur, and the aquatic idea of the whole place.

The grotto survives and one finds that Pope's own description is, if anything, too prosaic, for it is a strange and exotic little spot, quite as bizarre as any garden ornament you could find. One cannot help feeling that if Pope had not made it, he would have thoroughly enjoyed ridiculing it. In fact, it was the forerunner of a large number of grottoes, but none which can quite match the eccentric charm of the original.

One notable grotto continues the Pope connection. The gardens at Stourhead in Wiltshire are justly famous, and contain a remarkable collection of ornaments and monuments, including a vaulted grotto over one of the sources of the River Stour. In among the reclining statuary is an inscription, translated from the original Latin by Pope:

> Nymph of the Grot these sacred springs I keep
> And to the murmur of these waters sleep.
> Ah! spare my slumbers, gentle tread the cave,
> And drink in silence or in silence lave.

The title of 'largest and most beautiful in the world' was given to the grotto at Goldney House, Clifton by, of all people, John Wesley: not a gentleman whom one would normally associate with being a keen judge of such matters. It is a grotto with a marine theme. Walls,

The grotto at Stourhead as it appeared in the eighteenth century. 'The Nymph sleeping over a Little Cascade; the light falls in often very pleasingly upon her from an unseen side window above' *(National Trust)*

ceiling, supporting pillars are all thickly encrusted with seashells, while the timber supports are generally believed to be ships' timbers. This is all quite appropriate, for the grotto was constructed in the eighteenth century for one of Bristol's prosperous shipowners, Thomas Goldney.

Grottoes today are, alas, seldom seen except as Fairy Grottoes which appear in large department stores at Christmas, the modern name for a period extending from around October to the following spring. Indeed, the whole taste for exotic garden ornaments seems to have suffered a decline. Who now would dream of building a great pagoda

The splendidly rich and elaborate grotto at Goldney House, Clifton *(Reece Winstone)*

such as that at Kew? But then the taste for chinoiserie was short lived and not every example of the exotica from the brief period of its flourishing has survived. John Nash designed a pagoda, which was built in St James's Park in 1814. It was seven storeys high, brilliantly illuminated by night and in that Jubilee year was made the centrepiece for a grand fireworks display. Alas, the pyrotechnic plans proved over-ambitious and at the height of the affair the tower caught fire and disappeared for ever from the London scene. Not that that has meant an end to the Oriental influence in that part of London. Even today, in spite of the best efforts of modern planners and builders to ruin the London skyline, the view from St James's across towards Whitehall is still one of strange domes and minarets. The same influence can be

The Orient comes to London: the famous pagoda in Kew Gardens *(British Tourist Authority)*

seen at work in many gardens, especially those of the Regency. There was a fashion for Indian cloths, Indian designs and Indian architecture, which blended with native extravaganzas to produce a style that came to be known as Hindu-Gothic. This can be seen at its most elaborate at Sezincote in Gloucestershire, in the little garden temple and, more especially, in the conservatory. The latter is like an imitation Brighton Pavilion, reduced in size and dropped into an English country garden. It sits there, somewhat uncomfortably, among the more familiar urns and formal flower beds, a piece of the Mystic East settled in among the hydrangeas.

The pagoda is as obviously anachronistic in a British garden as a Hindu temple, yet one can also find a whole selection of other

'Hindu Gothic' at Sezincote conservatory *(British Museum: supplied by National Monuments Record); (opposite)* a beautifully preserved dovecote at Erddig House *(Country Life: supplied by National Trust: photo Alex Starkey)*

buildings which seem to have been built in more obviously native styles, yet which also seem to perform no very obvious function. More curiously, a building which might be thought to be just another decorative feature in the landscape, a pavilion or summer house, may turn out to serve a very practical purpose. At Linley Hall in Shropshire, a classical temple stands overlooking the ornamental lake. No surprise here, one might think, just another example of the taste for dropping classical buildings down to embellish the parkland. It turns out, however, to be a façade behind which is a very practical device: the ice house. In the days before the refrigerator and the deep freeze, Nature was the only ice-making agent to be found. Ice was collected from the lake in winter, and kept frozen in a dark, cold, dry pit in the ground. Linley Hall's ice house is exceptional in that it is so heavily disguised, though many were covered by pleasing little circular buildings. They are often found in a ruined condition, for in the age of the fridge their usefulness came to an end. The unwary explorer of the grounds of older houses can find himself entering an apparently innocuous building only to be faced by a deep, dark pit.

The Tudor gazebo at Melford Hall *(British Tourist Authority)*

Other familiar features of the park or garden include the dovecotes, of which there were once literally thousands. They too served an entirely practical purpose, for the dovecote supplied pigeons for his lordship's table. Like the ice house, the dovecote could be beautiful as well as practical. At one time, it has been estimated, there were something in the region of 25,000 such buildings, providing homes for a million birds. As there are still hundreds of survivors of these structures, it would take a large volume to list and describe them all, but anyone wanting to see a perfectly preserved example in a superb setting could do no better than to visit Rousham Park in Oxfordshire. Another example is notable for its many interesting and original features. It stands in the grounds of Erddig House, near Wrexham in Clwyd. The house and grounds here have been preserved to show many different aspects of life on a country estate. The dovecote has a revolving ladder attached to a central post, and up this ladder the servants would go and from it they could reach all the nesting boxes to collect the eggs or a few plump young birds for the table.

Another type of building which might seem to require no special explanation is that forerunner of the summer house, the gazebo. Yet it too has its curiosity value. The first gazebos were built when the country was beginning to settle down to the peace of the Tudors – a peace which was not perhaps entirely convincing for everyone. The wealthy might have abandoned their old, heavily fortified and usually uncomfortable homes, but they still felt somewhat safer if they could stay behind high protective walls. At the same time, they wanted to look out on the world – so little houses were built as look-out posts where the ladies and gentlemen could sit in comfort and security and view the passing scene. Since they were designed to combine a practical purpose – safety – with the pursuit of pleasure, there was often a tendency to minimise the former and emphasise the latter by making the gazebo attractive as well as functional. A splendid gabled Tudor gazebo survives at Melford Hall in Suffolk.

One final example of a class of garden building that has produced some quite remarkable structures is the conservatory. The earliest were probably those of the seventeenth century designed for growing oranges, of which there is a splendid example designed by Sir Christopher Wren at Kensington Palace. The conservatory's finest hour, though, arrived in the nineteenth century, thanks to the application of a new technology. Cast iron and glass were combined to produce beautiful, light, airy structures that seemed to float over the ground rather than sit on it. Sir Joseph Paxton was the great pioneer of the technique, and he went on to apply what he had learned from building greenhouses and conservatories to construct one of the most astonishing buildings of Victorian Britain, the Crystal Palace. That, sadly, is no more, but one can get a notion of what it must have been like from the many surviving iron and glass conservatories, such as those of the Botanic Gardens in Glasgow, so grand that the main building is known as the Kibble Palace.

It is sad that the Crystal Palace has gone – sadder still to think that the combination of iron and glass that produced the garden palaces of a century ago have led us to the unlovely steel and glass boxes which dominate so many of our towns and cities. Somewhere along the way, the sense of fantasy got lost. Over-elaboration was condemned – but instead of attempting to modify and simplify, architects threw all elaboration out of the door. The results can, in every sense, be all too plainly seen. However, there are signs that attitudes are changing again. In the gardens of Britain there is no need to change back, for the new style was never accepted in the first place. The Municipal Parks still boast their floral clocks and their fountains, boating pond and ornate bandstand. It is the great house park given to the people – and people, it seems, still like the elaboration, the grand gesture and, of course, the surprise.

*(opposite)* Neither a stately home nor a cathedral, but the Victorian pumping station at Papplewick *(Harold Crew)*

*(overleaf)* A delightful prospect tower, the Round House on the Kymin, near Monmouth *(National Trust: photo Roy J. Westlake)*

*(above)* Visitors listening to a German fair organ from the 1920s, part of Paul Corin's Musical Collection *(Paul Corin)*; *(below)* the sinister entrance to the catacombs in Highgate Cemetery *(Phillip Lloyd)*

# 7

# Squirrels and Other Animals

A house can be reasonably conventional, set in well-ordered grounds, and still be a place that will amaze and astonish us, simply because it once housed a collector and still houses a collection. Now collectors come in various guises. Some appear in mortar board and gown, clothed in full academic respectability, while others if they do not exactly prance in wearing cap and bells, certainly do not approach their task with undue solemnity. Many of the latter are the true addicts, those who seem unable to stop themselves collecting, and really do not care too much what they collect as long as it interests them at the time. These are what you might call the squirrel collectors, storing up a mixture of goodies for the future to enjoy.

Just such a collector is Paul Corin of St Keyne, though he does specialise in his collecting habits. It is tempting not to mention his museum to anyone, so that they too can have the delight of stumbling upon it by accident. St Keyne is a tiny village in southern Cornwall, and until I met Mr Corin my only knowledge of the place came from the fact that it once stood on the long vanished Liskeard and Looe Canal. Hunting for a crumbling lock chamber in the undergrowth, I was astonished to hear the unmistakable sounds of a fairground organ − and not just one but several, following on each other in succession, to which were soon added the sounds of an electric piano. I had found Paul Corin's Musical Collection.

The collection would be extraordinary anywhere, let alone in the depths of the Cornish countryside. There are street organs from Europe, a fairground organ and a pair of Belgian café organs, the latter being a sort of cross between a live band and a juke box. Rather more serious in intent, though equally fascinating, are the Welte reproducing pianos. Unlike the pianolas which simply banged out a tune in a very mechanical, featureless way, these pianos are electrically driven and can reproduce fine nuances of tone and expression. The pianist played the piece, and a series of pens marked notes and expressions, which could then be transferred to a roll of paper which was then fed back into the machine – the resulting playback is a faithful reproduction of the original performance. With such an instrument you can hear Paderewski play again or Debussy interpreting his own work. And if the classics are not to your taste, you can always turn instead to the Welte Jazz Piano, which comes complete with mandolin, drums, cymbal and wood block. And for those who like music every hour on the hour, there is the Orphonian Disc Music Box. When the discs are inserted into the clock, it not only strikes the hour but plays a tune for the hour as well.

This part of Cornwall boasts another extraordinary collection, though perhaps collection is not quite the right word. On the coast to the east of Looe is a woolly monkey sanctuary. Not a zoo: many people build cages to put animals in, but this is quite different. It is, in effect, a colony of wild monkeys, free to go where they please, but being sensible creatures they stay in the place that they recognise as home and where they are well looked after. Although the monkeys are well fed and cared for, there are a few restraints: and the restraints that you will find are not there to keep the monkeys in. They are there to keep us, the humans, out. The monkeys represent no threat to their visitors, generally greeting them in a friendly and dignified manner. The humans, however, are not always so sensible. In spite of being warned, they will wander up to a sedate grandmother monkey and try to poke her in the tum while making those coo-cooing noises generally considered appropriate to conversation with very tiny babies. Grandmother tends, not surprisingly, to dislike this sort of treatment, and the monkeys seem to have developed their own peculiarly effective antidote. They grab the offender's nose and hang on, until someone persuades them to let go. Treat the monkeys with respect, however, and you will have the rare privilege of sharing in their lives for a short time. You will see monkeys in Cornwall behaving as naturally as if they were back home in the Amazonian forests.

There are many who start animal collections, but not all have the necessary understanding and sympathy to keep the animals at least as contented as – and one would hope more contented than – their human visitors. Bristol Zoo has an entrance marked 'Most Dangerous Animal in the World'. Walk inside and you find yourself confronted by a mirror. The exhibit is all too accurate. Some collectors see the animals merely as items placed on earth for man's amusement. Lionel Walter, second Baron Rothschild, rode around the grounds of his house at Tring in Hertfordshire in a carriage pulled by zebra, while other exotic animals, such as giant tortoises, roamed the grounds like mobile garden ornaments. Today, the house is home to the Tring Zoological Museum with animals, birds and insects beautifully displayed – but dead. Taxidermy has a role to play in properly organised scientific museums such as Tring – even if the museum's origins were notably less organised and considerably less scientific. But what is one to make of Potter's Museum of Curiosity at Arundel, West Sussex?

Walter Potter was a taxidermist who founded his museum in 1862. Where most Victorian taxidermists were content to mount yellowhammers on branches and cover them with a glass dome, Mr Potter had grander ideas. He produced a series of tableaux. 'The Rabbits' School' has a score of genuine stuffed rabbits sitting on benches, reading books, doing their sums. The extraordinary thing about it is that they all do look so natural – if a rabbit standing on its

Duelling squirrels at Potter's Museum *(Sydney W. Newbery)*

JOHN HUNTER.

BORN
14TH FEBRUARY 1728.

DIED
16TH OCTOBER 1793.

hind legs with a book in its paws can ever be completely natural! The kittens' tea and croquet party has thirty-seven furry friends gathered for these delights. The kittens – ladies in jewels, gentlemen in cravats – sit up to table where they are served by the maids who pass round such culinary delights as baked mouse tart. Other tableaux represent traditional stories, such as the death of Cock Robin. There are conventional exhibits as well, but it is the tableaux that draw the visitors. This riot of anthropomorphism either attracts or repels utterly.

Another collection which many people find quite repulsive, yet which nevertheless was based on serious, and often brilliant, scientific work, can be seen in the Hunterian Museum at the Royal College of Surgeons in London. It contains the collection of John Hunter, one of those remarkable polymaths who flourished in the eighteenth century. He was one of a group of 'scientific and literary men' who met regularly to exchange ideas in the coffee houses of Soho, a group which included such eminent individuals as Sir Joseph Banks and Captain Cook. Hunter himself was a brilliant anatomist and researcher. His own work was too far ahead of its time to earn him very much in the way of recognition during his lifetime – he moved a long way towards establishing a theory of evolution before Charles Darwin was even born. His pupil Jenner left the world the techniques of vaccination: Hunter left his strange and wonderful collection.

Many of the specimens, pickled and bottled, are just what you would expect to find in the collection of a man concerned with the complexities of Nature, over 3,000 of them carefully arranged to show that interdependence among animals that is the basis of evolutionary theory. The pickled portions make it seem like a cross between an exotic delicatessen – woodpecker's tongue is, no doubt, a delicacy somewhere – and Frankenstein's laboratory. Then there are the freaks and aberrations. There is the 8ft tall Irishman who actually left a plea in his will that his body should be kept out of the hands of the anatomists. His efforts were in vain. Five hundred pounds to the

*(opposite)* John Hunter casts an appraising eye over the Irish Giant, the pride of his collection *(Medical Illustration Support Service)*

The old operating theatre of St Thomas's Hospital, London *(Guy's Hospital)*

undertakers and Hunter had the giant's skeleton for his collection. There are other macabre remains, from the double skull of a child to examples of the ravages and deformities caused by venereal disease. The Hunterian Museum is quite definitely not the place for those with weak stomachs. If, however, your digestive system is able to cope, then why not try another medical museum: the old St Thomas's Hospital in Southwark.

The old operating theatre at St Thomas's was closed down when the hospital was moved to Lambeth in 1862. It has now been preserved and restored to give visitors an indication of what surgery was like in the days before anaesthetics, an indication which some of us would be much happier not to be given at all. The operating theatre is a theatre indeed, with steeply raked tiers of seats for the students who came to watch the operations. On the floor, or stage, is the wooden operating table with a tray of sawdust underneath to soak up the blood. A mop and bucket stand nearby to deal with more vigorous splashing about. Many of the operations were amputations. The half-drugged patients, well supplied with alcohol or opium, were brought in blindfold, to save them from a view of the instruments, which look horrifyingly similar to the implements in a butcher's shop. Then it was all a question of speed – completing the operation before the patient died of surgical shock. Survivors then had to face the risks of infection, for hygiene was not a word much heard in those days.

An almost equally grisly museum can be found at Beaumaris on the Isle of Anglesey. Again it gives us a glimpse of the past which, mercifully, is no longer with us. The local gaol was built in 1829 by Joseph Hansom, inventor of the hansom cab. In some ways it was a model for its day, and for ours. Cells were of a reasonable size and even furnished with such luxuries as wash basins and flush toilets, which is more than can be said for many cells in use today. Other aspects are less enticing. There is the corridor along which the last walk was made. It ends at a door, above which the gallows stands. There is a treadmill, where prisoners walked for hours on end, pumping up water for the prison. If they worked especially hard and raised all the water they needed in record time, there was still no respite – the excess simply ran back to the well to be pumped up again. Other jolly attractions included the punishment cells where prisoners subsisted on a diet of bread and water, and – saddest of all – the nursery. The cradles were attached to ropes which could be pulled periodically by the women in the workshop below to rock their children to sleep.

After that spate of rather grim museums, perhaps we ought to turn to something a little more cheery, and what greater contrast could one find than the Battle of the Flowers Museum in St Ouen, Jersey. The Battle of Flowers takes place every August, when massive floats are pulled through the streets, each decked out in flowers arranged in many fanciful shapes. Florence Bechelet has been designing floats for nearly fifty years, and has carried off prizes in all but two of the years in which she entered, and in the museum is a record of her work. Here are animals and birds, creatures real an fantastical. The best are amazingly realistic give the materials. The grassy lion stalking a reedy gazelle convinces you that is might get there one day. The rest of the menagerie looks on. It must rank among the world's most charming museums.

There is an obvious rationale behind the Jersey Museum: the exhibits are beautiful and deserve to be preserved, but who in his right senses would start a dog collar museum? The collection consists of canine wear rather than clerical dress, but that scarcely makes it any less remarkable. It is only when one sees it that one becomes at least partially convinced that the thing was worth doing at all. Here is a truly amazing variety of dog collars, ranging from collars for hunting dogs with protruding spikes to prevent the hunted damaging the hunter to baroque masterpieces in brass, wrought iron and even silver and gilt. There are even occasional forays into wit, even if on occasion the witty inscriptions are blatant plagiarisms. Alexander Pope had the following lines engraved on a collar which he presented to the Prince of Wales for his pet pooch:

> I am his Highness' dog at Kew;
> Pray, tell me sir, whose dog are you?

The downmarket version in this collection reads: 'I am Mr Pratt's dog, King St, Nr Wokingham, Berks. Whose dog are you?' Somehow Pope's version has more of a swing to it. The collars are on display at Leeds Castle, Maidstone, Kent.

One of the dog collars in the museum at Leeds Castle *(Clark Nelson Ltd)*

Almost as odd is the House of Shells at Buckfastleigh in Devon. This is not merely a collection of seashells, but a collection of things made out of shells. Everyone must have seen the souvenirs on sale at every seaside resort: fishes made from shells, animals made from shells, shell ladies in shell crinolines. It might be something of a surprise to discover that we have been making objects out of shells for at least four centuries, and surviving examples display rather more imagination than is on view in most gift shop windows. Here we have shell pictures and shell valentines, shell jewellery that really could be worn with style, and even shell drinking cups. Such a collection could only have been put together by an individual obsessed with these objects, and so it was – the collector being Mr Cecil H. Williamson.

Anything is seems is collectable, provided it takes the collector's fancy, and if the collection grows to suitable proportions then eventually it might be opened to the public. Sometimes manufacturers rather than individuals take on the task, and if Avery of Smethwick had not taken on the job of collecting together ancient weighing machines and scales who else would have? Once having seen these objects brought together the appeal is obvious, and it does not come just from the appeal of the rich and ornate scales. One soon begins to realise what an important part such an apparently simple act as weighing plays in the community – whether it is in establishing an accurate coinage or balancing off an Indian prince against a pan full of gold.

Rather less important, and of considerably less antiquity as far as this country is concerned, is Anthony Irving's collection at the House of Pipes at Bramber in West Sussex, where anything and everything connected with smoking the noxious weed is displayed. There are ash trays made out of wrecked zeppelins, ornate tobacco jars and, of course, a vast array of pipes – little pipes and huge pipes, straight or twisted pipes, pipes in every conceivable shape and form.

Pipes of a quite different kind are displayed at Newcastle-upon-Tyne – bagpipes. Now there is nothing intrinsically strange about a bagpipe museum – in fact some unkind folk have been heard to remark that all bagpipes should be on display in locked cases. But why Newcastle? Why not Scotland? There is no obvious answer, but there it is – a thoroughly comprehensive collection of bagpipes on Tyneside.

An equally, if not more, unlikely setting has been found for Lady Bangor's Fairground Collection. She began the collection in the 1960s, when the old wooden carved and painted fairground objects began to disappear in favour of easily maintained plastic and metal. Collecting such marvellous, rich objects needs no excuse, for they are wonderful in a very real sense, their sole purpose being to instil a sense of wonder in the fair's visitors. They succeeded when they were first built as much as a century ago and they still succeed today. Lady

Fairground animals preserved in Lady Bangor's Fairground Collection *(Wookey Hole Caves Ltd)*

Bangor had originally intended to display the collection herself, but in 1974 she sold it to Madame Tussaud's, and they added it to another of their attractions – the Wookey Hole Caves in Somerset. So the bioscope and the fairground organ, the gallopers and the spinner have left the open air where they spent their working lives and have a new home underground. And they have some odd companions. Madame Tussaud's is celebrated for its waxwork figures of the famous. But fame is transitory, and Wookey Hole is full of likenesses of the once-glamorous, forlornly waiting in the hope that one day their originals' reputations will revive and they will return to glory in the Marylebone Road showrooms.

Today, the trend in museums is towards neatness and order, the use of modern display materials, continuity of theme. In the best cases, this has resulted in museums which tell an interesting story better and more coherently than ever before – in the worst, institutions which offer all the glamour and excitement of a night out in the staff canteen. There is still a place for the quirky collection, where themes are less important than the Aladdin's cave of wonders that is put on view – museums like the Pitt-Rivers in Oxford, where shrunken human heads jostle for space with shadow puppets from Indonesia. Even museums which appear to have a unified theme can emerge as glorious jumbles, often because the curator has too many objects, not enough space and is so in love with the collection that he simply cannot bear to leave anything out. You can find just such a museum in the railway station at Shackerstone in Leicestershire. It now stands on a preserved steam line, which itself has a splendid history of mild dottiness. An occasional visitor to the area was Edward VII who attended hunting parties at a neighbouring stately home. The station master decided that such a special traveller deserved special treatment. A mounting block was built on the platform and a red carpet laid on top of it. The royal carriage duly stopped at the appointed place, at which point the dignified ceremonial collapsed into farce. The block had been built too high and the door simply could not be opened – the royal party was left desperately shoving and heaving in an attempt to get out of their carriage. Eventually the train was moved on and the door could be opened at last. Such a station with such a history deserves a special museum and it has it, housed in the old booking hall. Everything is

Tussaud rejects: heads of the once famous at Wookey Hole *(Wookey Hole Caves Ltd)*

Samurai warriors ready to invade the Cotswolds from Snowshill Manor *(National Trust)*

crammed in. There are ticket machines and signs from the Gents', signal frames, lamps, postcards, timetables, ancient staff captured in fading sepia, whistles, flags, badges and all the minutiae of railway life. It is quite glorious and it is there because it was built up, and is still being built up, as a labour of love. It is there because the Shackerstone Society contains individuals deeply bitten by the squirrel instinct, genuine collectors.

If the title of King Squirrel was ever to be handed out, then it would have to be awarded to Mr Charles P. Wade of Snowshill Manor in Gloucestershire. He was a scholar, an architect and an artist, but above all he was a collector. He bought the old house in 1919 when it was in a shocking state of disrepair, restored it to its former glory and set about filling it with whatever took his fancy. If he saw something he fancied, then he bought it and brought it back to the lovely old Cotswold manor. He ended up with what must be the least coherent collection in the country. Some of the items do look at home in a Tudor home – old musical instruments, for example. There is a whole room full of those. Spinning and weaving tools have relevance in an area that once had a thriving wool trade. Toys and clocks might just about get by as well. But why bicycles? The Great Garret, also known as 100 Wheels, boasts a huge collection, and why a collection of things nautical in a house as near to the centre of the country as you can get? The answer is simple – Wade liked the sea, and several of the rooms have been given nautical names by him: Admiral, Top Royal, Top Gallant, Mizzen. It all starts to seem reasonably logical after all – until one comes across the Samurai warriors, a small army of them huddled together in martial conference, their weapons around them. It appears that Mr Wade was walking past an antique shop when he saw a suit of Samurai armour. He liked the look of it so he went inside. The shopkeeper, catching the powerful scent of a collector, casually remarked that this was just one suit but there were several more to be had. The hint was sufficient: Wade bought the lot, and began collecting Japanese weapons and armour on the spot. This was the true squirrel at work. No doubt, somewhere there are collectors even now putting together objects which the rest of us pass by without a glance. In time, their collections too might go on display. Long may the squirrels thrive.

# 8

# Burning the Clavie
# and Whuppity Stourie

Just as museum exhibits and collections have become, over the years, more and more rigorously catalogued and shut off into neatly labelled compartments, so too our sports and our pastimes have become detached from their origins in the wider world. They have been tidied away as 'leisure', something which has nothing to do with the all too real and earnest affair of living. Sports have become either the preserve of the new demi-gods, the sports superstars, or they have been passed to the amateur who plays for the fun of it. Either way, the activity seems to have little or nothing to do with the serious business of getting on in life.

Football is a splendid example. Millions turn up every Saturday, festooned with the colours of their favourites, to watch the professionals play. Others take to muddy municipal pitches or slither among the cow pats of some village field, taking part in their local teams' efforts. The latter are certainly closer to the old tradition. It is only very recently that football has become a 'spectator sport' – and it is not all that long ago that there was no sort of formal game at all, with its fixed and complex rules. There were no footballers as such, for specialisation in that sense is really quite a modern concept. Not so very long ago, a football match was something in which the whole community could participate. It was a glorious, muddy brawl, a free-for-all, a cross between a monumental booze-up and mass mud wrestling. But the old style of game has not quite disappeared, even if its origins are not always remembered.

The traditional date for football matches was Shrove Tuesday, which as it was the day before the beginning of a six-week fast was a suitable occasion for fun and games, not to mention food and drink, to set everyone up for the weeks ahead. Football games were played all over the country: there was seldom any limit to the number of players, frequently no time limit set for the playing, and not very much in the way of rules for anyone to worry about. The only point of certainty was that there should be a ball and some sort of goals. Usually two neighbouring communities were involved and the object was to get the ball, by any means whatsoever, into the goal – though, unlike the modern game, it was usual to try and fetch the ball back to your own goal. The wrestling throng made their way, assuming that they could make any way at all, up hill and down dale, through village streets and, for a really good game, through a few streams as well. And although other forms of football may have overtaken the Shrovetide game, it has not yet died out.

Quite the most energetic of the surviving games must be that played at Ashbourne in Derbyshire, between the Up'ards and the Down'ards. The dividing line between the two teams is a brook, and as you either live up to the north of it or down to the south of it, so you have the two teams. The goals are mills, set three miles apart, and at two o'clock in the afternoon the game gets under way. It goes on through the afternoon and frequently into the evening as the players rampage through the brook and splash through several other streams until they eventually reach one or other of the goals. It is all such good fun that they come out and do it all over again the next day.

Up at Alnwick in Northumberland, they have taken the game out of the streets and put it in a special field, bringing it that much closer to our modern notion of what a sport should be. Here it is at least begun in high style, the ball being piped in procession from Alnwick Castle. But for those who feel that no ancient 'sport' is complete without a full set of rituals and archaic titles, then the best game of 'football' of them all must be the Hood Game of Haxey in Humberside. It is not, however, played on Shrove Tuesday, but on the other traditional day for such games, Christmas Day – not 25 December as we modernists have it, but the old Christmas Day, as it was before the new calendar came in in 1752, which now falls on 6 January.

The ceremony starts with a Fool accompanied by twelve Boggars, what one might call the official team. The Fool is allowed to kiss any woman he meets, while the Boggars are busy getting bruised and muddied, suggesting that though he may be a Fool, he is certainly no fool. He does, however, have to suffer in the cause as well, since before the game begins, he has to make a speech to the crowd, reminding them of the simple rules of play, which amount to little more than 'every man for himself' and if anyone gets in your way knock him over. While he delivers this speech, a fire is lit behind him, but suitably damped down so that the Fool is soon enveloped in smoke. In former times he was actually suspended over the fire by a rope. The game can now begin.

The hoods are not hoods at all, but bundles of canvas or – in the case of the main hood for the main game – a piece of thick rope bound in leather. The object of the game is to get the hood to one of the goals – in this case, pubs. As the hood cannot be kicked or thrown forward, this involves a huge, heaving crowd trying to go in several directions at the same time. Eventually, they reach one of the pubs and that hostelry then holds the prize for a year. Many theories have been put forward to explain the origins of this strange pastime, but no one now remembers why they play the game every year.

Football is only one of the games played on Shrove Tuesday. In Cornwall, at St Ives and St Columb Major, they go in for 'hurling' – not the Irish game, but one in which, as the name suggests, the ball is thrown and not kicked. Up at Jedburgh in Scotland, the traditional game is Jethart Ba', which is played at Candlemas and on Shrove Tuesday, but they calculate their Shrove Tuesday according to their own rules, so that it sometimes coincides with the generally recognised day but sometimes does not. It began as a particularly violent football game, but kicking was later banned in the hope of reducing the incidence of broken legs in the local population. It is very much a street game. Shopkeepers and householders board up their property for the day as the whole town is given over to this game which goes back many centuries.

Some places have rather more peaceful Shrovetide occupations. Down at Scarborough, they have the pleasant notion that the best way to celebrate the occasion is to go down onto the shore and skip. At noon, a bell is rung and everyone meanders down, in their own good time, for a little skipping practice. They are not the only Great British Skippers. Others congregate at Alciston in East Sussex, but on Good

Friday. There was a time when skipping had a magical, ritual meaning and skippers would travel to particular sites – often very ancient ones, such as burial mounds. It is not difficult to see the connection between the traditional magic circles and an activity which involves making great circles in the air through which the participant must jump.

The best known event associated with Shrove Tuesday is the little ritual carried out in homes throughout the country – the making and eating of pancakes. The idea of eating your fill of tasty pancakes before starting a long fast requires no explanation, but at Olney in Buckinghamshire feasting and fun have joined together to produce the annual pancake race. Only local women may compete and, unlike the football matches, the race has quite definite rules. The women must arrive at the start wearing an apron and some sort of headgear, usually a scarf, and they must have a pancake in a frying pan. The course is just over 100yd long, and the pancake must be tossed at least three times during the course of the race. A local event, it has received national and even international fame – a rival race over the same length of course is run in Kansas.

Other traditional games and sports have their own special days. Some, as in the case of Whuppity Stourie or Scourie, have become such a mixture of game and ritual that it has become all but impossible to disentangle the various strands. This takes place on 1 March at the parish church in Lanark. The bells are rung and the local children, armed with home-made weapons of paper balls on strings, pursue each other three times round the church, beating each other over the head as they go. That completed, the town officials, who have been watching the proceedings from the safety of a raised platform, throw down handfuls of pennies and the children all dive in for what they can grab. Once, the weapons were rather more potent – screwed-up hats and caps – while the participants were also a good deal larger. The grand finale was a battle between the lads of Lanark and those of New Lanark. But as New Lanark was only built in the eighteenth century, and the custom goes back further than that, there must have been earlier 'battles' fought between other factions.

*(opposite)* Two winners of the Olney pancake race demonstrating their skill *(British Tourist Authority)*

Good Friday, being the other end of the Lenten fast from Shrove Tuesday, has many games in common with the latter. It also marks the end of the marbles season. Those who think of marbles as a game for small children have clearly never been to Tinsley Green in West Sussex on Championship Day. Good Friday sees teams from all over the country competing not just for the local nor even the national championship, but what is generally regarded as the world marbles championship. The centre of activity is the circular rink where the coloured glass balls are propelled towards their targets. It is a very serious matter.

Whit Monday is another occasion for games though many old customs have now died, just as Whit Monday itself has gone to be replaced by the new, dull Spring Bank Holiday. However, some games have survived to the new date, including the most spectacular of them all: the cheese rolling on Cooper's Hill at Brockworth in Gloucestershire. The hill is decidedly steep, and the object of the exercise is to chase after a cheese rolled down the hill, which tends to involve rather more tumbling and rolling than actual running. Amazingly, serious injuries are very rare. The downhill dash is rather reminiscent of another hillside sport, the fell racing of the Lake District, where competitors run up hill at the risk of bursting a lung and then pelt down again at the even greater risk of breaking a leg. Cheese rolling was once much more widely spread and involved a certain amount of ritual. Old ceremonials and special rituals are generally associated with specific dates, but before turning to those we shall just take a glance at some uncommon ancestors of our now common games.

There is no way in which one could begin to list 'odd' games, since all games are by their very nature fundamentally absurd. If anyone doubts the truth of that statement then let them try a simple test. Imagine you are talking to someone who has never seen or played any game, then select any game you like and try to explain what it is and why people play it. Or, if that seems too complex, try taking an American to Lords. Some games, however – even if they are no more curious than any others – do have a certain rarity value, including some which, like Shrove Tuesday football, are forerunners of sports we now accept as all too ordinary. Tennis, for example, only acquired

In hot pursuit of cheeses down Cooper's Hill *(British Tourist Authority)*

its present form of lawn tennis quite recently. Long before that, there was Real or Royal Tennis, a sport which is beginning to enjoy a mild revival.

There is a splendid old tennis court in a suitably royal setting at Falkland in Fife. The court was built at the Royal Palace for James V in 1539. Tennis has the distinction of being one of the very first ball games to be given formal rules, and very complex rules they were at that. Quite when or where the rules were formulated is uncertain, but the game is generally thought to have originated in medieval France. Shakespeare's mention of the game in *Henry V*, when the English king is taunted by a gift of tennis balls, could well be based on an historic incident. Certainly, the Falkland court is very much the traditional court. Essentially, it consists of a closed court, along one side of which is a covered area for spectators. The sloping roof of the stand is actually used in the game, the ball being bounced off it during service, and is one of the main differences between real tennis and the later version. Originally, the ball was hit with the hand, giving it the French name of *jeu de paume*. That name, is, in fact, continued in the Parisian art gallery which houses the work of the Impressionists, which was originally a tennis court. The British game developed through the use of bare hands to the use of racquets, but real tennis has retained its identity – distinguished from the more familiar game with its argumentative professionals, by the way in which players use roofs and walls. In this, it might be thought of as the forerunner of other closed court games, such as squash and our other old ball-and-racquet game – fives.

Fives, like real tennis, has never quite faded away. But whereas the oldest surviving tennis court is in a royal palace, the oldest fives courts are attached to pubs. The origin of the term 'fives' is uncertain, but is possibly derived from the fact that, as in real tennis, the ball was hit with the five fingers of the hand. The main feature of the court is the wall, some 30ft high and 20ft wide against which the ball has to be played. There are three examples in Somerset – at the Crown Inn, Petherton; the Poulett Arms, Hinton St George; and the Bell Inn at Curry Rivel. Other games, too, have their origin in earlier pastimes which have all but slipped out of sight. Croquet which, as all who have played it will agree, is a game that brings out the worst, most vindictive sides of humanity, has its origin in the earlier game of mall or pall-mall. That game has gone, but the avenues in which it was once played, where elegant ladies and gentlemen strolled along, tapping at wooden balls with their mallets, have remained in London – the Mall and Pall Mall; the name is also continued in a pub in Notting Hill Gate. Another ancient game, knurr and spell, would seem to have given birth to not just one but two pastimes. A wooden ball, the knurr, is thrown into the air by a mechanical device, the spell, and the spectator must then try to hit it as far as possible with a wooden stick – making the game a cross between clay pigeon shooting and hockey. It was once very popular in Yorkshire and Lancashire, but has now virtually disappeared.

These sports were all, like modern games, to be played whenever the players fancied. Others were tied to special dates, and with these there is no more than a thin division which marks off something done just for the fun of it from solemn ritual. Some have, over the years, lost the ritual element, and simply become games with formal rules, played for no better reason – or perhaps one should say, no worse reason – than that people enjoy them. Lately, it sometimes seems that much of the pleasure provided by games has been lost in the encroachment of professionalism, and sometimes the same is true of other special rituals and pastimes. It usually ends up as less fun than it used to be – but a lot more expensive. Easter eggs are an excellent example. During my childhood, Easter eggs were hard-boiled hens' eggs, decorated by the family in whatever style was fancied: some were given bright, abstract patterns, others given faces, and the best of them were true works of art. Once completed, they could be shown off in egg-rolling ceremonies. The brightly coloured eggs were taken to an appropriate hill and put through their paces on the slope. There were no winners and no losers, but it was considered a good omen if your egg got to the bottom unbroken. The custom is not yet dead and there are several spots, ranging from the royal grandeur of Arthur's Seat in Edinburgh to the municipal splendours of Avenham Park in Lancashire, where eggs are still rolled. In other spots, egg rolling has disappeared along with the decorated eggs. No one, after all, wants to roll their expensive chocolate concoctions through the dirt.

There are many old traditions associating Easter and eggs, not surprisingly perhaps if one thinks of Easter as a spring festival and the egg as an obvious symbol of fruitfulness and birth. The most attractive custom is pace egging. Originally, groups would roam a district, begging for eggs in return for which they would perform the mumming play. These are plays which date back beyond written records and which, it seemed, were destined to die away and be forgotten. But the recent increased interest in folk history and folklore has led to the re-establishment of mummers' companies. A recent example is the group formed at Knaresborough in Yorkshire, which was certainly never there in my childhood. Other companies have more continuous traditions, and associations with other dates (see p. 223). And there are always mummers to be seen at big folk festivals, such as that at Towersey in Oxfordshire. The sentiments of the plays might be naive, the comedy broad, but they have a directness and immediacy which is very appealing. One might imagine that there could be no less auspicious time for a revival of such simple pleasures. Yet it is perhaps the very sophistication of the modern entertainments that has helped to arouse interest in older and simpler pastimes. So, perhaps, pace egging and egg rolling have survived simply because they are rather more satisfying activities than stuffing oneself with the manufactured chocolate product.

There is a strong appeal in any ritual that has survived for long periods: it forms a definite link with the past, providing a sense of continuity in a world of rapid change. Today, we are all much more mobile than our ancestors: not only dashing around the country and travelling abroad, but also moving house with an unconcern which would have astonished our forebears as recently as a century ago. Yet there is a paradox here. We welcome our new mobility, yet at the same time yearn for a sense of belonging, being a part of some stable community. Old customs and rituals help us to achieve that feeling of belonging to a particular place, even when we are not altogether sure what the rituals are supposed to be celebrating.

Some rituals are preserved even though their intrinsic value might seem to be limited and even when, in some cases, the ritual and the context seem hopelessly at odds. Dicing and drawing lots are, as a whole, rather frowned on by religious bodies – though bingo may not be entirely unknown at church fêtes and the parish raffle is considered fairly harmless. But dicing for a prize in church? Not the sort of thing one could expect to start up today, but when it is part of an old tradition, why then it can become perfectly acceptable. At St Ives in Cambridgeshire, dice are rolled by the church steps to decide which six out of a dozen children will receive prizes. This has been going on for 300 years, ever since Robert Wilde left a legacy at his death in 1675, which stipulated that this curious form of ecclesiastical gaming should take place every year. It could never happen now, but tradition is its own justification and the prizes are, after all, Bibles.

On this occasion, the tradition can be traced back to the whim of one man: the origins of most local traditions are not so easily established. Take, for example, the large number of ceremonies connected with

May Day and other springtime festivals. There are many May Day customs which are peculiar to particular places, but perhaps the most widespread of all is that of dancing round the maypole. Nowadays, we tend to regard it as a charming entertainment, as often as not laid on by the children of the local primary school. The maypole is usually a manufactured one: brought out every year to be festooned with ribbons. The children dance, the May Queen and her attendants look on, while proud parents clap enthusiastically and try to understand why that ghastly Mary, who isn't even pretty, was chosen as queen instead of their Jane. This is all very different from earlier May Days when a tree, specially cut that morning, was trimmed and brought to the green for the dancing that celebrated spring. It was such an obviously pagan ritual that it inevitably attracted the extreme displeasure of the Puritans who, whenever they had the opportunity, banned the practice. Some communities had permanent maypoles, and many of these were destroyed. Of course, they came back eventually, but there are now very few places where the maypole can be seen all through the year. This is rather a shame, because they were often very impressive and brightly coloured. Visitors to Barwick-in-Elmet in West Yorkshire can see the country's tallest, all 86ft of it, rising high above the village square. The locals who have the job of decking it out each year need a good head for heights.

Many another old May Day custom has either vanished or now only appears in a rather debased form. The surviving customs may still have charm, in the sense that people will remark how charming they are, but there is no longer any belief in a real charm. No one now believes that the rituals can have a direct effect on their lives. Garlands are still made up, and dolls dressed in their best and settled into beds of flowers as May Dolls, but none of it has any real significance. There are, however, still a few places where the old rituals are carried through with something like the old fervour. We may have long since given up the pagan beliefs which are at the heart of May Day celebrations, but down in the West Country, at least, they still act as if it all matters. The best known and most popular of all the May Day ceremonies takes place at Padstow in Cornwall.

The ceremony starts on the eve of May Day, when the Mayers go from house to house throughout the town, serenading the inhabitants

– flattering the lady of the house with a traditional song of good fortune, and inviting her to join the celebration of the coming of summer:

> Rise up, Mrs —, all in your gown of green,
> For Summer is i-comin' in today.
> You are as fair a lady as waits upon the Queen,
> In the merry month of May.

The male members of the household are given a very similar song, except that the third line is changed to a clear hint that they are expected to dip their hands into their pockets to pay for the compliments to their ladies:

> You've a shilling in your pocket, and I wish it were in mine.

Any suggestions that the references to coinage should be decimalised have so far been resisted and one hopes that we shall never hear 'You've five pee in your pocket' being sung in the streets of Padstow. There are many verses and many variations, but all contain that essential reference to the merry month which heralds the coming of summer.

The next morning sees the arrival of the Hobby Horse. The man who gets to act the part of the horse has to be fit and especially strong on stamina. His costume consists of a great hoop, about 6ft in diameter, covered by a tarpaulin, at the front of which is a horse's head. The man himself is all but invisible, his face being covered by a mask while a tall hat crowns his head. Accompanied by another strange figure, the Club Man, who wears a variety of strange clothes and carries a special, soft club, the Hobby Horse sets off in the early morning for his dance around Padstow.

The horse whirls and gyrates through the streets, occasionally pausing to submerge a young woman under his voluminous skirt. The enveloped young ladies are assured of a husband or, if already married, children. From time to time, the horse drops down as though dead, and a dirge is sung over him, but then the May song is resumed and he leaps back to life and the dancing continues. Apart from providing a welcome respite for the poor horse, it is an obvious symbol of the annual cycle of death and renewal. The Hobby Horse, with his great

The Padstow Hobby Horse *(British Tourist Authority)*

crowd of followers, dances on through the morning and into the afternoon when the day ends at the brightly decorated maypole in the market square. A similar custom takes place at Minehead in Somerset, where the Hobby Horse is known as the Sailor's Horse and has his home by the sea.

The Padstow Horse is now an intensely popular tourist attraction, and it might be thought that that is what ensures the survival of the custom. But as anyone who has ever been to Padstow on May Day can tell you, there is a good deal more to it than that. The tourists might come and line the route to watch, but the ceremony itself is not for them: they are always spectators, never participants. The Hobby Horse is Padstow's Hobby Horse, and one has the feeling that they would go on just as they always have, even if not one tourist turned up. In fact, they might well prefer it that way.

The band and dignitaries leading the dancers in Helston's Furry Dance *(British Tourist Authority)*

The same is true of another famous Cornish celebration, held not on May Day itself, but on 8 May, the feast day of St Michael the Archangel, patron of the local parish church. The place is Helston; the ceremony the Furry Dance. The origins of the ceremony take us right back to those standing stones which the Devil was inclined to hurl somewhat indiscriminately around the countryside. The Devil and St Michael fought for the souls of the people of Helston, and the Devil being a poor loser hurled a huge boulder which St Michael caught and gently lowered to the ground. The stone, or part of it, can be seen in the yard of the Angel Hotel. There is nothing, however, that is very Christian about the ritual itself, which is very much – as at Padstow – a celebration of the death of winter and the rebirth of summer. It is not perhaps too surprising to find this mixed up with the other story of the triumph of good over evil.

Helston's Furry Dance is unlike the Padstow celebrations, however, in that the dance involves the whole community. It is not strictly accurate to speak of the Furry Dance, for there are several dances. At seven in the morning, the young people dance through the town; later come the children, dressed in white and wearing or carrying lilies-of-the-valley. There is then one main dance when, led by the mayor in full regalia, all the people of Helston join in. The couples are very formally attired, the men traditionally in morning coats and top hats, the women in their best dresses. The couples dance through the streets and on through gardens, shops and houses, bringing good fortune wherever they go. And all the time the band plays the traditional Furry Dance music. At the end of the day any visitors may join in, but for the main dance they must remain as spectators while the natives of Helston perform their very own rituals.

Music as well as dance has always been associated with the celebration of May Day. The best known, and certainly the most attractive of May Day musical celebrations, is that of Oxford. You have to be up early in the morning to hear it, but every year thousands are present. The ceremony takes place at Magdalen College promptly at six in the morning. The College choristers climb to the top of Magdalen Tower to sing the hymn *Te Deum Patrem colimus*. After that the bells ring and Morris dancers, including one of the most famous of all groups – the Headington Men – dance off down the

Morris dancers in Oxford on May morning *(British Tourist Authority)*

street. This is the signal for more general music making, with everyone from folk groups to – in recent years – rock bands adding their bit to a very festive morning. The actual music to be heard on an Oxford May Day morning may not always be traditional, but the idea of everyone dashing off to make music has been part of the Oxford celebrations for a very long time.

If more rituals have survived around May Day than around most other days in the calendar, that does not mean that other dates are without their special and sometimes very unusual ceremonies. So, here are a few ceremonials spread throughout the year. There were once many more, and all would once have had more significance to the local community than they have now. Some old traditions have been absorbed into what one might call the modern commercial festivals. St Valentine's Day, 14 February, was once an important date when a number of serious rituals were performed; now it is just a bit of a joke, and an occasion for buying and sending mass-produced cards. The card makers, dissatisfied with such traditional dates as Christmas and birthdays, have become assiduous manufacturers of new anniversaries, such as Father's Day. Perhaps in time these dates, too, will be seen as traditional, but there will always be a distinction between those dates which have great religious significance (even if the religion might change from time to time) and those promoted to make a profit. The list that follows is a selection of particularly interesting customs and rituals, most of which are now so ancient that their origins might be deduced, but seldom absolutely known. They are also events which can seem strange and bizarre to outsiders, but which, tied to a particular spot for centuries, seem part of the normal pattern of life to the locals.

This extraordinary year could well begin on 11 January at Burghead in Grampian. Strictly speaking, the old custom practised here represents the end of the old year, for 11 January would have been New Year's Eve before the calendar changes of the eighteenth century. The locals decided simply to ignore the changes and continued their old rituals on the day on which they had always been performed. So, New Year's Eve old style – or plain boring 11 January new style – is the day for the Burning of the Clavie. The Clavie itself is like a great torch, prepared and lit according to rigid rules. The basic holder is made up of the bottom of the barrel nailed to a long pole, which sounds straightforward enough, but even here strict regulations are applied. The pole or spoke has to be a salmon fisherman's stake; the nail is specially forged for the occasion and hammered into place with a stone instead of the conventional hammer. The container is strengthened by the addition of parts of a herring barrel, and the clavie is filled with wood from the same barrel that forms the firebasket. The whole assembly is controlled by a Clavie King, who has the responsibility of ensuring that everything follows the correct pattern. When evening comes, burning peat is brought out from one of the cottages, the clavie is lit and then smothered in tar so that flames shoot up to the sky. It is carried in procession to a headland where it is set on a special stone pillar. After it has burned for a while, the clavie is smashed into pieces, at which there is a mad rush for the smouldering fragments which are supposed to bring good luck. It might be thought of as a ceremony to bless the New Year, but it was originally marking an end not a beginning – the end of Yule, and the end of the old year.

A far more famous ceremony marks the end of Yule in the Shetland Islands – Up-Helly-Aa, which falls on Twenty-fourth Night, now reckoned as the last Tuesday in January. It is another of the festivals which attracts national attention, though mostly through television. Early summer visitors might swell the crowds for the Maytime celebrations in Cornwall, but there are rather fewer prepared to make a winter excursion to the Shetlands. The festival has changed a good deal over the centuries, but in its present form it emphasises the islands' connections with the Norsemen who settled here more than 1,000 years ago. The model of a Viking long boat, some 30ft long, is constructed and dragged through the streets by torch bearers in Viking costume. At the climax of the ceremony, the torches are hurled into the boat and the result of a year's work goes up in flames. As the boat burns, the crowd sings a Norse song, and then the next stage of the proceedings begins – dancing, singing and a fair bit of drinking. So the old year ends and continuity with the Norse past is retained.

Quite where the next burning ceremony originated is uncertain, and it is, in any case, rapidly dying away. The figure that is burned is not the effigy of some old Viking warrior chief, but that of Judas Iscariot and the scene is now the centre of Liverpool's decaying dockland. At first light on Good Friday morning, the local kids take to the streets with their Judas figures, straw dummies dressed in old cast-offs. They knock up the households demanding money, and when their pockets are full – or they decide they are not likely to get any more – Judas is set up on the bonfire and duly burned. The custom of burning Judas is more common in Catholic Europe and it seems likely that it was sailors who were responsible for bringing the practice to Liverpool.

The week after Easter, on the two days following Low Sunday, once saw some of the year's most boisterous feasting. This was Hocktide, all but forgotten now, but still an important time in the affairs of Hungerford in Berkshire. Hungerford is one of those towns which, instead of being run by Mayor and Corporation, is controlled by a Sheriff or Constable and Court. The officials are always elected at a Hocktide Court, which is all very proper and solemn, while elsewhere in the town other business is carried on which, if not improper, is at least a good deal less solemn. Two Tutti-men and an Orange Scrambler set off on their tour. The Tutti-men were the old town

Hungerford's Tutti-men claiming their Hocktide kisses *(British Tourist Authority)*

wardens who kept watch over the place throughout the year, and collected their dues of a penny per head at Hocktide. They each carry staffs decorated with ribbons and flowers and topped with an orange. Fully arrayed, they set off to claim their dues: though the women of the house have the right to offer a kiss instead of a penny. If the kiss is accepted, an orange is offered in return. The Orange Scrambler has the busy task of sticking new oranges on the staffs. Kisses are also demanded of non-Hungerfordians who happen to take the Tutti-men's fancy. The morning ends with a luncheon at the Three Swans, presided over by the newly elected Constable, at the end of which the Tutti-men and the Scrambler shower down the remaining oranges on a waiting crowd of children. There is one other ceremony to the day, an initiation ceremony, but that is strictly reserved for Hungerford men and those who are joining the community. Like all the best ceremonies, Hocktide at Hungerford still retains significance for the local community: it has not degenerated into a mere show.

Ascension Day, which follows on fifty days after Easter, is another of those fixed points in the Ecclesiastical year which once had special significance for the community as a whole, but now go largely unmarked. It is, however, marked in Whitby, where on every Ascension Eve the Penny Hedge is planted out as it has been since – it is said – the twelfth century. It was originally a ceremony which ensured that certain tenants of Whitby Abbey could continue in their tenancy. Its origin goes back to a dastardly deed, when three huntsmen chased a boar which ran into a hermit's chapel. The hermit closed the door behind it, at which the infuriated huntsmen beat the old hermit to death. This early and extreme example of the clash between huntsmen and their opponents had long-term effects. Before the hermit died, he forgave his assailants but insisted that, in future, they should hold their lands only as tenants of the Abbey, and would have to reaffirm their rights in an annual ceremony. The pact was sealed, the hermit died and ever since the hedge has been planted on Ascension Eve. There is a complicating factor in this annual replanting: the hedge has to be planted on the shore below high-water mark, and must stand for three tides. When the hedge is completed the Manor Bailiff blows a horn and shouts, 'Out upon ye! Out upon ye!' which is said to recall the original incident.

From hedges to trees might seem a small step, but the Arbor Tree ceremony dates back far further than the Whitby hedge planting, right back to the ancient British religion of tree worship. Very little of that old cult survives, though it turns up again with Christmas holly and, more especially, the mistletoe bough. At Aston-on-Clun in Shropshire, a tall poplar in the centre of the village is decked out in flags on Arbor Day, 29 May, and the flags remain throughout the year. No one is quite sure why it is done, but it is generally said locally that it commemorates an eighteenth-century wedding. It most certainly goes back further to tree worship, and the more modern story simply provides a rationale for the custom. It is, after all, somewhat unlikely that there should be many active tree worshippers in twentieth-century Aston.

At least one can make a reasonable assumption about the origin of the Arbor Tree, but once a year, on the Saturday nearest to St Bartholomew's Day, the folk of West Witton in Wensleydale burn an effigy of a character known as 'Bartle' – and no one seems to have the least notion of just who the original Bartle was. Nevertheless, the figure is carried around the village and displayed to everyone along the way. A splendidly enigmatic verse is then declaimed, describing a series of calamities that befell Bartle, starting at Pen Hill where he 'tore his rags' and finishing with 'At Grassgill End he made his end', having broken his knee and his neck along the way. And at Grassgill he does indeed make his end, on the bonfire. Bartle's identity seems lost for ever, and those who visit this lovely part of Yorkshire will find that other things have been lost as well – most notably the famous Wensleydale cheese. The stuff produced these days under the name Wensleydale is nothing like the original, made in local farms for centuries. No doubt it still would be made if some busybody from The Ministry had not arrived one day and informed the astonished locals that their delicious cheese did not comply with some petty regulation, and production must stop on the instant. There was a certain amount of 'cheese bootlegging' after that, but the great days of a great cheese were over. If the ceremony was not known to be somewhat older, one might well believe that Bartle was The Man from The Ministry.

The strangest of all August rituals takes place on the day before the Ferry Fair at South Queensferry in Lothian. This is, in fact, one of the strangest and most mysterious of all old British customs, and there is something very satisfying to find it carried out in the shadow of one of the great monuments to Victorian rational thought, the railway bridge across the Firth of Forth. Each year on this day one man is dressed in a white flannel costume, with just his eyes visible, and burrs are then stuck all over the flannel, so that he becomes like a moving bush. In his outstretched hands he carries two staves, decked with flowers and he wears a headgear made up of roses. The strange creature makes his slow progress around the town, with two attendants who help to take the weight of the staves. Seven miles he walks, arms outstretched all the time, stopping at each house but never speaking. People come out to give him gifts, but the Burryman merely stands there. The origins of this ceremony have long been lost but are clearly very ancient, and one can only marvel at the persistence of such strange rituals which have lasted down through the centuries.

September sees another, almost equally strange, custom – the Abbots Bromley Horn Dance. The dance takes place on the Monday after the first Sunday after 4 September, and it begins outside the vicarage at eight in the morning. Six sets of reindeer antlers are handed out from the church, the largest having a spread of 2ft and going to the chief dancer. The six dancers wear a form of Tudor costume, and they carry the antlers in such a way that they appear to belong to the human figures. They are joined by Fool, hobby horse, bowman, a man dressed in women's clothing and known as Maid Marian, and two musicians. Such dances are very ancient, and can even be seen depicted in cave paintings, though some of the attendants may have been added on over the years. Quite why Tudor dress is worn is uncertain. It is possible that the earliest dancers were nude, and that this represents the first costume worn, and has been kept on in much the same form ever since.

The period around Hallowe'en is one featured particularly in old customs, but mostly not connected with any one place – everyone can join in. It is a time for ghosts and spirits, when mischief is abroad in the land. Nowadays the spirits tend to be no more frightening than children in masks and turnip lanterns. The degree of mischief involved is also variable. Children in Yorkshire celebrate 4 November as Mischief Night. As children we used to enjoy having semi-official

The Horn dancers of Abbots Bromley *(British Tourist Authority)*

licence to run riot – later, as adults, we tend to suffer from lapses of memory and regard the whole thing as an anti-social nuisance. The following day is, of course, associated with Guy Fawkes, bonfires and fireworks – but there are other strange ceremonies on the same day. At Ottery St Mary in Devon, the bonfire is enlivened by the addition of tar barrels. The barrels are lit, then rolled or carried through the streets to end up on the fire. Not so far away in Shebbear there is a quite different event – Turning the Devil's Boulder. Once again, the Devil has been littering the landscape with rocks: this particular example stands just outside the churchyard and, because of its Satanic associations, the annual ritual has to be performed to keep evil at bay. Quite what form the diabolic association takes is unclear. One story has it that the boulder was dropped by the Devil on his flight from heaven to hell. Another has it that the stone was quarried locally for rebuilding a church, but was returned to this spot every night after it had been moved during the day – the Devil, not wanting to see the church completed, being the culprit. In either case, the Devil has to be kept at bay by ringing a discordant peal on the church bells, while two men with crowbars turn the boulder over.

November, with its fireworks and discordant chimes, is then an unusually noisy month. There is a further eruption of noise on the 11th at Fenny Stratford in Buckinghamshire, when the Fenny Poppers are fired. These are six miniature cannon, which are fired three times during that day, which is the feast day of St Martin. St Martin is the patron saint of the local church which was built largely through the efforts and benevolence of Dr Browne Willis. When he died in 1760, the cannon firing was introduced in his memory and has continued ever since.

December brings Christmas and the familiar traditions, but few which have any local peculiarities. Some old traditions are kept on, such as the mummers' play performed on Christmas Eve at Marshfield in Avon, but mostly the season is celebrated by families in their own homes. For end of the year celebrations there is really only one place to be – Scotland, where apart from drinking out the

*(opposite)* Guy Fawkes' Night in Ottery St Mary features burning tar barrels carried through the streets *(Exeter Express & Echo)*

old year they also burn it out. There are many variations on this old practice of lighting fires to mark the end of winter and darkness and the coming of light, spring and renewal. At Biggar they light a giant bonfire. At Comrie in Tayside the citizens dress up in all kinds of costumes and parade through the streets carrying flaming torches. But for quite the most spectacular end to the year, and to this look at the year's customs, one should travel to Stonehouse in Grampian for the fireball parade. The balls are made of cloth soaked in tar and are held in a wire cage at the end of a long wire. They are lit and then whirled round their heads by the young men in the procession. It looks spectacular and downright alarming, but is actually safer than it appears. It is intended to keep the evil spirits at bay and send them scurrying back to the graveyard where they belong. There, if they have nothing better to do, they can contemplate some of the strange ways men have chosen to commemorate the dead.

# 9
# Memento Mori

Graveyards are little used these days – land for the living being considered too scarce and expensive a commodity to be squandered on the dead. The crematorium with its neat rows of urns and crosses has taken over from the old, cluttered churchyard and no doubt it all adds up to a good thing. Death can be safely tucked away behind high walls and hedges and even those who venture inside the boundaries can be reassured by the impersonality of the scene, which seems to have so little to do with the messy realities of life and death. It is removed from the world we know, it is remote, almost inhuman. One cannot imagine anyone sitting down to pen lines in a country crematorium.

It was not always so. Our ancestors proved as quirky in their commemoration of death as they ever were in their celebration of living. The British have never been great ones for elaboration in their graveyards: compared with the cemetery in even the most modest French village, all but the grandest of our tombs might seem insipid. Just occasionally, there have been moves towards establishing grandiose cemeteries complete with great mausolea in the continental style. You can see such grand, not to say grandiose, schemes in London – in Kensal Green and, most dramatically, in Highgate Cemetery.

Highgate must be the least British of all British cemeteries – and it often seems more so today when the visitor is very liable to find troops of solemn-faced Chinese and Russians on their way to pay homage at the tomb of Karl Marx. If, however, one penetrates deeper into the cemetery one comes across a section of mausolea which look for all the world – or should one say all the other world – like imports from Transylvania. Behind an entrance in the Egyptian style lie the catacombs, vaults through whose crumbling, weed-covered walls one catches unnerving glimpses of coffins. It is, without question, the

The catacombs at Highgate in their days of Victorian splendour *(BBC Hulton Picture Library)*

spookiest, most unnerving spot in London. Forget the Chamber of Horrors, forget the Dungeons. If you really want to have your spine chilled, then visit Highgate on a misty November evening.

Not surprisingly, a number of strange stories surround this eerie spot – and not merely tales of events long gone. In 1970, there was a great furore over evidence of black magic and satanic rites at the catacombs. There were also stories of a mysterious apparition and at least one vampire was reported. All kinds of people from sensation seekers to amateur exorcists and television teams swarmed around the area of the catacombs, and in the end the authorities were forced to close off this area of the cemetery. The stories all seem incredible, just so much mumbo-jumbo, when read in a nice, warm, comfortable arm-chair. But in the cemetery, when the mist is just beginning to smoke around the crumbling vaults . . .

A reminder of one of the grimmer episodes in history can be found in some churchyards in the measures that were taken to thwart the resurrectionists, those grave robbers who disinterred newly buried corpses to sell to the anatomists at the local medical schools. The most famous of these somewhat unsavoury gentlemen were Burke and Hare who, failing to find enough bodies to satisfy the Edinburgh doctor Knox, solved the shortage problem by creating corpses for themselves. There was a rhyme that became popular after their crimes were discovered:

> Down the Close and up the Stair
> But and ben wi' Burke and Hare.
> Burke's the butcher, Hare's the thief,
> Knox the man that buys the beef.

Most resurrectionists stopped short of murder, and it could be argued that they performed a public service by aiding medical research. Grieving relatives took a less altruistic view, and took steps to ensure that once they had buried their kin, their kin should remain buried.

One solution was to hire a watchman to guard fresh graves, and at Wanstead in London you can still see the stone sentry box where he kept his vigil. Another solution was to make it as difficult as possible for the resurrection men to get into the graves. At Aberfoyle in Scotland, one grave is most securely guarded by a vast iron mortsafe, a contraption placed over the grave which is so heavy that it could only be lifted off again with the aid of a block and tackle. Even the most enthusiastic grave robber would have second thoughts about arriving in a churchyard at midnight with a small derrick.

Other, apparently equally impregnable, graves are not always quite what they seem. A monument in Pinner churchyard would appear to have a coffin set half way up a great stone pyramid – but the coffin, too, is stone and empty. John Claudius Loudon, the landscape gardener and publisher of Humphrey Repton's work, was not noticeably whimsical in his working life, but when it came to executing his father's will he showed that he possessed a somewhat bizarre imagination. He had been presented with something of a problem, for his father had expressed the desire to be buried above ground – hence, as they say, the pyramid. The 'coffin' was buried within the pyramid, well above ground level. It was, however, no more than a gesture, for there is no body in that airy resting place.

An equally strange stone pyramid can be seen in Sharow churchyard in North Yorkshire, marking the grave of Charles Piazzi Smyth, a former Astronomer Royal for Scotland. He was a most distinguished holder of that office, and did a great deal for the science, though none of his official work had anything to do with pyramids. His private work did – he was one of the principal explorers of the Great Pyramid at Giza, and in his exploration of its many intricate passages and tunnels he reached the conclusion that the pyramid's measurements had some special significance. Scientists of the day refused even to consider his evidence, but the notion that pyramids might be something more than arbitrarily piled-up blocks of stone has gained considerable currency in recent years. Smyth would no doubt have been pleased by the news that the special properties of pyramids built to the same ratios as the Great Pyramid have been officially recognised. A radio engineer from Prague claimed that a razor blade placed under a cardboard pyramid built in these proportions would sharpen itself. His claim was tested, declared officially proven and the Cheops Razor Blade Sharpener was dignified with the designation Czech Patent No. 91304. This was some time after Smyth's death, and he had to content himself with a pyramid over his grave. If other theories about the special powers of pyramids are true, then his body might by now have become mummified.

The great pioneer of the iron industry, John Wilkinson, was less fortunate in his choice of memorials. When he died in 1801 he had to his credit the invention of a machine for boring through iron, making it possible for steam engine cylinders to be bored with accuracy; he had built the first iron boat, a barge which was launched on the Severn

*(opposite)* Classical dignity at All Saints, Sandon in Staffordshire *(National Monuments Record)*

HI[C]

...verendi Johannis Cotton

...ielmi & Mariæ Cotton

de Cotwalton pii filii;

...non hujus Eccleshæ Vicarii.

...Deo...obiit...Feb: 1745

near the Wilkinson works, and he played a part in the construction of
the famous iron bridge over the Severn at Ironbridge. Not
surprisingly, he wanted an iron memorial. He was buried in the
garden of his house and an iron obelisk was erected to mark the spot.
The house was then let, and the new tenants were reluctant to include
the late Mr Wilkinson in the inventory. The church was happy to
accept his remains, but was less happy about taking in the obelisk. So,
iron master and monument were parted: master settled inside Lindale
churchyard, near Grange-over-Sands; monument left outside hallowed
ground.

The Lindale obelisk is not the only monument to be found outside
the normal confines of the churchyard. A number were set up on the
sites of some unfortunate tragedies, generally those in which the
victim met a notably violent end. Murder was often marked by a stone
at the site of the deed. Some record the date of the death, and the
names of both victim and perpetrator. At least one, however, contains
just the one name. 'Scotsman's Stump' on the moors above Rivington
in Lancashire marks the spot where a wandering Scottish pedlar was
killed and robbed. His murderers were never discovered and, not
surprisingly, the pedlar's ghost is said to wander the moorland, still
waiting for revenge.

Accidents are also recorded by stones. A small stone cross by the
roadside at Ganton, just south of Scarborough in North Yorkshire,
shows where, a century ago, a huntsman was thrown and killed. But
what do you do when someone meets his death in the middle of a river?
Stage coaches used to cross the river Wylye in Wiltshire by a ford,
and one unfortunate postillion died in the crossing. He was not struck
by lightning, the traditional fate of his clan, but washed off the coach
in a flood and drowned. There was only one place to erect the
monument, and there it was duly set, in the middle of the stream by
Wylye Mill. An even odder monument can be seen in the river Ouse at
Turvey in Bedfordshire. It certainly fits its watery stance, for it is a
statue of a man holding a fish. It is a work of some antiquity and of
uncertain origins, for it was found in the river. It was generally
thought to be a representation of the Fisherman Peter, which would
originally have been housed in some church. But how did it get into
the river? The coroner sat on the stone corpse and recorded a verdict

Rising up at the last trump: a headstone from the churchyard at St John sub Castro, Lewes *(National Monuments Record)*

There's no mistaking the former occupation of the inhabitant of this grave in the churchyard at St John sub Castro, Lewes *(National Monuments Record)*

of 'found drowned', and the suicidal statue was restored to stand in midstream.

Most memento mori do not occur in such odd surroundings. The traditional country churchyard is the place where family goes to remember family, a homely place with homely gravestones carrying simple messages. Some, however, are more homely than others. Among the most fascinating of gravestones are those which show some aspect of the occupant's former working life. Mark Sharp was a carpenter who died at Lewes in Sussex in 1747 and carved on his headstone one can see all the tools of his trade – plane, saw, axe, set square, chisel, calipers and many more to a grand total of fourteen different tools. An equally appropriate memorial can be seen at Kildwick in Yorkshire, where the grave of a former church organist is marked by a beautifully carved church organ. but what should one make of another Yorkshire monument, at Kirkheaton? This one is in the form of a beer barrel. Was the occupant of the grave a brewer perhaps, or a cooper? Or was he, as local legend has it, the town drunk whose widow chose the barrel as a last revenge on her feckless husband? If the latter, then one can at least say that he died in the pursuit of pleasure rather than profit, as did the unhappy Miss Lily Cove, commemorated in yet another Yorkshire monument. She ascended in a balloon, piloted by a Captain Bridmead, in order to give a demonstration of her parachuting skills. The balloon went up, Miss Cove came down, but sadly the parachute failed to open – the fatal balloon is pictured on her gravestone. At least she had the honour of burial in one of the most famous churchyards in the land, the churchyard at Haworth overlooked by the parsonage which housed the remarkable Brontë family. She must however, concede the prize for the most evocative 'hobby' stone to that which stands above the grave of Harry Bagshaw in Eyam, Derbyshire. Bagshaw played cricket for both Derbyshire and England, but was finally bowled out in 1924. His tombstone shows a bat – far from straight, it must be said – behind which the ball can be seen neatly removing his middle stump. Lest anyone be in any doubt as to what happened, above that is a finger forever raised – indicating that Harry Bagshaw was indeed 'out'. This is matched by the memorial at Petersfield, Hants, to the last survivor of that noble band from Hambledon who set the great

An old Norfolk couple buried side by side in Ashby churchyard *(National Monuments Record)*

game on its way. The inscription is simple, recording the fact that in 1826, John Small had been finally 'bowled out by death's unerring ball'.

John Small played long before the days when cricket was a profession, so let us return to those graves which showed their occupants earning an honest crust. Quite the most attractive examples are those of George and Ann Basey at Ashby St Mary in Norfolk. They were a farming family and the delightful carvings on their headstones show them going about their work. Ann was the first to die in 1868 at the age of seventy-one, and she is shown feeding a flock of turkeys – and fine, plump Norfolk turkeys they look too. Her husband leans over the fence, watching her. He died eight years later at the age of eighty-two, and he too is shown at work. A few of the same turkeys appear, but they are outnumbered by the sheep, which were clearly George's main concern. Norfolk has traditionally been the land of the sheep and the turkey and in the memorial to this sturdy yeoman and his wife there stand monuments that speak not just for two individuals but for a whole region.

The Baseys epitomised the best of old rural Britain; the railway navvies who helped to change the face of the country epitomised the new. They too have their own memorial, and one which speaks just as strongly of their way of life as the other does for the Baseys. The navvies were an itinerant work force, known only as a group, seldom recognised as individuals – and it is as a group that they are commemorated in Otley churchyard. The present main line from Leeds to Harrogate – the old Leeds and Thirsk Railway – passes through a long tunnel at Bramhope, the northern entrance of which was described in Chapter Four. This same design is repeated at Otley – a tunnel in miniature, with all the castellations and towers of the entrance in place. Tunnelling was a dangerous business and many died in the years from 1845 to 1849 when Bramhope was being built. No individuals are named, for it is doubtful if anyone knew their names. The inscription speaks for all the navvies, who left their homes to die an anonymous death beneath a hill in Yorkshire: 'I am a stranger and a sojourner with you.'

The early railways saw more than their share of fatal accidents. It began with the navvies who built the line and continued with the men who ran the locomotives. Those early engines were by no means completely safe, and the engineers themselves added to the risks by such dangerous practices as screwing down safety valves to get more pressure and thus more power. Too often, the result was a boiler explosion and it was an exploding boiler on the Birmingham and Gloucester Railway that killed the two men on the footplate of a locomotive in 1840. They were buried side by side in Bromsgrove churchyard, each headstone carrying a representation of the locomotive. An anonymous friend added these lines on the memorial to one of the engineers, Thomas Scaife:

> My *engine* now is cold and still.
> No water does my *boiler* fill:
> My *coke* affords its flame no more,
> My days of usefulness are o'er.
> My *wheels* deny their noted speed,
> No more my guiding hand they heed.
> My *whistle* too has lost its tone,
> Its shrill and thrilling sounds have gone.

My *valves* are now thrown open wide,
My *flanges* all refuse to guide.
My *clacks* also, though once so strong
Refuse to aid the busy throng.
No more I feel each urging breath,
My *steam* is now condens'd in death.
Life's *railway*'s o'er, each *station*'s past,
In death I'm stopp'd and rest at last.
Farewell dear friends and cease to weep.
In Christ I'm safe, in Him I sleep.

For some reason, railway disasters seem to have evoked elaborate epitaphs, full of railway metaphors which might seem slightly comical to us today, but which were deeply felt by those who wrote them. A tablet in Ely Cathedral pushed the imagery even further in one of the

A railwayman's grave and the locomotive whose exploding boiler put him there: Bromsgrove churchyard *(Reece Winstone)*

most extraordinarily long epitaphs of the country. It is dedicated to
William Pickering, driver, and Richard Edgar, fireman, two more
victims of boiler explosions:

> The line to heaven by Christ was made
> With heavenly truth the Rails are laid.
> From Earth to Heaven the Line extends
> To Life eternal where it ends
> Repentance is the Station then
> Where Passengers are taken in.
> No fee for them is there to pay
> For Jesus is himself the way
> God's word is the first Engineer
> It points the way to Heaven so dear.
> Through tunnels dark and dreary here
> It does the way to Glory steer.
> God's Love the Fire, his Truth the Steam,
> Which drives the Engine and the Train,
> All you who would to Glory ride,
> Must come to Christ, in him abide
> In First and Second, and Third Class,
> Repentance, Faith and Holiness.

There is quite a deal more of this eptiaph, which is entitled 'The
Spiritual Railway', and it is quite the most elaborate of all such
exercises. Other trades and professions also ended up providing
material for headstones and memorial plaques, and here is one of the
very best from Lydford in Devon:

> Here lies, in horizontal position
>   the outside case of
> George Routleigh, Watchmaker;
> Whose abilities in that time were an honour
>   to his profession,
> Integrity was the Mainspring, and prudence the Regulator,
>   of all the actions of his life.
> Humane, generous and liberal,
> His Hand never stopped
>   till he had relieved distress.

So nicely regulated were all his motions,
    that he never went wrong,
    except when set a-going
    by people
    who did not know his key;
Even though he was easily
    set right again.
He had the art of disposing his time so well,
    that his hours glided away
    on one continual round
    of pleasure and delight,
Until an unlucky minute put a period to
    his existence
He departed this life
    Nov. 14, 1802:
    aged 57:
    wound up,
In hopes of being taken in hand,
    by his Maker;
And of being thoroughly cleaned, repaired,
    and set a-going
in the world to come.

There is more than a touch of humour in the epitaph. The touch is firmer in the lines to Joseph Wright, auctioneer of Corby Glen, Lincolnshire. He was killed when he fell from his trap and was dragged along behind the horse, until:

    grim Death, with visage queer,
    Assumed Joe's trade of Auctioneer,
    Made him the Lot to Practice on,
    With 'going, going' and anon,
    He knocked him down to 'Poor Joe's gone'.

Humour is surprisingly common in epitaphs. It is perhaps not so astonishing, and certainly not as irreligious as it might appear. In past ages, religious faith was a good deal stronger than it is today, so that death was not necessarily seen as a total calamity. It was an entrance to a better world. So epitaph writers could cheerfully indulge in thoroughly bad puns, as in these lines to a boy named Calf, written in the seventeenth century and found in Gloucester Cathedral:

Oh cruel Death, more subtle than the Fox,
To kill the Calf, e'er he became an Ox.

But for an absolute welter of punning, one cannot beat the lines to Sir
Richard Worme in Peterborough:

Does Worm eat Worme? Knight Worme this Truth confirms,
For here with Worms, lies Worme, a Dish of Worms.
Does Worm eat Worme? Sure Worme will this deny,
For Worme with Worms, a Dish for Worms don't lie.
'Tis so, and 'tis not so, for free from Worms,
'Tis certain Worme is blest without his Worms.

The quirkiest epitaph must surely be that at Bampton in Devon,
dedicated simply to the memory of 'The Clerk's Son'. It reads:

Bless my i.i.i.i.i.i.
Here he lies
In a sad pickle
Kill'd by an Icicle.
In the year, 1776.

There is no name, nor any indication of how the icicle helped the
youth on his way out of this world.

Memorials are not limited to recording the doings, or goings, of
Homo sapiens. Other animals are occasionally introduced and seem at
least as important to the memorialist as the human element. John
Wyard, who died in 1867, was buried at Offton in Suffolk and was
clearly a notable horseman. Above his grave is a sculpture showing his
wife leading his favourite horse to mourn for his old master. Other
memorials go further. They do not show animals grieving for man,
but are instead monuments to the animals themselves. The most
famous is in Edinburgh, a memorial to the dog which never forgot its
master – Bobby of Greyfriars. Others are even simpler, expressions of
a human's love for his animal, whether workmate or friend. Not too
surprisingly, horses feature prominently in such dedications. One of
the most famous horses of recent years has an impressive memorial on
an impressive site. The horse is Foxhunter, a great show jumper
which carried its rider Harry Llewellyn to three victories in the King
George V Gold Cup. His memorial is to be seen on open moorland,
high in the Brecon Beacons in Wales.

The most famous of all canine monuments — the statue of Greyfriars Bobby in Edinburgh *(British Tourist Authority)*

A simple gravestone at St Mary Redcliffe, Bristol *(British Tourist Authority)*

Dogs are also well represented in the ranks of animal memorials. Tell's Tower at West Kirby in Merseyside stands 25ft high, a suitably large monument for a very large dog, for Tell was a Saint Bernard. Hounds also figure largely, though generally in the metaphorical rather than, as in Tell's case, the literal sense. 'Trouncer', the one-time scourge of Suffolk foxes, has a commemorative tablet, recording his death in 1788, set up in the wall at Euston Park. It carries the message: 'Foxes Rejoice: Here Buried Lies Your Foe'. More foxes slept easily in the vicinity of Rousham, the fine Oxfordshire house, when the best hunting hounds' days came to an end, and these hounds were also given a grand memorial in the grounds. Cats are, for some reason, less well represented – perhaps because it might seem an impertinence to attempt to do anything for such independent creatures. An exception can be seen in a splendid cat monument, with the animal crouching on a high pillar, in the grounds of Shugborough

IN
MEMORY
OF THE
OLD FISH

UNDER THE SOIL
THE OLD FISH DO LIE
20 YEARS HE LIVED
AND THEN DID, DIE
HE, WAS SO TAME
YOU, UNDERSTAND
HE, WOULD, COME, AND
EAT, OUT OF, OUR HAND
DIED April the 20th 1855
Aged 20 YEARS

Hall in Staffordshire. A still more unusual pet is commemorated in a stone beside the main road from Manchester to Halifax. It records the sad demise of one Dick, who died at the age of twenty-three in 1923 – Dick was a pet gander. Odder still is the memorial found by a stream at Blockley in Gloucestershire. The epitaph speaks for itself:

> In
> Memory
> of the
> Old Fish
> Under the soil
> The Old Fish do lie
> 20 years he lived
> And then did die
> He was so tame
> You understand
> He would come and
> Eat out of our hand.

It is said that the world's most impressive memorial is the Taj Mahal in India, and no doubt it is. The idea of a great palace which serves no function other than to record a bereavement seems strange to us. Yet if Britain cannot boast anything to match this beautiful memorial, it can at least boast one which attempts the task.

Any visitor to the city of Lancaster cannot fail to notice the Ashton memorial, which stands on top of a hill surrounded by the formal gardens of Williamson Park. It quite dominates the city. Lord Ashton made his fortune from linoleum, and a very considerable fortune it must have been to allow him to spend £87,000 in 1906 for this memorial to his wife. It is a tall building, colonnaded at the base and topped by a dome, and it fulfils no practical function whatsoever. Dedicated as it is to the wife of one of the great Victorian industrialists, it is perhaps not altogether surprising to find some odd little details lurking in among the strictly classical forms of the main structure. They certainly help to make the memorial unique, for how many other Victorian ladies could boast a monument across which a 4-4-4 locomotive steams in perpetual stone?

*(opposite)* The fish monument at Blockley *(British Tourist Authority)*

Having started with standing stones and arrived at gravestones, this might seem an appropriate place to end this brief survey of oddities and curiosities. Everything has found its place, neatly confined within a chapter, labelled and stowed away. Yet surely one of the great attractions about oddities is that they are not so easily disposed of. So let us have one more chapter, a rag-bag of favourites that belong here for no better reason than that they do not belong anywhere else either. And we shall simply call it . . .

*(opposite)* Lancaster's answer to the Taj Mahal: the Ashton Memorial *(British Tourist Authority)*

# 10
# Odds and Ends of Oddities

The world is full of little oddities which it is all too easy to pass by without a glance. Perhaps oddity is not quite the right word, since they were often put there in the first place for sound, practical reasons, but their usefulness having ended long ago we look at them with bewilderment. What are they? Who put them there and why? It is their role as functional objects without a function which makes them seem somehow strange.

Street lighting is a case in point. The ubiquitous electric light made the gas lamp obsolete, just as the gas light had once superseded the lanterns and flaming torches of the link men. Yet even these older lights have left physical evidence of their use behind. In Georgian Bath you can see examples of decorative wrought-iron gateways with a loop for a lantern and an iron cone which looks like, and indeed is, an overgrown candle snuffer, for it was used to snuff out the link men's torches. The ornate gas lamp is still with us, if only just, but is still sufficiently common not to be thought of as especially strange – though not in every case. Gas lamps can be seen in Carting Lane off the Strand in London, but these lamps were not run on the old town gas nor even on modern North Sea Gas. They are examples of J. E. Webb's Patent Sewer Lamps, and they ran on the gas produced in the sewers below the street.

Sewers are themselves fascinating places, great works of civil engineering which few of us get the chance to see or explore. It has to be admitted that not everyone would wish to do so. Everyone, however, has added his or her share to the underground flow via a public lavatory. The Victorians who were the builders of the huge and ornate sewage pumping stations were also the great providers of the public loo. There was, in fact, an appalling shortage of such institutions before the middle of the nineteenth century. When they did arrive, the gents, as always, got the best of the deal, thanks largely to their anatomy – the stand-up urinal being much cheaper to install than those which had to be fitted with seats. Victorian urinals still linger in our cities, often lurking down back alleys. The simplest are no more than screens, shoes visible below and hats above. These shelters could be quite ornate and decorative, particularly when the screen was made from cast iron. The design at its simplest can be seen, for example, in Birmingham where the screens are no more than a rectangle of metal, curved round at either end and set up against the street wall. At the opposite end of the ornamental scale are the circular loos of Bristol, looking like miniature temples or even – since there is an Oriental feel about the decoration – miniature Taj Mahals. Unlike most such edifices, they are dignified with roofs in the shape of open-work domes. Nowadays, there are so few really good examples of the cast-iron pissoir that they have even found a place in the nostalgia industry. The Severn Valley Railway, one of the many devoted to preserving and running old steam locomotives, has specialised in re-creating stations as they would have been in the days when steam power ruled the system. At Bewdley Station they have added a fine cast-iron Gents' to the platform furniture.

In the case of the cast-iron Gents', the decoration is intended to give propriety to the scene, to disguise the function. With public lavatories now reasonably common, decorum is preserved by supplying a discreet entrance with an equally discreet sign to indicate what is what. There was quite a vogue at one time for making discretion doubly discreet by building the loos underground. Occasionally the entrance steps are marked by ironwork or even ceramic surrounds to the doorway, but in general the greatest glories were reserved for the interior. The extravagant loo, replete with shining brass, coloured tiles and glass cisterns, can happily still be found, sometimes as a solitary reminder of former glories in the world outside. The seaside town of Rothesay on the Isle of Bute has seen better days and its pier is no longer as busy as it used to be: it has the faded charm of a neglected maiden aunt. The busy pleasure boats from Glasgow no longer ply with their crowds of holidaymakers, but the splendid Gents' is still there waiting for their return.

One can expect many things from the municipal loo but not, one

The cast-iron urinal in all its glory in Bristol. This particular example has sadly been demolished, but an identical one stands at Horfield in the same city *(Reece Winstone)*

would think, official humour. There is, however, one such establishment which not only shows humour but subtle humour at that – assuming it is a joke. A Gents' in south-west London boasts an entrance decorated by tiles depicting the first eight bars of Beethoven's setting of Schiller's 'Ode to Joy' from the last movement of the Ninth Symphony. The poem contains two lines which are especially apt:

> Wir bertreten Feuertrunken
> Himmlische, dein Heiligtum.

which could be translated as 'We walk into your heavenly shrine, dazzled by your brilliance.' It ends:

> Alle Menschen werden Brüder
> Wo dein Sanfrer Flügel weilt.

'All men become brothers under your tender wing.' Certainly there are few places where men could be said to be more equal.

If official humour is rare, the public loo remains the greatest repository for unofficial humour. Graffiti have advanced somewhat since the days when the best that could be hoped for in the way of mural inscription was the announcement of the presence of the ubiquitous Kilroy, an exhortation in favour of United, and anatomical sketches in which the vigour of the style was matched only by the inaccuracy of the detail. Nowadays it is not unknown for genuine wit to appear, and even the 'Manufacturers of Porcelain Sanitary Ware' have themselves become the butt of the jokes. One of the best known of such manufacturers is Messrs Armitage Shanks. Above their name in an Oxford loo some puzzled writer has penned the question, 'Who's Armitage? And what's Shanking?' But such messages are, by their nature, ephemeral – and made more so by the growing habit among publicans in particular of providing blackboard and chalk, thereby saving money on redecoration. If such a practice were to become universal, we could be blessed with a whole new medium for casual reading, a sort of combination of public functions. A loobrary perhaps?

The public lavatory provides a first-class illustration of the fact that oddities surround us on all sides, if only we know where to look. Several strange phenomena can be observed in areas not entirely unrelated to the subject of lavatories and sewers. Even so humble an object as the domestic drainpipe can have its surprises. Bucklers Hard on the Beaulieu River in Hampshire was once a great shipbuilding centre, a fact still remembered through the maritime museum there – and through that drainpipe. Look at the top of the pipe on the master builder's house and you can see a fine ship under sail.

Continuing the liquid theme, a great repository of the curious is the inn sign. The name of the pub and the painting on the sign can often give anyone with the time and the patience – or the thirst – an opportunity to get a short lesson in local history. The Cuckoo Bush at Gotham in Nottinghamshire is a perfect example. Gotham is the legendary city of fools and the men of this Gotham, though acting the part, showed that they were in no way short of grey matter in good working order. King John decided that this neighbourhood would make an ideal spot for a hunting lodge, a view not shared by the locals. A royal hunting lodge meant royal rights over the game for miles around, so they set out to persuade the king's men that the local inhabitants were all dangerous lunatics. One trick was to build a fence round a bush, and when anyone enquired why the fence was there they replied that there was a cuckoo in the bush and they wanted to keep it in so that it would sing to them all the year round. This is the scene depicted on the inn sign, yet another example of the traditional antipathy between the men of Nottinghamshire and that most unjustly maligned monarch, John. It is an antipathy perpetuated in the very many signs showing the King's foremost enemy, in mythology if not in fact – Robin Hood. Sometimes the name and the sign have a very obvious derivation. The Barge Inn at Seend stands beside the Kennet and Avon Canal, and the sign shows a canal narrow boat, all very appropriate. But there is more to it than that. The boat on the sign is *Friendship*, the last canal boat in Britain to be worked by 'Number Ones', owners who lived on their boats and plied for trade all over the canal system. These particular owners, Joe and Rosie Skinner, are both dead, and although the boat has gone to a museum it is in a sorry state. But it floats on in all its glory on the pub sign at Seend.

The name of a pub can often tell a story, though it may not always be deciphered with ease. Is the Elephant and Castle in London really a corruption of the Infanta de Castille? It seems a little far fetched. In other cases, the derivation is simpler to trace. What would one make, for example, of the Swan with two Necks on the Thames? Is it a reminder of some obscure mythical beast? The name is in fact a corruption of the swan with two *nicks*. All Thames swans are marked annually, and have been since medieval times, in the ceremony of swan upping. Various owners who had the privilege of keeping swans on the river distinguished theirs from the unmarked royal birds by marking their beaks. Two nicks are the mark of the Vintner's Company, so what could be more appropriate for an inn sign? And what could be more appropriate for a pub entrance than that at the Dragon at Batheaston, Avon? A thousand-gallon barrel has been let into the wall, half sticking out into the street, half intruding, providing a perfect draught-free doorway.

The pub is also one of the great repositories for local games and customs. This may mean no more than that the local is home to the football team and cricket team or that it runs its own darts team. It can, however, be a place where very local games are found, and any particular game can appear in a wide variety of different forms. Take the game of skittles or Aunt Sally. In essence, it involves competitors throwing one object in an attempt to knock over another object. But how you throw, what you throw and what you throw at depend very much on which part of the country you happen to be in at the time. The traditional skittle alley involves throwing a spherical ball at a group of vertical pegs, usually arranged in a triangle – the forerunner of American ten pin bowling. If you are in Staffordshire, however, you will probably find the game reduced to table-top proportions. The ball is hung from a pole by a chain and is swung round to knock down – or not knock down – the skittles. Its small scale makes it ideal for playing in front of a large fire on a cold winter evening when indoor sports come into their own. The Warwickshire version requires rather more space. Here the missile is not a ball, but a thick wooden disc, known by the very descriptive name of 'the cheese'. It is thrown at the skittles using a backhand action. In Oxfordshire, Aunt Sally is an outdoor summer game, requiring a good deal of room. Here the target is 'the dolly', a wooden peg which is balanced on a hoop on top of a metal pole. The ammunition consists of half a dozen sticks, like large batons. It seems the easiest thing in the world to knock the dolly off with one of these large hunks of wood – until you come to try it. So the variations go on.

The oddest of all pub games is dwyle flunking, which is either a new invention by a modern idiot or a very old invention by an ancient idiot. Idiotic it certainly is. There are rules, though few seem to know them, and as any game involves the consumption of vast quantities of ale, those who knew them at the beginning can seldom remember them at the end. In essence, it involves one team dancing round a member of the opposite side, who holds a beer-soaked sponge at the end of a broom handle. The sponge has to be flicked at the dancing team and points are scored depending on the part of the anatomy hit. Failure to score a hit of any kind involves the thrower in downing a large quantity of ale, usually from a chamber pot. It is not unknown for both teams to end the evening insensible – which goes down in the books as an honourable draw. Few other results have ever been recorded.

Games once had a more serious purpose. Pub darts is no more than an indoor, scaled-down version of archery, and there was a time when a man's livelihood, even his life, might depend on his skill with the bow. The archer was once an important part of the nation's army, as was the soldier on horseback. And just as shooting arrows at a target helped to foster the one skill, so tilting at the quintain helped to foster the skills of the cavalryman. There is only one surviving quintain in Britain, and it stands on the village green at Offham in Kent. It consists of a high wooden post, on top of which is pivoted a board, one end of which is marked with five rows of dots and from the other end of which is suspended a heavy bag of sand. The object was for the horseman to gallop at full speed – full tilt – and attempt to hit the dotted end of the board. He was jeered at if he missed, and his troubles were not over if he hit, for unless he was agile the board would swing round and the sandbag knock him off his horse. It thus provided a splendid training in both attack and defence, and kept everyone amused at the same time.

In appearance, the quintain could be mistaken for a gibbet, a grisly pole from which felons' bodies were hung and left to rot as a warning to passers-by. A few of the vile structures remain and those who enjoy such things will, no doubt, have little difficulty in locating

The Coleshill pillory *(British Tourist Authority)*

them. Other survivors of punishments past were no doubt miserable enough places in their day, but are not so grim as the reminders of the noose. The pillory was hardly a joyous spot for those who were placed in it. There is a fine example at Coleshill, near Birmingham, a two-man – or two-woman – pillory. The malefactors stood on a platform some 6ft above the ground, and their hands and heads were then clamped into a board, providing an excellent target for sour fruit, rotten eggs, soggy cabbage or anything else with which the local populace might choose to pelt them. The victims were, in fact, worse off than those placed in the more familiar stocks: here only the ankles were pinioned, giving the victim enough freedom of movement to duck and weave in an attempt to avoid the missiles. Today, they are harmless bygones and tourists photographed in the stocks can smile happily in the knowledge that they can release themselves whenever they choose. As children, we used to play around the stocks at Ripley in North Yorkshire, sitting at the foot of the market cross being pelted by our friends, until shooed away by our elders and betters.

No doubt many of those who occupied pillory or stocks in earnest were there as a result of having drunk too much, and no doubt they received the standard admonition to stay with water in future. That commodity was available through pumps and wells, and among survivors there are some particularly odd examples of water-supply mechanisms. The strangest well must be that at Stoke Row in Oxfordshire. It was presented to the village in 1864 by the Maharajah of Benares, and has a very strong Oriental look to it, which makes it seem quite a bizarre addition to a peaceful rural scene. The actual winding mechanism is, however, very much home produced, built at nearby Wallingford. The well was in the care of a wellkeeper, who had his own little octagonal cottage which was graced by a tall chimney springing up from the centre of the roof.

The wells of Derbyshire are rather more famous, since this is an area which still practises the ancient custom of well dressing. Most famous of all are the wells of Tissington, on the edge of the Peak District National Park. There are five wells in the village – Coffin Well, Hands Well, Hall Well, Town Well and Yewtree Well. Each Ascension Day, the wells are decked out with a biblical scene made up of thousands of flower petals pressed into damp clay. No one seems quite certain where the custom originated, nor even whether it was originally Christian or goes back to pagan times. All, however, are happy that the custom survives in Tissington and the surrounding villages.

Other wells to attract the visitor can be found in the many spa towns from Buxton to Bath. Harrogate in North Yorkshire, for example, is one where the waters are supposed to provide a cure of a number of ailments, especially rheumatism. The old pumps still exist and on the

The village stocks at Ripley *(Reece Winstone)*

One of the wells of Tissington dressed in flowers for Ascension Day *(British Tourist Authority)*

Stray, a large grassed area surrounding the town, there are a number of wells where visitors can sup the waters. The taste is disgusting, thereby reinforcing the idea that it must be doing you good. One advantage of these wells, or disadvantage depending on one's point of view, is that they never close, the beverage being available day and night through taps on the outside of the well buildings.

Inns and pubs are, of course, subject to licensing laws and opening hours. We are used to these restrictions, yet they date back no further than World War I, when it was deemed necessary to restrict drinking hours for the good of the war effort. Indeed, preoccupation with time keeping is an essentially modern phenomenon, and the idea that the time kept in place A should coincide accurately with that of place B is even more modern. Until the advent of the railways and the railway timetable, local differences in time keeping had little practical significance. The passage of the sun determined the work of the day: noon was noon, and the fact that when noon was reached in London it was still half an hour away in Land's End had no effect on anyone. Travel between the two places was so slow that the differences were simply lost along the way. Then we reached the day when the 8.15 from Paddington was expected in Bristol at 11.47 – and now Bristol time had to coincide with London time. Standardisation had arrived, hauled in behind an asthmatically wheezing engine. The old measurers of time began to disappear, gradually vanishing from the scene until those that are left are regarded as merely quaint and picturesque. Yet once they measured off the passage of time for the whole community, and they were undoubtedly as useful in their day as the digital watch is in ours. Old clocks survive in many places, as do the recorders of time which date back to the Roman occupation – the sundials.

The sundial is, in fact, a simple enough device. We all know that the sun rises in the east and sets in the west, throwing a steadily moving shadow across the land. Set up a pole and mark off the shadows at different times and you have a clock. What could be simpler? Alas, it is nowhere near that easy. This is not the place for a technical discussion of sundials, though it is perhaps worth remarking that there are a number of quite difficult problems to be solved by the dial maker. There is a difference between what one might call 'sun time' and 'clock time', for the passage of time and solar movements are not quite the constant factors we might like to think they are. Anyone wanting to learn the practicalities of sundialling – while receiving entertainment with their instruction – could do no better than to get hold of a copy of A. P. Herbert's *Sundials Old and New*. And if anyone then decides to take up the task of dial construction he will be joining an illustrious company, for many eminent men tried their hand at the work, and their efforts have often survived their passing. The sun dial on the cottage at Killingworth, Northumberland is a good example, for the cottage in question was the home of the great railway engineer George Stephenson. He built a dial with the help of his son Robert, and placed it over the front door. It was a plain, unsophisticated device, which would have been just another small, domestic time keeper if it had not had such illustrious builders. Other dials are fascinating in their own rights.

The Stephensons had no great pretensions when it came to sundial construction: not so William Watson, when he built one on his cottage at Seaton Ross, Humberside. He was a true enthusiast for dialling, a fact recorded in his epitaph in the local churchyard, erected at his death in 1857:

> At this church I so often
> With pleasure did call
> That I made a sundial
> Upon the church wall.

The cottage sundial occupies most of the front of the building, with the dial itself forming a semicircle some 12ft in diameter which starts under the eaves and reaches to the top of the ground-floor windows. It might well be the largest sundial in the country, though it is quite insignificant by international standards. When the Rajah of Jeypore constructed his dial at Delhi in 1724, he built it with the gnomon – the part in the centre that casts the shadow – in the form of a triangle with a base over 100ft long and a 56ft perpendicular.

To return to more modest offerings at home, one often finds a connection between sundials and epitaphs. One of the finest combines the function of time-keeper and memorialist to perfection. It stands at East Tytherton in Wiltshire and is a memorial to Maud Heath who

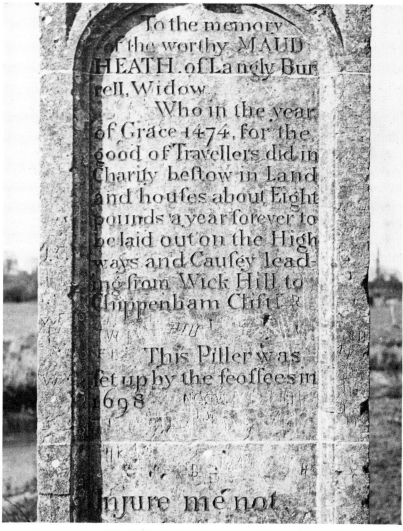

Maud Heath's monument *(Reece Winstone)*

died in 1474 and in her will left a legacy to pay for a causeway across the flood plain of the Avon to help her old neighbours to reach the local markets. Maud Heath's causeway still stands, as does the memorial put up in 1698. This consists of a sundial mounted on a column, the dial occupying three faces of a cube. The south-facing part has the familiar triangular gnomon, while the east and west faces have bell-shaped gnomons, giving an appropriate ecclesiastical air to fit the monumental function. Around the dial are suitably moral homilies, such as:

> Haste Traveller the Sun is sinking now
> He shall return but never thou.

These lines were presumably not intended to cheer the lonely traveller.

Another multi-purpose dial tower can be seen at Blaise Hamlet (see p. 148). It was the work of John Nash. As with the Maud Heath memorial, the sundial is mounted on a high column, on top of which is a weather-vane and at the bottom a pump. The pipe of the latter emerges through a carved lion's head, making it appear as if the beast is sticking its tongue out and spitting at the same time. At least this has not suffered the fate of an equally elegant if older sundial, the so-called Countess Pillar put up in memory of Lady Anne Clifford at Brougham in Cumbria. It has lost the gnomon from the south face, thus rendering the monument timeless.

The most elaborate of the high-perched dials is atop a column at Barrington Court in Somerset. The column ends in grand style with a heraldic lion rampant at the very pinnacle. An elaborate dial in a different sense is to be seen over the doorway of Eyam church in Derbyshire. Not content with telling the local time, it also informs passers-by of the local times in other spots as far apart as South America and India, though what use the inhabitants of this delightful village are supposed to make of the information is far from clear.

An extraordinary Elizabethan sundial can be seen at Madeley Court in Shropshire, though it is in a rather sorry state of repair. Holes cut in the stone block are used for other astronomical calculations, such as the positions of the planets. It is too heavily damaged to be of any practical value, even if one could work out how it was used in the first place.

The same cannot be said of the dial in the churchyard at St Neot, Cornwall, which is beautifully made and is, one is assured, remarkably accurate. Unfortunately, this would-be teller of the time was wholly defeated by its intricacies and had, and has, not the least notion of how to read it. This at least makes it not just the most modern but also the

The elaborate sundial at Barrington Court *(National Trust: photo Jeremy Whitaker)*

most curious sundial to be seen in the country. It is possible that when I visited St Neot I was distracted by arriving at the church on the day of a strange annual ceremony. On Oak Apple Day, a whole young oak tree is hauled up to the top of the church tower, where it stays for a full year until it too is replaced.

Leaving St Neot's complex sundial, we can move on to other time-keepers – clocks. The name comes from the same root as the French work 'cloche' or bell, for early clocks were unlike modern versions in that they were without hands and relied on striking bells to tell the hours. Chiming and striking clocks still provide some of the most interesting timepieces to be seen. Examples of handless clocks are comparatively rare – if one discounts the very modern clocks with

*(left)* The King Henry clock at Exeter *(British Tourist Authority)*; *(right)* the blacksmith ready to sound the hours at Abinger Hammer *(British Tourist Authority)*

their digital displays – though there is a very fine one in the Thames valley at Cookham church. The fifteenth century saw the introduction of 'jacks', mechanical figures which trundled out every hour, or even every quarter, to strike the bell. In truth, the very best of these are to be seen in continental Europe, but Britain can boast a few of these charming and fascinating devices. The parish church at Rye in East Sussex, for example, has a clock from the sixteenth century in which a pair of cupids emerges every quarter to sound the bell – a most unsuitably pagan motif one might think for a pious church to possess. The tradition of striking jacks has lasted right through to modern times. A blacksmith most appropriately strikes the hours at Abinger Hammer in Surrey. Elsewhere heralds, knights, tradesmen, all can be seen striking merrily away at the top of country bell towers.

The clock jacks did not last, but their passing did not mean the end of interesting clocks. Inevitably, the Victorians added their fair share of ornate clocks, particularly those put up in public places to record public events as well as time. Seaside towns, especially, have some remarkable clock towers. Weymouth's clock is probably that town's outstanding landmark. Brighton's Jubilee clock tower is not so much a support for a timepiece as a quick course in architectural history. The top is Baroque – all twiddles and urns, the tower is Renaissance and the base Classical, complete with Grecian-style pediments and statues – not to mention a styleless loo underneath. It is not, however, nearly so fine as the Diamond Jubilee clock put up in Chester for Victoria in 1897. It stands over the walkway along the city walls, and is supported by some of the most complex iron work one could ever hope to see.

There are so many clocks in so many styles that one could go on for ever, so here to end the list are two personal favourites. Iron work seems to go so well with clocks that it is a pleasure to find that the warehouse of the most famous ironworks in Britain – possibly in the world – the Darby works at Coalbrookdale in Shropshire, is topped by a quite magnificent clock. It is housed in a multi-coloured tower and now stands guard over the new museum at the works. The second choice is more modest but has fine surroundings. One of the great features of the city of Leeds is the system of shopping arcades, each arcade being a lovely tunnel of glass and decorative iron work. In one of these you can find a watchmaker advertising his presence through a splendid bracket clock which contains the motto of all horologists – *Tempus Fugit*.

As this is a rag-bag of a chapter, no one will, I hope, object too strongly if we stuff the subject of clocks back in the sack and pull out the topic of trees. There is no connection whatsoever between the two subjects: indeed, there could scarcely be a greater contrast. Clocks show us what the ingenuity of man can achieve: trees show us what Nature can manage without our intervention. The 'scissors tree' at Dawlish in Devon is a good example. It has grown in such a way that the lower part of the trunk has developed into a remarkable likeness to a pair of scissors, complete with symmetrical handles. Was no human hand involved in training the tree to this shape? If it was, no record of it has ever appeared. Great age is another tree characteristic, though any claimant for the title of oldest tree in Britain will have to compete with the Cowthorpe Oak of North Yorkshire, which seems to be over 1,500 years old – though, truth to tell, it is long past its prime and all

Victorian ironwork at its most elaborate supports Chester's Jubilee clock *(British Tourist Authority)*

The famous Cowthorpe oak *(BBC Hulton Picture Library)*

but dead. Other ancient oaks can be seen at Tilford in Surrey, a mere 500 years younger than its Cowthorpe rival, and the Cressage Oak of Shropshire could join in the contest. The latter might be ruled out of order. It is said that it was under this tree that St Augustine met the British leaders in the sixth century AD, so it must already have been well grown. It began, however, to age and crumble, so an acorn was taken from its branches and planted in the centre of the rotting trunk. Soon a new tree began to grow. But was it new or a continuation of the old? That would be a good topic for a late night discussion.

Some trees do owe their peculiarity to man's interference. In Chandos Street in London a plane tree grew up from the basement and round the iron railings. As the tree grew, so the iron work was lifted upwards until the owners had no option but to cut off the railing section and leave it embedded in the tree. Every year the tree carries its unique iron branch a little further away from the railings where it started. The next group of trees have no obvious distinction in themselves, though the story of their planting makes them interesting.

Queen Elizabeth's oak preserved – though only just – at Hatfield House, Hertfordshire *(British Tourist Authority)*; *(opposite)* the Woodbridge steelyard – an overgrown weighing machine *(Reece Winstone)*

Gilbert White, whose great book, *The Natural History and Antiquities of Selborne* (1788) is one of the very few works to be lauded as both a literary and a scientific classic, planted these trees. As an animal lover, he loathed the sight of blood at the butcher's shop in the village, so he planted the trees which stood as a sightscreen between himself and the Selborne slaughterhouse.

Nearing the end of this travelogue of curiosities, the problem arises – where and how to stop. There seems no logical reason why one should not go on for ever. Why not, for example, write about the last two big steelyards in Britain – at Soham in Cambridge and Woodbridge in Suffolk? Yet they are after all no more than overgrown

One of East Anglia's many attractive village and town signs *(British Tourist Authority)*

weighing machines, used for weighing in tons rather than pounds and ounces, for they weighed loaded waggons. They do look odd when you first see them, but they are really just forerunners of the familiar public weighbridges of today. What then of the wreckers' window at Shaldon in Devon? That presents a quite opposite case, a simple round window that would attract no one's attention today. Yet in the eighteenth century it was part of a nefarious trade. Lanterns were set there to imitate the lighthouse and to lure ships onto the rocks.

The list goes on and on and one hopes it never will end. New curiosities and new delights are appearing all the time. The village signs of East Anglia, for example, show aspects of the life of the village and form a new and welcome addition to the scene. In time, they will be cherished as antique survivors from the distant past.

It was never the intention of this book to supply a comprehensive catalogue of strange sites. It is in any case not merely the strangeness that attracts: the element of surprise also has a part to play. I have no doubt at all that after the book is published I shall find a new and amazing site which I had never known of before. Even as I write, someone somewhere is perhaps providing a new wonder – painting a bizarre mural on a terrace end or constructing a maze. Elsewhere someone is rediscovering a long-forgotten wonder, perhaps an eighteenth-century folly that the rest of us had ignored. The best the author of such a book can do is to wish the reader Good Hunting. May your oddities get ever odder, your curiosities more curious, and long may they all be with us.

# Gazetteer

Inclusion of buildings etc in this gazetteer should not be taken as an indication that they are open to the public. Those marked NT and NTS are the properties of the National Trust and National Trust for Scotland respectively.

## AVON

**Banwell** *(5 miles E of Weston-super-Mare)* Banwell Castle, a typical Victorian castellated house privately owned and notable for a belvedere in the form of a round tower.

**Bath** Ralph Allen's sham castle, one of the best sham ruins in the country, stands on Bathwick Hill. *Pages 55–6*
  Beckford's Tower, Lansdown Hill, stands 130ft high and offered its builder a view of his old home at Fonthill Abbey.

**Batheaston** The George and Dragon Inn has a curious beer barrel entrance. *Page 251*

**Bathford** *(3 miles NE of Bath)* Brown's Folly, a tower built to provide work for the poor in 1842.

**Blaise Hamlet** *(near Henbury)* A picturesque village built to enhance the view for the owners of Blaise Castle. Also has a fine sundial. (NT) *Pages 84, 148–50, 260*

**Brislington** Arno's Castle, a gloomy sham castle built out of slag from a copper smelter.

**Bristol** Goldney House, Clifton, has a fine grotto in the grounds (now part of Bristol University). Can be visited on open days. *Pages 176–7*
  Horfield Common: ornate cast-iron Gents'. *Page 247*

St Mary Redcliffe Church: church cat memorial and look for maze carved inside the church, on roof boss in north aisle.

**Hawkesbury** *(4 miles NE of Chipping Sodbury)* Tower of 1845 to commemorate the Duke of Somerset.

**Marshfield** A mummer's play is performed on Christmas Eve. *Page 223*

**Midford** *(3 miles S of Bath)* Roebuck's Folly, a castle-like building shaped in plan like the Ace of Clubs – the card that made its owner's fortune.

**Stanton Drew** *(6 miles S of Bristol on B3130)* The toll house is unusually rural in having a circular thatched roof.

**Weston in Gordano** Walton Castle, a particularly convincing sham ruin built in a mixture of styles. *Pages 50–1*

**Worle** (Weston-super-Mare) The folly tower has now been incorporated into the local golf club.

## BEDFORDSHIRE

**Harrold** Small stone lockup near market house still has its original giant padlock.

**Turvey** Statue of fisherman can be seen in the centre of the river Ouse. *Page 230*

Mid-river memorial beside the old mill at Turvey *(National Monuments Record)*

**Willington** *(4 miles E of Bedford, just N of A603)* Sixteenth-century dovecote is all that remains of a large estate. (NT)

**Woburn Abbey** The house and grounds have a fine collection of oddities including a grotto and shell room, a Chinese dairy and a timber pagoda in a hedged garden maze.

## BERKSHIRE

**Aldworth** The remains of a 1000-year-old yew can be seen in the churchyard, and outside the Bell Inn is the massive well head standing over a 370ft well, which is now capped.

**Bisham** A circular dovecote stands close to the former abbey, now a physical recreation centre.

**Cookham** A lot of curiosities in a small place. The church has a handless clock, there is fine topiary in the churchyard, an ancient boundary stone can be seen at the top end of the High Street, and excitable visitors are given warning in a High Street notice: 'All fighting to be over by 10 pm'. *Page 262*

**Hungerford** On the second Monday after Easter the Tutti Men and the Orange Scrambler make their way through the streets. *Pages 217–18*

**Hurley** A circular dovecote stands beside the tithe barn.

**Remenham** On a ridge overlooking St Bride's Church stands, in solitary splendour, the original spire.

**Winterbourne** Hop Castle folly, a flint-walled hunting lodge with a grotto in the basement.

## BORDERS

**Jedburgh** Jethart Ba', the traditional ball game, is played on Candlemas Day and Fastern Eve, the latter a moveable feast. *Page 201*

**Traquair** The gates of the Traquair estate are kept closed, waiting to be opened when a Stuart king returns.

## BUCKINGHAMSHIRE

**Ascott** *(½ mile E of Wing)* Ascott House has a topiary sundial in the grounds (NT) *Page 174*

**Beaconsfield** Topiary in churchyard.

**Buckingham** The old gaol, a castellated folly, stands in the market place. *Page 61*

**Cliveden** *(off B476 2 miles from Taplow)* The grounds contain a pagoda, a fountain of Siena marble, seventeenth-century yew hedges and a gazebo. (NT)

**Dinton** *(3 miles W of Aylesbury)* A mock castle, originally designed as a fossil house, stands beside the A418. A circular dovecote can be seen at Dinton Hall. *Page 61*

**Fenny Stratford** On 11 November, six miniature cannon are fired in the churchyard. *Page 223*

The railway station is an elaborately half-timbered cottage. *Page 122*

**Frieth** The Yew Tree Inn has a yew tree sign.

**Hartwell** *(2 miles W of Aylesbury)* In the woods just outside Lower Hartwell there is an Egyptian-style well head.

**Hedsor** *(3 miles SW of Beaconsfield)* Hedsor Priory, a huge mock castle also known as

Midday recorded on the topiary sundial at Ascott House *(British Tourist Authority)*

Lord Boston's Folly, lies immediately to the north of the B476.

**Horsenden** *(1 mile W of Princes Risborough)* A timber dovecote of 1550 built over archway.

**Ivinghoe** A thatch hook hangs on the churchyard wall. *Pages 8–9*

**Long Crendon** A medieval square dovecote at Notley Abbey.

**Medmenham** Medmenham Abbey incorporates a mock ruin and is famous as home to the Hell-Fire Club. *Page 67*

**Monk's Risborough** *(adjoining Princes Risborough)* Dovecote in field behind church square.

**Olney** A pancake race is held here every Shrove Tuesday. *Page 202*

**Stoke Poges** 1,000-year-old yew in churchyard and topiary in Memorial Gardens.

**Stowe** The grounds of Stowe School boast a variety of follies designed by William Kent including a splendid Gothic temple and a temple of British worthies. (NT)

**West Wycombe** The church is topped by a golden ball which was used by the Hell-Fire Club. There is also a mausoleum close by and a mile post topped by a stone pudding. There are a number of follies in West Wycombe Park. (part NT) *Pages 68–9*

## CAMBRIDGESHIRE

**Cambridge** Hobson's conduit at the corner of Lensfield and Trumpington roads was built by the Hobson who gave his name to Hobson's Choice.

**Caxton** A gibbet stands beside the A14 Huntingdon–Royston road.

**Ely** Memorial tablet in Ely Cathedral contains a long poem to two dead railwaymen. *Pages 236–7*

**Eversden** *(6 miles N of Royston)* A sham castle by Sanderson Miller graces the view from Wimpole Hall.

**Hilton** *(4 miles SW of St Ives)* A turf maze with a pillar to mark the centre. *Page 168*

**Kirtling** *(5 miles SE of Newmarket)* Kirtling Tower stands alone – a three-storey semi-moated gatehouse, all that remains of a big estate. (NT)

**St Ives** Each Whitsun local children dice for Bibles on the church steps. *Page 208*

**Soham** A steelyard can be seen at the rear of the Fountain Inn. *Pages 266–8*

**Wisbech** A castellated flint house now used as offices, 67 King's Lynn Road.

## CENTRAL (SCOTLAND)

**Aberfoyle** A mortsafe, protection against grave robbers, in churchyard. *Page 227*

**Airth** A building in the form of a pineapple, Dunmore Park. (NTS) *Page 146*

## CHANNEL ISLANDS

**Alderney** Fort Clonque on the western tip of the island, a nineteenth-century fort, now a most unusual holiday home. *Page 142*

**Jersey** St Ouen's Battle of Flowers Museum where exotic animal creations from the annual procession are kept. *Page 191*

## CHESHIRE

**Anderton** The Anderton boat lift carries boats between the River Weaver and the Trent and Mersey Canal. *Pages 116–17*

**Bollington** White Nancy, a sugar-loaf-shaped folly on the hill-top overlooking the town. *Page 64*

**Chester** Ornate jubilee clock, Eastgate. *Page 263*

**Disley** Lyme Cage, a hunting lodge in Lyme Park, which was also used as a prison.

**Rode Heath** Thurlwood steel lock, a bizarre structure on the Trent and Mersey Canal. *Pages 119–20*

**Tatton Park** *(2 miles N of Knutsford)* Topiary garden by Repton. (NT)

## CLWYD

**Erddig** *(near Wrexham)* Erddig House, dovecote with revolving ladder. (NT) *Page 183*

**Marford** *(4 miles N of Wrexham)* Early example of planned village. *Pages 147–8*

**Moel Famma** At the top of the mountain is the stump of the jubilee tower.

## CORNWALL

**Bodmin** The town car park contains a memorial to Prince Chula of Siam's dog.

**Calstock** Danescombe Mine engine house, downstream of the village, has been converted into a holiday home.

**Castle-an-Dinas** Roger's Tower, a sham tower on Castle Downs, near St Columb Major.

**Cremyll** *(on the Tamar opposite Plymouth)* Mount Edgcumbe obelisk and a sham ruin.

**Durgan** *(4 miles SW of Falmouth)* Beautiful maze in the grounds of Glendurgan House. (NT) *Page 170*

**Helston** The Furry Dance takes place on 8 May. *Page 213*

**Lanhydrock** Topiary in the formal gardens of Lanhydrock House. (NT) *Page 172*

**Looe** The Monkey Sanctuary, home to a colony of wild monkeys, is signposted out of Looe. *Page 186*

**Minions** There are three interesting features on the moor but the OS map is needed to find them. The Hurlers stone circle is at SX 257 713, the Cheesewring rocks are at SX 258 723, and the South Phoenix mine engine house, once converted to a home, is at SX 260 718. *Pages 22–3, 138*

**Morvah** The starting point for a hunt for some ancient stones: Lanyon Quoit (NT) SW 430 337, Chun Quoit SW 402 339, Men-an-Tol and Men Screfys SW 43 35. *Pages 20–1*

**Morwenstow** The rectory has five chimneys in the form of church towers and the churchyard has a figurehead memorial from the wreck of the *Caledonia*.

**Padstow** The Hobby Horse dances through the streets on May Day. *Pages 209–12*

**Penzance** The exotic Egyptian House in Chapel Street. *Page 141*

**Polperro** A house on props stands over the river, while in the Warren is a house encrusted with shell designs. *Pages 138, 154*

**Porthcurno** A house is built into the foot of the cliffs, while halfway up the cliffs is the Minack Theatre. *Page 137*

**Porthtowan** A converted engine house stands on the beach. *Page 138*

**Portquin** Doyden Tower, a Gothic folly, overlooks the bay. (NT) *Page 97*

**Roche** *(5 miles N of St Austell)* A fourteenth-century chapel-cum-hermit cell on Roche Rock.

**St Buryan** The Merry Maidens are an impressive group of nineteen standing stones in a circle. *Page 22*

**St Cleer** *(3 miles N of Liskeard)* Trethevy Quoit, one of the most impressive ancient monuments in Cornwall, SX 260 688.

**St Columb Major** Nine Maidens, a line of ancient stones SX 827 630. 'Hurling', a hand ball game is played on Shrove Tuesday. *Pages 22, 24, 201*

**St Ives** The Knill monument, a stone pyramid, can be seen on the hill to the south of the town. Shrove Tuesday hurling (see above). *Pages 64–5, 201*

Shells decorate the outside of this house at Polperro *(British Tourist Authority)*

**St Keyne** *(2 miles S of Liskeard)* Paul Corin's collection of mechanical musical instruments. *Pages 185–6*

**St Mawgan** Churchyard memorial, like a boat stern, to sailors who froze to death.

**St Michael Caerhays** *(Veryan Bay)* Caerhays Castle, a Gothic masterpiece by John Nash. Privately owned.

**St Neot** Twentieth-century sundial in churchyard and oak tree on church tower. *Pages 260–1*

**Trewoofe** *(4 miles SW of Penzance)* Near the Merry Maidens stone circle (St Buryan) are the Pipers stones, SW 433 245.

**Veryan** Round houses in the village, designed to keep the Devil at bay. *Pages 139, 141*

**Werrington** *(2 miles N of Launceston)* Three stone sugar loaves decorate the hillside in Werrington Park.

## CUMBRIA

**Ambleside** Bridge house across the river. (NT) *Pages 158, 161*

**Brougham** *(2 miles SE of Penrith)* Lady Anne Clifford's sundial, Brougham Castle. *Page 260*

**Carlisle** Citadel station is a fine example of railway Gothic.

**Castlerigg** *(1½ miles E of Keswick)* Stone circle with stone rectangle inside. (NT) *Page 37*

**Greystoke** *(5 miles W of Penrith)* An extraordinary collection of farms commemorating American battles: Bunkers Hill, Fort Putnam and Jefferson Farm. There is also a farm with a spire. *Pages 57–8*

**Levens** *(5 miles S of Kendal)* Levens Hall, topiary garden.

**Lindale** *(2 miles N of Grange-over-Sands)* Cast-iron obelisk by church to commemorate the iron-founder John Wilkinson. *Page 230*

**Little Salkeld** *(4 miles NE of Penrith)* Long Meg and her daughters – a stone circle in a dramatic setting, NY 57 37.

**Penrith** Easter eggs are rolled in the castle moat.

**Ulverston** A lighthouse, the Hoad Hill monument, overlooks this inland town. *Pages 61–2*

**Workington** A communal game of football is played on Good Friday and on the following Tuesday and Saturday.

## DERBYSHIRE

**Ashbourne** Football in the old style is played here every Shrove Tuesday. *Page 200*

**Baslow** The tiny building at the end of the bridge over the Derwent is said to be either a toll house or lockup.

**Buxton** A folly tower known as Solomon's Temple stands on Grinlow Barrow.

**Chatsworth** Chatsworth House boasts an impressive fountain *Pages 163–5*

**Derby** Easter eggs are rolled on Bunker's Hill.

**Elton** Nine Stones; the name is misleading, since only four ancient stones remain on the site on Harthill Moor, SK 226 626.

**Elvaston** A nineteenth-century topiary garden in the grounds of Elvaston Castle.

**Eyam** A village with a wealth of interest, famous for its inhabitants' heroism during the plague years. There is a fine sundial in the churchyard, a splendid cricketer's grave, village stocks and a mechanically operated sheep-roasting spit. *Pages 233, 260*

**Matlock** A prospect tower on the Heights of Abraham. *Page 95*

**Old Brampton** *(4 miles W of Chesterfield)* The church clock is divided into 63 minutes.

**Renishaw** A splendidly elaborate Gothic building, the Renishaw arch stands in the grounds of the old Hall. *Pages 51–2*

**Rowsley** A grand sham castle, now ruined, stands in the grounds of Riber Castle Fauna Reserve.

**Tissington** On Ascension Day the five wells in the town are dressed with pictures made up of flowers. *Page 234*

## DEVON

**Ashburton** The stones of Buckland Beacon are inscribed with the Ten Commandments.

**Bampton** Odd churchyard monument to 'The Clerk's son'. *Page 239*

**Brixham** The Old Coffin House, so known simply because it is coffin-shaped. *Page 153*

**Buckfastleigh** A collection of objects made from shells can be seen at the House of Shells. *Pages 192–3*

**Chagford** *(4 miles NW of Moreton-hampstead)* Rushford Tower is, in fact, two mock towers.

**Combe Martin** The Pack o' Cards Inn, an architectural celebration of the original owner's good fortune. *Pages 153–4*

**Doddiscombsleigh** Haldon Belvedere is a tall prospect tower also used as a home. *Page 80*

**Exmouth** Summer Lane, ornate circular house decorated with shells and known as A La Ronde. *Page 154*

**Honiton** Castellated toll house 1 mile west of the town on the A373.

**Lydford** Churchyard memorial to a watch-maker. *Pages 237–8*

**Merrivale** Stone row, 1 mile east of the village just south of Princetown Road. *Pages 24–5*

**Offwell** Bishop Copplestone's Folly, an 80ft prospect tower. *Page 87*

**Ottery St Mary** On 5 November, barrels of burning tar are rolled through the streets. *Page 223*

**Powderham** Powderham Castle belvedere looks down over the River Exe.

**Shaldon** In the eighteenth century, lanterns were set at the 'wrecker's window' to lure ships onto the rocks. *Page 268*

**Shebbear** The annual ritual of Turning the Devil's Boulder. *Page 223*

**Tavistock** Octagonal slate-hung toll house on the A384 Launceston road.

**Tiverton** Knightshayes Court, 2 miles north, topiary garden. (NT)

## DORSET

**Cerne Abbas** Giant cut out of the hillside. (NT) *Pages 39–40*

**Creech** *(3 miles W of Wareham)* Creech Grange arch, an eighteenth-century eye catcher. (NT)

**Godmanstone** The Smith's Arms, the smallest pub in Britain. *Page 161*

**Horton** Sturt's Folly, a huge triangular tower used originally for watching deer. *Pages 82–4*

**Kimmeridge** An attractive prospect tower overlooking the bay. *Page 82*

**Lyme Regis** Umbrella Cottage, actually an umbrella-shaped toll house near the main road junction on the edge of the town. *Page 153*

**Portisham** Hardy monument on the road to Martinstown, not a monument to Dorset's literary genius but to the admiral. (NT)

**Weymouth** Splendidly ornate clock tower on sea front. *Page 263*

## DUMFRIES AND GALLOWAY

**Tongland** Castellated bridge over the River Dee. *Page 116*

Cerne Abbas' hillside giant. The enclosure above him is known as the Frying Pan (*Dr J. K. S. St Joseph: supplied by National Monuments Record*)

## DURHAM

**Bishop Auckland** Mock cloisters under castle wall for deer watching. *Page 61*

**Sedgefield** Communal football played on Shrove Tuesday.

**Staindrop** A splendid Gothic folly on a hill behind Raby Castle, 1 mile north of town.

**Sunderland** The Penshaw memorial in the Greek style at Kingsley Hill has been absorbed into the suburbs.

## DYFED

**Brynberian** Pentre Ifan cromlech, arguably the most impressive prehistoric monument in Wales. 1 mile north of village. *Pages 21–2*

**Lampeter** A tall brooding monument known as Derry Ormond tower, 2 miles north of the town.

**Llanarthney** An impressive prospect tower built by Sir William Paxton stands 1 mile south of the town (NT) *Pages 91–2*

## ESSEX

**Colchester** A ruined arch is all that remains of a sham castle in the castle grounds.

**Henham** Anti-bodysnatcher cage in churchyard.

**Pentlow** *(3 miles W of Long Melford)* Bull's Tower, a 70ft prospect tower.

**Saffron Walden** Bridge End gardens have a decaying hedge maze, and a turf maze can be seen on the common.

**Wanstead** Stone sentry box for guarding the graves in the churchyard. *Page 227*

## FIFE

**Anstruther** Village house decorated with shells. *Page 154*

**Colinsburgh** Balcarres Craig, a splendid castellated folly to the north of the town. *Page 49*

**Falkland** *(11 miles N of Kirkcaldy)* Real tennis court at Falkland Palace. *Pages 205–6*

**Kinglassie** *(2 miles SW of Leslie)* Blythe's Folly, prospect tower on the hill overlooking the town.

## GLAMORGAN

**Pontypridd** Glyntaff Towers, 1 mile south-east of the town, was built as a grand entrance to a palace which never materialised.

## GLOUCESTERSHIRE

**Bishop's Cleeve** *(4 miles N of Cheltenham)* Toll house on the A435 still has a list of charges for horses, chaises, curricles etc.

**Blockley** Fish memorial beside the stream. *Page 243*

**Brockworth** Cheeses are rolled and pursued down Cooper's Hill every Spring Bank Holiday. *Page 204*

**Cirencester** Alfred's Hall, magnificent sham ruin complete with stained-glass window, stands in Oakley Wood. *Pages 49–50*

**Gloucester** Humorous epitaph in the cathedral to a boy named 'Calf'. *Pages 238–9*

**Hidcote Bartrim** *(4 miles NE of Chipping Campden)* Hidcote Manor topiary garden with a pair of gazebos. (NT)

**Leckhampton** Devil's Chimney, a tall pinnacle on the escarpment to the south of Cheltenham. *Page 15*

**Sapperton** Ornate classical entrance to tunnel on Thames and Severn Canal.

**Sezincote** Sezincote House and pavilions in the Hindu-Gothic style. *Page 179*

**Snowshill** *(3 miles S of Broadway)* Snowshill Manor contains an amazing collection of objects from ancient bicycles to Samurai armour. (NT) *Pages 197–8*

**Wyck Rissington** *(2 miles S of Stow-on-the-Wold)* Maze in the rectory gardens. *Page 168*

## GRAMPIAN

**Aberdeen** Large maze in Hazelhead Park. *Pages 169–70*

**Alves** *(5 miles W of Elgin)* York Tower is said to be where Macbeth met the witches.

**Burghead** Each year on 11 January the Clavie, a great burning torch, is carried through the town. *Pages 215–16*

**Craigellachie** Castellated road bridge designed by Telford across the Spey. *Page 116*

**Stonehouse** Fireball parade on New Year's Eve. *Page 224*

**Udny Green** *(5 miles E of Oldmeldrum)* The village contains a mort house, a circular stone building where bodies were kept safe from the resurrectionists.

## GREATER MANCHESTER

**Manchester** Heaton Park has a row of ionic columns, the remains of the old town hall.
   Ducie Street: a car park stands next to the Rochdale Canal which here disappears under an office block. *Page 121*

## GWENT

**Abergavenny** Clytha Castle, 6 miles east of the town on the A40, a sham castle now a holiday home. *Page 146*

**Kemey's Inferior** *(6 miles NE of Newport)* Originally built as a sham castle, Kemey's folly is now a private house.

**Monmouth** The Kymin, 1 mile east of the town, is a hill topped with a circular pavilion and a rustic temple dedicated to the Navy and once visited by Nelson. (NT)

## GWYNEDD

**Barmouth** Circular lockup by the harbour. *Page 130*

**Beaumaris** The old gaol is now a museum with grisly relics. *Page 191*

**Beddgelert** The grave of the dog Gelert killed in error by the thirteenth-century prince Llewellyn can be seen by the river. Story and grave are equally false, having been invented to promote tourism.

**Bull Bay, Anglesey** Remains of 'Roman baths' built in the last century.

**Conwy** Two castellated bridges, one for rail and one for road, stand beside the real castle. In Lower Street is what claims to be the smallest house in Britain. *Pages 114–16, 124, 137, 161*

**Portmeirion** *(2 miles SE of Porthmadog)* Amazing Italianate village. *Page 63*

**Llanuwchllyn** The Bala Lake Railway, a preserved steam line, boasts a unique halt where trains were stopped by flag signal from across the lake. *Page 75*

## HAMPSHIRE

**Breamore** *(3 miles N of Fordingbridge)* Breamore House has a museum of carriages, and a turf maze in the grounds.

**Bucklers Hard** *(2 miles SE of Beaulieu)* The Master Builder's House, now a hotel, has a ship-decorated drainpipe and an eyrie from which the owner overlooked his works. *Page 250*

**Farley Down** *(3½ miles NE of Braishfield)* A pyramidal monument to a horse that saved its owner's life.

**Fawley** Luttrell's Tower, Eaglehurst, an interesting prospect tower. *Pages 87–8*

**Hambledon** Topiary in churchyard. The Bat and Ball Inn is a reminder of the famous Hambledon Cricket Club.

**Petersfield** Churchyard memorial to the last of the Hambledon cricketers.

**Selborne** Trees planted outside the butcher's shop by Gilbert White to shield him from the sight of slaughter. *Page 266*

Little Italy in Wales: Clough Williams-Ellis' extravaganza Portmeirion *(British Tourist Authority)*; *(below)* trees outside the butcher's shop at Selborne, planted by Gilbert White to hide the slaughterhouse from view *(National Monuments Record)*

**Sway** Peterson's Tower, a tall folly tower built of concrete. *Pages 99–100*

**Warblington** *(1 mile W of Emsworth)* Shelter in the churchyard for watchmen guarding against grave robbers.

**Winchester** Square turf maze, St Catherine's Hill.

## HEREFORD AND WORCESTER

**Abberley** *(5 miles SW of Stourport)* A monumental clock tower stands in the grounds of the local prep school.

**Bewdley** Ornate cast iron Gents' on platform of Severn Valley Railway station. *Page 247*

**Broadway** Prospect tower off the A44 1 mile east of the town in the Country Park. *Pages 89–91*

**Bromsgrove** Churchyard monuments to victims of early train accident. *Pages 235–6*

**Defford** *(3 miles SW of Pershore)* Sham castle on Defford Common.

**Eardisley** Great oak, last survivor of vast forest, ½ mile east of the village at Hurstway Common.

**Garway** Close to the church is a fourteenth-century dovecote built by the Knights Templar.

**Hagley Park** *(2 miles S of Stourbridge)* Grounds contain sham castle, obelisk and classical temple.

**Little Comberton** Medieval dovecote at Nash's Farm and seventeenth-century dovecote at Manor House. A 39ft tower on 961ft Bredon Hill raises the summit to 1,000ft.

**Ombersley** Plague stone in centre of village and sixteenth-century Hawford dovecote 1 mile south of village. (NT)

**Rous Lench** Village post boxes enclosed in little half-timbered building by nineteenth-century parson, Dr Chaffy, who also built a prospect tower in his grounds.

**Shobdon** *(6 miles W of Leominster)* Eye catcher created out of salvaged Norman arches.

**Wichenford** *(5½ miles NW of Worcester)* Unique timber-framed dovecote at Wichenford Court. (NT)

**Wolverley** Cottage carved out of the rock, another claimant for the title of smallest house. *Page 137*

## HERTFORDSHIRE

**Aldenham** *(2 miles NE of Watford)* The medieval farmhouse was given a mock Gothic frontage and further embellished with a sham ruin in the grounds.

**Ashridge Estate** *(3 miles N of Berkhamsted)* The Bridgewater monument in the centre can be climbed by means of its 172 steps. (NT)

**Benington** Benington Lordship, a Georgian house by the pond, is attached to a sham castle. *Pages 54–5*

**Brookmans Park** *(2 miles N of Potters Bar)* Isolated arch entrance to Gobions Park. *Page 51*

**Hatfield** Hatfield House. Maze in the grounds and Queen Elizabeth's somewhat dilapidated oak. *Page 170*

**Knebworth** Knebworth House. Sham Gothic church in the grounds. *Page 52*

**Leverstock Green** (Hemel Hempstead) Combative dog and cat topiary on main road.

**Little Berkhamsted** Admiral Stratten's observatory, a charming Georgian prospect tower. *Pages 85–7*

**Northchurch** Norcott Court, brick and timber Tudor dovecote.

**St Albans** The Fighting Cock claims to be oldest pub in England.

**Shenley** Village lockup with moral inscriptions. *Page 128*

**Tring** Zoological Museum based on second Baron Rothschild's exotic collection. *Page 187*

## HIGHLAND

**Auldearn** *(2 miles E of Nairn)* Boath Doocot, a seventeenth-century dovecote (doocot being the Scottish name). (NTS)

**Kinloch, Isle of Rhum** Kinloch Castle, an Edwardian mock castle in the grandest of styles; now a hotel.

**Lybster** Hill o' Many Stanes, an extraordinary ancient site on a minor road off the A9 4 miles north of the village. *Page 28*

## HUMBERSIDE

**Alkborough** A collection of mazes. The original turf maze, Julian's Bower, cut circa 1200. Three replicas in church – one cut into porch, one in stained-glass window and one on tombstone.

**Haxey** The game of Haxey Hood, a form of football with many odd ceremonies, is played on 6 January. *Pages 200–1*

**Rudston** A monolithic stone stands within the churchyard. *Page 19*

**Seaton Ross** A 12ft diameter sundial on cottage wall, and the builder's churchyard memorial records his enthusiasm for dials. *Page 258*

**Sledmere** A mock castle now a farmhouse on the estate of Sledmere House. *Page 58*

## ISLES OF SCILLY

**St Agnes** A stone maze made in 1726.

**St Martin's** A modern maze constructed to amuse the tourists.

## KENT

**Biddenden** A stained-glass window in a High Street restaurant is in memory of some twelfth-century Siamese twins.

**Birchington** Quex Park, 1 mile south-east of the village, contains an ethnographic museum and a tall structure like a miniature Eiffel Tower. *Pages 92–4*

**Hadlow** Hadlow Castle, May's Folly, the splendid Gothic extravaganza in the form of a tower 170ft high. *Page 95*

**Maidstone** Dog Collar Museum, Leeds Castle. *Page 192*

**Margate** Lord Holland was responsible for a number of follies here, including Kingsgate Castle (now a hotel) and a round tower in the grounds of his home which is now a convent.

**Offham** A quintain stands on the village green. *Page 252*

**Sevenoaks** Knole Park, in the grounds of which stands a tiny Gothic folly house built as a home for birds.

## LANCASHIRE

**Bacup** The Coconut Dancers clog dance in bizarre apparel. *Pages 11–12*

**Colne** The churchyard has an unusual set of mobile stocks on wheels.

**Lancaster** Ashton memorial, Lancashire's answer to the Taj Mahal, dominates the town. *Page 243*

**Ormskirk** The Sisters' Folly, a church built with both tower and spire. The sisters, who endowed the church, disagreed over which was more appropriate so decided to build both.

**Preston** Egg rolling takes place every Easter at Avenham Park. *Page 207*

**Rivington** Lord Leverhulme built a replica of Liverpool Castle in Lever Park and a folly tower on the top of Rivington Pike. Scotsman's Stump on the moor commemorates a murder. *Page 230*

The quintain at Offham, where would-be knights could practise their jousting skills
*(Batsford: supplied by National Monuments Record)*

## LEICESTERSHIRE

**Bradgate** *(5 miles NW of Leicester)* The Park contains an eighteenth-century folly tower known as 'Old John'.

**Breedon on the Hill** Village lockup with weathercock on roof.

**Burley-on-the-Hill** Hermitage built in the grounds of Burley House by the Earl of Nottingham. *Page 76*

**Burton Lazars** Churchyard memorial – a pyramid raised over a pedestal base.

**Exton** Exton Park contains a pavilion known as the Bark Temple, and a Gothic summerhouse.

**Hallaton** On Easter Monday a hare pie is shared out, followed by a boisterous game of bottle kicking. *Page 12*

**Leicester** Abbey Mills pumping station, a fine example of Victorian industrial extravagance, is now a museum. *Page 111*

**Measham** Model cathedrals decorate Mr Bill Talbot's garden. *Page 167*

**Shackerstone** The little station has what must be, if not the smallest, then the most crowded of railway museums. *Pages 195, 197*

**Wing** Turf maze at the rear of the church. *Page 168*

## LINCOLNSHIRE

**Corby Glen** Auctioneer's gravestone with rhyming epitaph in churchyard. *Page 238*

**Deeping St James** Village lockup, circular with a little spire. The stone walls are lined with brick with three niches into which prisoners were squeezed.

**Dunston** Alongside the main road, 4 miles to the west, is Dunston Pillar, an eighteenth-century beacon for travellers.

**Eagle** Eagle Moor, 1 mile north-east, boasts an amazingly convoluted farmhouse known as The Jungle.

**Fillingham** Fillingham Castle has an isolated Gothic gateway on the edge of the A15.

**Grantham** The Beehive Inn has a living sign, a beech tree with a beehive in its branches.

**Great Limber** *(5 miles N of Caistor)* Pelham's Pillar is a monument erected to Charles Pelham who at the end of the eighteenth century planted over 12 million trees.

**Lincoln** The Glory Hole or High Bridge; houses, spanning the Witham. Aaron the Jew's House, claimed to be the oldest house in the country. *Pages 157–8*

**Witham on the Hill** Stocks on the village green are covered by a canopy. One mile from the village is the Bowthorpe Oak said to be 500 years old.

## LONDON

**Barnet** House in Barnet Lane with whalebone entrance to the garden.

**Camden Town** Camden locks on the Regent's Canal, castellated lock cottage. *Page 116*

**Carting Lane, WC2** Old gas lamp was originally one of Webb's patent sewer lamps. *Page 246*

**Chandos St, W1** Plane tree has grown through iron railings. *Page 265*

**Gunnersbury Park, W3** Sham ruin and tower in the grounds laid out by William Kent.

**Hampton Court** Britain's best-known maze in the grounds. *Page 167*

**Highgate Cemetery, N6** More interesting than Marx's tomb are the spooky catacombs. *Pages 225–7*

**Kensington Palace, W8** Fine ornate orangery. *Pages 183–4*

**Kenwood, N6** Sham bridge over the lake in the grounds.

**Kew** Botanic gardens have the famous pagoda and the magnificent palm conservatory. *Page 178*

**Leinster Gardens, W2** Numbers 23 and 24 are façades covering the railway. *Pages 62–3*

**Lincoln's Inn Fields, WC2** Hunterian Museum, Royal College of Surgeons, a private museum with some extraordinary specimens. *Pages 189–90*

**Mornington Crescent, NW1** Egyptian-styled factory. *Page 109*

**Pinner** Churchyard monument to the gardener Loudon with a sarcophagus embedded in a pyramid. *Pages 227–8*

**St John's Wood, NW8** The branches of a churchyard tree have been trained downwards to form a tent.

**St Pancras, NW1** The Railway Hotel represents Victorian Gothic at its most exuberant. *Page 122*

**Shooters Hill, SE3** Sevendroog Castle in Castlewood Park is an eighteenth-century prospect tower.

**Soho Square, W1** Tiny mock Tudor toolshed in centre of square. *Page 110*

**St Thomas Street, SE1** Old St Thomas' Hospital operating theatre. *Pages 190–1*

**Thamesmead** Crossness pumping station, one of the great Victorian industrial monuments. *Page 111*

**Tottenham, N17** Bruce Castle (now a Postal Museum) in Lordship Lane has a mysterious tower in the grounds.

**Twickenham** Pope's Grove, Alexander Pope's house, has gone but the exotic grotto he fashioned in the garden still exists. *Pages 49–50, 175–6*

A rare example of elaboration in canal building in the lock cottage at Camden Town *(Derek Pratt)*

Strawberry Hill: Walpole's Gothic fantasy which is now the home of a Catholic training college.

**Western Avenue, Greenford** A multicoloured factory in the Art Deco style built for Hoover.

## LOTHIAN

**East Linton** *(5½ miles W of Dunbar)* Phantassie Doocot is a massive stone dovecote with a sloping roof. It is a close neighbour to beautiful Preston Mill. (NTS)

**Edinburgh** Arthur's Seat: egg rolling at Easter. *Page 207*

Calton Hill has a number of monuments including an incomplete Acropolis – the money ran out.

Monument to the dog, Greyfriars Bobby, at Greyfriars Church. *Page 239*

**Oldhamstocks** Watch house in the graveyard for guarding bodies.

**South Queensferry** *(south end of Forth bridge)* A strange figure, the Burryman, parades the streets on Ferry Fair Eve, generally during the second week in August. *Pages 219–20*

## MERSEYSIDE

**Liverpool** Albert Dock. The dock office has a huge portico constructed from cast iron.

Royal Philharmonic Hotel: remarkably palatial loos.

The decaying dockland is the scene of a Good Friday burning ceremony. *Pages 216–17*

**West Kirby** A 25ft tower commemorating Tell, a St Bernard dog. *Page 241*

## NORFOLK

**Appleton** *(1 mile SE of Sandringham)* Water tower converted into a holiday home.

**Ashby St Mary** Churchyard memorials to a farmer and his wife. *Page 234*

**Briningham** *(4 miles SW of Holt)* Belle Vue Tower, originally used as a beacon, now a private home.

**Grimes Graves** *(3 miles NE of Brandon)* Neolithic flint mines.

**Walsingham** A combination of lockup, beacon and conduit, all in the same tiny building. *Page 130*

## NORTHAMPTONSHIRE

**Finedon** *(3 miles NE of Wellingborough)* A round tower, part of a house and dedicated to the victory at Waterloo.

**Harrington** The vicarage has a chimney pot in the form of a steeple. *Pages 146–7*

**Holdenby** *(6 miles NW of Northampton)* Two solitary arches in a field, sole remnants of a sixteenth-century house.

**Lyveden New Bield** *(4 miles SW of Oundle)* A house built for Sir Thomas Tresham, full of Catholic symbolism but never completed. (NT)

**Rushton** The triangular lodge, another work by Tresham and again full of symbolism. *Pages 65–6*

## NORTHUMBERLAND

**Alnwick** Brislaw Tower, a prospect tower overlooking the town. Tenantry column erected by the tenants for the Duke of Northumberland who thanked them by increasing their rent. Shrovetide football is played, starting with a procession from Alnwick Castle. *Pages 66–7, 200*

**Branxton** Animal garden at The Fountain. Hundreds of concrete animals and over 200 garden gnomes. *Pages 166–7*

**Elsdon** *(2½ miles SE of village on the Newcastle road)* A replica gibbet – though why a replica gibbet is wanted is the biggest mystery.

The palatial Gents' in the Liverpool Philharmonic Hotel *(British Tourist Authority)*

**Ford** Village smithy with a horseshoe-shaped entrance.

**Rothley** *(4 miles NE of Kirkwhelpington)* Rothley Castle, a sham castle with two prominent towers.

**Warden** *(2 miles NW of Hexham)* Hoops over grave to foil grave robbers, and hexagonal toll house by the Tyne bridge.

**Whitton** *(just south of Rothbury)* Tower built to provide work for the unemployed.


## NOTTINGHAMSHIRE

**Beeston** Anglo-Scotian mill in Wollaton Rd has a false castellated front. *Pages 106–7*

**Gotham** Cuckoo Bush Inn named after pretended lunatics. *Page 250*

**Newstead** Newstead Abbey has little forts on the lake built for Lord Byron.

**Nottingham** Trip to Jerusalem, Castle Road, an old pub carved out of the rock of Castle Hill. *Page 161*

**Ravenshead** Papplewick Pumping Station, Longdale Lane – Victorian beam engines in an amazingly exotic setting. *Pages 112–13*

**Scarrington** An obelisk built up from 35,000 horseshoes. *Page 77*

**Sherwood Forest** *(½ mile N of Edwinstowe)* Off the B6034 is the Major Oak which is claimed as the largest tree in Britain.


## OXFORDSHIRE

**Chastleton** *(2 miles W of Chipping Norton)* Opposite Chastleton House, a gabled dovecote built on massive pillars.

**Chipping Norton** Bliss Tweed Mill, on the A40 to the west of the town, has a factory chimney popping up out of the middle of the domed roof. *Page 107*

The Theatre: a converted Salvation Army citadel. *Page 146*

**Coleshill** Strattenborough Castle Farm, 1½

miles south of the village, is an ordinary farm lurking behind a castle façade.

**Faringdon** Lord Berner's Folly is one of the rare twentieth-century follies, a prospect tower of 1935. *Page 101*

**Great Milton** Circular stone dovecote in the churchyard.

**Harpsden** Opposite the church is a barn with walls made up of old printing blocks. *Page 157*

**Henley-on-Thames** Park Place, a private house near Marsh Lock, has a miniature stone henge in the garden which can be glimpsed from the river. *Page 46*

**Little Haseley** Haseley Court has a topiary garden with topiary chess set.

**Little Rollright** The Rollright stones, ½ mile north-east of the village, consisting of King's Stone, King's Men and Whispering Knights, are standing stones around which a wealth of legend has gathered. *Pages 23, 28–9*

**Long Wittenham** Tudor dovecote behind the church.

**Mapledurham** The statue of Old Palm sits high on a brick plinth overlooking Mapledurham House and is said to come visiting at Christmas.

**Middleton Stoney** Manor House contains the remains of a motte and bailey within the grounds so has suitably castellated entrances. *Page 58*

**Oxford** The Pitt-Rivers and University Museums in Parks Road are alike extraordinary: the former for its odd collection, the latter for its architecture. *Page 195*

Magdalen College: the choristers sing each May morning. *Pages 213–15*

**Rotherfield Greys** Grey's Court, 3 miles west of Henley on the road to Rotherfield Greys; the well house has a huge wheel which was turned by a donkey to raise water from the well. (NT)

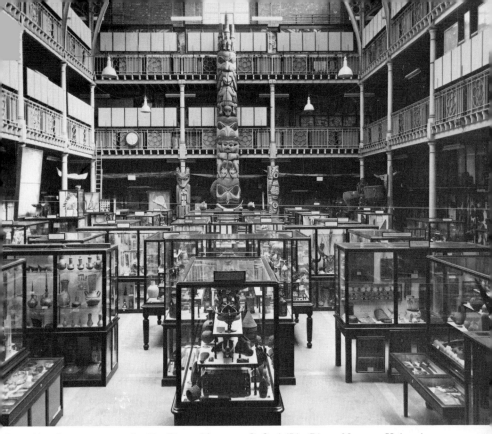

Something for everyone at the Pitt Rivers Museum, Oxford *(Pitt Rivers Museum, University of Oxford)*

**Rousham** *(4 miles W of Middleton Stoney)* The grounds contain a dovecote and an elaborate memorial to a favourite hound. *Pages 183, 241*

**Shirburn** A medieval fortified house was altered in the nineteenth-century to become a mock castle, Shirburn Castle, still a private home. Thus a genuine antiquity was transformed into a fake.

**Somerton** Troy Farm has a turf maze; it is not open to the public. *Page 168*

**Steeple Aston** Rousham eye catcher, a solitary Gothic wall, stands in fields to the east of the village. *Page 7*

**Stoke Row** The ornate village well was a gift from the Maharajah of Benares. *Page 254*

**Sydenham** A small brass sundial now acts as a keyhole plate on the church door.

**Uffington** The white horse on the hill was galloped from Berkshire into Oxfordshire in a boundary change. *Page 41*

**Wheatley** Pyramidal stone lockup. *Page 125*

## POWYS

**Brecon Beacons** Memorial to Harry Llewellyn's horse Foxhunter. *Page 239*

## SHETLAND ISLANDS

**Lerwick** The ceremony of Up-Helly-Aa, when a Viking boat is burned, takes place on 29 January. *Page 216*

The Viking ship goes up in flames in the Shetland ceremony of Up-Helly-Aa *(British Tourist Authority)*

## SHROPSHIRE

**Alberbury** Princes Oak stands on the border with Powys. It was here that George IV was introduced as Prince of Wales.

**Aston on Clun** The Arbor Tree is decked out in flags each year on 29 May. The flags remain all year. *Page 219*

**Boscobel** The Royal Oak was grown from an acorn from the tree in which King Charles sheltered after the battle of Worcester.

**Claverley** A contender for the smallest house in Britain title, a thatched cottage measuring only 8ft by 10ft.

**Coalbrookdale** The Darby works boast a very ornate clock tower under which is a museum containing some of the more elaborate Victorian ironworks, including a cast-iron fountain. *Pages 165, 263*

**Cressage** The Cressage Oak is said to be one of the oldest trees in the country. *Page 265*

**Hodnet** Hawkstone Park follies. The sandstone cliff under the old castle has been transformed into a bewildering series of caves, grottoes and walks. *Pages 53–4*

**Ironbridge** The toll house on the end of the famous bridge still has its list of tolls. *Pages 113–14*

**Linley** Linley Hall grounds contain an ice house disguised as a classical temple. *Page 180*

**Madeley** Madeley Court, a privately owned house, has an Elizabethan sundial in the courtyard. *Page 260*

**Priestweston** One mile to the north-east is Mitchell's Fold, a stone circle high up the mountainside. *Page 28*

**Tong** The Egyptian Aviary, probably the most elaborate hen house ever built, stands off the A41, on the Shifnal road.

**Wenlock Edge** Flounders Folly is a massive prospect tower on the top of Callow Hill.

## SOMERSET

**Barrington** *(3 miles NE of Ilminster)* Barrington Court has an elaborate sundial perched on a high column. (NT) *Page 260*

**Barwick** A collection of follies can be found in Barwick Park, all credited to George Messiter. There are towers, pinnacles and an obelisk and, perhaps most curious, a monument to Jack the Treacle Eater – a gentleman of uncertain origin.

**Bruton** Half a mile south of Bruton is an unusual gabled dovecote from the sixteenth century. (NT)

**Burrow Bridge** *(4 miles NW of Langport)* On Burrow Mump, the medieval church was rebuilt in the eighteenth century but never completed.

**Castle Cary** Circular lockup on the A371, so tiny it was said to be built for eighteenth-century juvenile delinquents.

**Chard** An attractive thatched Gothic toll house stands in the angle between the A30 and a minor road to Axminster, west of the town.

**Combe Florey** *(6 miles NW of Taunton)* A mock church tower in Combe Wood, built as a keeper's lodge.

**Crowcombe** The Heddon Oak is the tree from which followers of the Monmouth rebellion were hanged.

**Curry Rivel** *(2 miles SW of Langport)* The Burton Pynsent Column was once climbable by a spiral staircase. It was closed after a cow walked up and fell from the top.

The Bell Inn has a fives court. *Page 206*

**Dunster** An eighteenth-century folly tower stands on the top of Conygar Hill.

**Hemington** Ammerdown Park Column, a monumental column with a view from the top. *Page 99*

**Hinton St George** Punkie Night, the last Thursday in October, is the occasion for a parade of turnip lanterns. There is a fives court behind the Poulett Arms. *Page 206*

**Kingsbury Episcopi** Octagonal lockup with heavily studded door, tiny ventilation grilles and conical roof.

**Minehead** May Day is celebrated with the arrival of the Hobby Horse, known as the Sailor's Horse. *Page 212*

**Montacute** Montacute House boasts two garden pavilions and a splendidly ornate lodge. A folly tower stands on St Michael's Hill. (NT)

**Stoke sub Hamdon** *(5 miles W of Yeovil)* A fives court wall with a shaped gable can be seen in the village.

**Wells** A folly tower 60ft high, known as Lax or Laxey Folly, stands on Knapp Hill.

**Wookey Hole** Besides its natural delights, Wookey Hole houses Madame Tussaud's waxwork rejects and Lady Bangor's Fairground Collection. *Pages 193–5*

## STAFFORDSHIRE

**Abbots Bromley** The ancient Horn Dance, in which the men wear Tudor costume and antler head pieces, takes place annually on the first Sunday after 4 September. *Page 220*

**Alton** Alton Towers' grounds contain a number of exotic garden ornaments including a corkscrew fountain, a Chinese pagoda and an imitation Stonehenge. *Page 165*

Alton Station built in the Italianate style, is now a holiday home. *Page 143*

**Biddulph** The gardens of Biddulph Grange now belong to an orthopaedic hospital. They include a fine Chinese garden and are being restored.

**The Bratch** *(4 miles SW of Wolverhampton)* On the Staffs and Worcester Canal are an odd group of locks graced by an octagonal toll house.

**Drayton Bassett** A funny little castellated footbridge crosses the Birmingham and Fazeley Canal.

**Enville** *(5 miles W of Stourbridge)* There is a triple-arch eye catcher in the park at Enville Hall.

**Gnosall** *(6 miles W of Stafford)* Nineteenth-century village lockup.

**Kidsgrove** Two miles north-east of the town is Mow Cop, crowned by a sham ruin. (NT) *Pages 47–9*

**Milford** *(4 miles SE of Stafford)* Shugborough railway tunnel has castellated entrances.

**Sandon** The old belvedere from the Duke of Sutherland's home now stands in the grounds of Sandon Hall. *Page 80*

**Shugborough** *(5 miles E of Stafford)* There are many intriguing monuments in the grounds of Shugborough Hall including mock ruins, a Chinese house, a commemorative arch to Admiral Anson and a rather smaller monument to a cat. Lichfield Drive is crossed by a highly decorated bridge carrying the old Trent Valley Railway. (NT) *Pages 241–3*

**Stoke on Trent** The railway station is built like a Jacobean manor. *Pages 121–2*

## STRATHCLYDE

**Glasgow** The Botanic Gardens off the Great Western Road contain a splendid glasshouse, the Kibble Palace. *Page 184*

The Templeton Carpet Factory on Glasgow Green is a riot of colour. *Pages 109–10*

Central Station includes a bridge section over the main road.

**Lanark** On 1 March local children pursue each other around the church in the ritual of Whuppity Stourie or Scourie. *Page 202*

**Oban** McCaig's Tower is a Colosseum-like building overlooking the town. *Pages 43–5*

**Rothesay, Isle of Bute** A splendid Gents'. *Page 247*

## SUFFOLK

**Aldeburgh** Martello tower, now a holiday home. *Page 142*

**Debenham** On the edge of the village is the groaning stone which is said to roll over and groan at midnight.

**Euston** A monument to a foxhound, Trouncer, in the wall of Euston Park. *Page 241*

**Freston** A sixteenth-century prospect tower. *Pages 79–80*

**Long Melford** Melford Hall has an octagonal gazebo with gables and pinnacles. (NT) *Page 183*

**Offton** Churchyard memorial to John Wyard with a monument to his horse. *Page 239*

**Rendlesham** *(3 miles SE of Wickham Market)* Rendlesham Hall has an extravagantly pinnacled Gothic lodge. *Pages 58–61*

**Somerleyton** Somerleyton House has a yew-hedge maze. *Page 170*

**Stoke by Nayland** Tiny brick lockup with a grating high in the wall, School Street.

**Tattingstone** Three cottages disguised as a church and known as the Tattingstone Wonder. *Page 146*

**Thorpeness** The new development contains some very odd features, including a water tower disguised as a house and partly habitable, giant tees on the golf clubhouse, and a Peter Pan boating lake. *Pages 104–5*

*(opposite)* Acres of glass shaped in spectacular fashion in the Kibble Palace, Glasgow Botanic Gardens *(F. G. Rodway)*

When is a water-tower not a water-tower? When it is also a home: House in the Clouds, Thorpeness *(G. C. Cook)*

**Woodbridge** A steelyard for weighing waggons stands beside the Old Bell and Steelyard Inn. There is a tide mill on the Deben. *Pages 266–8*

**Woolverstone** *(4 miles S of Ipswich)* The Cat House has a painted window complete with painted cat.

### SURREY

**Abinger Hammer** *(5 miles W of Dorking)* A blacksmith strikes the hours on a clock over the main road. *Page 262*

**Box Hill** A small circular flint tower, fulfilling no known purpose, stands overlooking Juniper Hall. (NT)

**Caterham** A castellated prospect tower on the North Downs.

**Egham** Beside Virginia Water is a set of classical columns in an unlikely setting.

**Esher** Claremont Park, 1 mile south of Esher, one of the earliest landscape gardens complete with pavilion, grotto and turf amphitheatre. (NT)

Churchyard monument: 'This tombstone is a milestone. How so? Because beneath lies John Miles who's miles below.'

**Guildford** Merrowgrange, once a convent and now a comprehensive school, possesses fantastic grounds full of grottoes, strange tunnels and walks.

**Leith Hill** The highest point in south-east England is topped by a prospect tower. The builder, Richard Hull, is buried underneath. (NT) *Pages 88–9*

**Lingfield** *(4 miles N of East Grinstead)* The village lockup is half engulfed in an oak tree struck by lightning.

**Nutfield** *(2 miles E of Redhill)* A simple two-storey tower in the grounds of Well House.

**Peper Harow** *(2 miles W of Godalming)* Has a fine sham church ruin.

**Reigate** The castle was pulled down and a false castle built in 1777.

**Tilford** *(3 miles SE of Farnham)* The oak tree by the green is nearly 1,000 years old. *Page 265*

# EAST SUSSEX

**Alciston** Locals skip on the ancient barrows each Good Friday. *Page 201*

**Battle** Railway station in an appropriately medieval style. *Page 121*

**Brightling** The whole district is imbued with the spirit of the great folly builder, Mad Jack Fuller, from the obelisk on Brightling Down to the pyramid tomb in the churchyard. *Pages 72–4*

**Brighton** Home of one of the country's most extravagant buildings, the Royal Pavilion, and a more modest piece of elaborate design – the Jubilee clock tower. *Page 263*

**Eridge** *(3 miles SW of Tunbridge Wells)* Saxonbury Hill has a splendid if somewhat decayed prospect tower.

**Lewes** St John sub Castro Church has a finely carved resurrection gravestone, and a carpenter's grave. *Page 233*

**Northiam** The oak on the green is said to have sheltered Queen Elizabeth I while Great Dixter, basically a fifteenth-century house, has a fine topiary garden.

**Pevensey** Has the oldest and the smallest town hall in Britain, incorporating a lockup with two tiny cells.

**Rye** Parish church has a sixteenth-century church clock with striking cupids. *Page 262*

**Westdean** *(6 miles E of Eastbourne)* Medieval dovecote in the grounds of Charleston Manor.

**Wilmington** The famous Long Man is carved into the hillside. *Page 38*

A suitably bizarre monument to a great eccentric. Inside the pyramid is Mad Jack Fuller, said to have been interred sat upright in his favourite chair *(Reece Winstone)*

## WEST SUSSEX

**Arundel** Potter's Museum of Curiosity at 6 High Street is famous for its well-dressed animal tableaux. *Pages 187, 189*

**Bramber** The House of Pipes on the A283 is a museum of smoking. *Page 193*

**Clayton** Clayton tunnel on the London–Brighton railway line has a castellated entrance with the tunnel-keeper's house above. Two windmills, Jack and Jill, stand on the hill above the tunnel. *Page 125*

**Henfield** A platoon of cats marches round the eaves of a sixteenth-century cottage in the lane leading to the church. *Page 154*

**Slindon** *(4 miles W of Arundel)* The Nore folly is a ruined arch to the north of Slindon Park. (NT)

**Tinsley Green** Marbles rink where the annual championship is held on Good Friday. *Page 204*

**Uppark** *(4 miles SE of Petersfield)* Uppark Tower was built in 1770 to commemorate the launching of the plan for a new American colony. The plan came to nothing.

## TAYSIDE

**Birnam** *(½ mile SE of Dunkeld)* The last oak of Birnam Wood; the rest presumably can be found at Dunsinane.

**Fortingall** In the churchyard are the remains of a great yew, believed to be 3,000 years old.

**Dunkeld** The Hermitage, 2 miles to the west off the A9, is a charming folly set on a rock overlooking the river. (NTS)

## TYNE AND WEAR

**Newcastle upon Tyne** The Bagpipe Museum, St Nicholas Street. *Page 193*

**Ryhope** Grand Victorian pumping station in Jacobean style, engines regularly steamed. *Pages 111–12*

**Sunderland** Monkwearmouth station, a fine example of classical railway architecture, is now a museum. *Page 122*

## WARWICKSHIRE

**Atherstone** The Shrovetide football game is played on Shrove Tuesday afternoon along the main street.

**Chesterton Green** A windmill designed in a picturesque style. *Pages 105–6*

**Coleshill** Two-man pillory attached to the wall on Church Hill. *Pages 253–4*

**Compton Wynyates** *(5 miles E of Shipston on Stour)* The gardens of this fine Tudor house contain a topiary chess set. *Page 172*

**Edgehill** *(7 miles NW of Banbury)* Sanderson Miller's folly tower is now the Castle Inn. *Page 47*

**Hockley Heath** Packwood House, 1 mile to the east, has a topiary garden representing the Sermon on the Mount. (NT)

**Kinwarton** *(1½ miles NE of Alcester)* A circular dovecote dating from the fourteenth century. (NT)

**Welford on Avon** A 70ft striped maypole.

## WESTERN ISLES

**Lewis** At the southern end of Callanish village are the mysterious old stones consisting of a circle and avenue. *Pages 26–8*

## WEST MIDLANDS

**Birmingham** Perrott's Folly, a seven-storey tower in Rotton Park, Edgbaston. *Pages 84–5*

Gravelly Hill: the famous Spaghetti Junction, seen at its best from underneath. *Pages 120–1*

Smethwick: the Avery Museum traces the history of weighing while on the nearby Birmingham Canal can be seen the Engine Arm aqueduct in cast-iron Gothic. *Pages 116, 193*

**Coventry** Cash's Top Shops in Cash's Lane – houses with a factory on top. *Pages 107–8*

**Dudley** The entrance to Dudley Tunnel is by the Black Country Museum. Boat trips enable visitors to see an underground world of caverns and arches. *Pages 117–19*

### WILTSHIRE

**Avebury** Arguably the most impressive set of prehistoric monuments in Britain consisting of the Avebury stone circle itself (NT), mysterious Silbury Hill, 1 mile to the south, and West Kennet Long Barrow to the south-east. *Pages 32–4*

**Bradford on Avon** The building on the bridge was a lockup, was used as a powder magazine and may once have been a chapel. *Pages 130–1*

**Devizes** Shane's Castle is in fact a toll house at the junction of the Chippenham and Trowbridge roads. *Page 114*

**East Tytherton** Maud Heath's monument and sundial commemorate the lady who endowed the causeway across the flood plain of the Avon in the fifteenth century. *Pages 258–60*

**Fonthill Bishop** Hermit's cave overlooking the lake. *Page 76*

**Great Wishford** Ancient plaques on the wall of St Giles Church record the changing price of bread.

**Seend** *(4 miles W of Devizes)* The Barge Inn's significant sign. *Page 250*

**Shrewton** Massive village lockup stands beside the bridge.

*(left)* Radway Tower – suitably militaristic architecture on the site of the battle of Edgehill *(BBC Hulton Picture Library)*; *(right)* the last of the owner-boatmen, the late Joe Skinner, sails on in a Seend pub sign *(Derek Pratt)*

**Stonehenge** Internationally famous but still mysterious monument. *Pages 32, 35–7*

**Stourton** Stourhead is famous for its landscape garden which includes several temples and a magnificent grotto. Nearby, on Kingsettle Hill, is the 160ft prospect tower known as King Alfred's Tower. (NT) *Page 176*

**Tollard Royal** *(6 miles SE of Shaftesbury)* Larmer Tree Gardens – park laid out by General Pitt-Rivers with some bizarre ornaments.

**Wardour Castle** *(2 miles SW of Tisbury)* Eighteenth-century grotto.

**Westbury** *(4 miles S of Trowbridge)* White horse on hillside. *Page 42*

**Whiteparish** 2½ miles west of the village is Pepperbox Hill, topped by the seventeenth-century folly which gave it its name. (NT)

**Wylye** Monument in the middle of the river to a drowned postillion. *Page 230*


### NORTH YORKSHIRE

**Boroughbridge** The Devil's Arrows, grooved standing stones between the town and the A1. *Page 16*

**Brandsby** Turf maze known as the City of Troy, on the edge of the village. *Page 168*

**Castle Howard** *(5 miles W of Malton)* The house has a belvedere and temple in the grounds but its most impressive feature is a vast mausoleum.

**Cowthorpe** *(3 miles NE of Wetherby)* The Cowthorpe Oak is reckoned to be 1,500 years old. *Pages 263–5*

**Grewelthorpe** *(3 miles S of Masham)* In Hackfell Woods, in the Ure gorge, are three fine sham ruins.

**Harrogate** Harlow Hill has a prospect tower which is now a public observation tower, while throughout the town are wells where visitors can taste the foul waters. *Pages 254–7*

**Helmsley** Some 2½ miles north-west of the town is Rievaulx Terrace, a grass terrace decorated with temples. (NT)

**Ilton** *(3 miles SW of Masham)* On the moors is a very convincing imitation of Stonehenge known as the Druids' Circle. *Pages 45–6*

**Knaresborough** A good collection of oddities. Beside the river are Fort Montagu, a house hewn out of the cliff, a petrifying well and Mother Shipton's Cave. The river is crossed by a castellated railway viaduct. *Pages 124–5, 133–4, 137*

**Pannal** In the graveyard there is a stone slab weighing a ton, hired by relative to put on top of graves to foil body snatchers.

**Pateley Bridge** Some 3 miles to the east of the town are Brimham Rocks, weathered into fantastic shapes and bearing names such as the Dancing Bear and the Yoke of Oxen. (NT) *Page 16*

Above the town are two ruined pillars, part of an eighteenth-century mock ruin.

**Richmond** About 1½ miles north of Richmond is Aske Hall which has a fine Gothic garden temple.

**Ripley** Hotel de Ville appears out of place in this Yorkshire village which has a set of stocks in the square. *Pages 148, 254*

**Scarborough** Locals go down to the shore to skip on Shrove Tuesday. *Page 201*

**Sedbury** *(1 mile NE of Hawes)* The watch tower, a mock ruin, stands on a rocky outcrop.

**Sharow** A pyramidal monument in the churchyard to Charles Smyth. *Page 228*

**West Witton** On 24 August an effigy is burned in the ceremony of Burning Bartle. *Page 219*

**Whitby** On Ascension Eve a Penny Hedge is planted on the shore. *Page 218*

The dropping well at Knaresborough and part of the weird array of objects being turned to stone *(British Tourist Authority)*

## SOUTH YORKSHIRE

**Birdwell** *(3 miles S of Barnsley)* A sham castle commemorating the Boston tea party.

**Penistone** *(7 miles W of Barnsley)* A circular tower, built in 1851, stands high on the moor.

**Wentworth** The eighteenth-century mansion Wentworth Woodhouse has three fine follies, Hoober Stand, Keppel's Column and the Needle's Eye. *Pages 69–72*

## WEST YORKSHIRE

**Barwick in Elmet** The tallest standing maypole in Britain. *Page 209*

**Bingley** On a hill above the town is a mock ruin known as St David's, built in 1796.
The lock cottage on the Leeds and Liverpool Canal contains traces of old lettering from its earlier days in Liverpool. *Pages 154, 157*

**Halifax** Wainhouse's Tower, a prominent landmark in the town, was originally built as a factory chimney. *Pages 102–4*

**Haworth** Among the Brontëana is the grave of Lily Cove, balloonist. *Page 233*

**Hebden Bridge** Strange houses built top to bottom rather than back to back on the hillside terraces. *Page 151*

**Kildwick** Organist's grave in churchyard with organ monument. *Page 233*

**Kirkheaton** Beer barrel monument in churchyard to a local boozer. *Page 233*

**Leeds** Marshall's flax mill – a textile mill built like an Egyptian temple, stands in Marshall Street. Glass covered shopping arcades with ornate signs are found off Briggate. *Pages 108–9, 263*

**Otley** Navvies' grave in the churchyard built as a representation of Bramhope Tunnel, complete with castellated entrances. *Page 235*

**Shipley** Incorporates the mill village of Saltaire, built in the Italianate style by Sir Titus Salt. *Page 151*

**Triangle** *(2 miles SW of Sowerby Bridge)* On the side of the Manchester–Halifax road is the gravestone of a pet gander. *Page 243*

# Further Reading

Barton, Stuart. *Monumental Follies: An Exposition on the Eccentric Edifices of Britain* (Lyle Publications, 1972)

Bland, John. *Odd and Unusual England: An Illustrated History of Curious Things* (Spurbooks, 1974)

Bord, Janet. *Mazes and Labyrinths of the World* (Latimer New Dimensions, 1976)

Bord, Janet and Colin. *A Guide to Ancient Sites in Britain* (Latimer New Dimensions, 1978)

—— *The Secret Country: Interpretation of the Folklore of Ancient Sites in the British Isles* (Paul Elek, 1976)

Clayton, Peter. *Archaeological Sites of Britain* (Weidenfeld & Nicolson, 1976)

Darley, Gillian. *Villages of Vision* (Architectural Press, 1975)

Edwards, Paul. *English Garden Ornament* (G. Bell, 1965)

Gaunt, Arthur. *Tourists' England: A Kaleidoscope of Oddities and Strange Places* (F. Graham, 1969)

Grigson, Geoffrey. *The Shell Country Alphabet* (Michael Joseph and Rainbird, 1966)

Herbert, A. P. *Sundials Old and New* (Methuen, 1967)

Hitching, Francis. *Earth Magic* (Cassell, 1976)

Hogg, Garry. *Facets of the English Scene* (David & Charles, 1973)

—— *Odd Aspects of England* (David & Charles, 1969)

—— *The Shell Book of Exploring Britain* (John Baker, 1971)

Hole, Christina. *A Dictionary of British Folk Customs* (Hutchinson, 1976)

Hunt, John Dixon, and Willis, Peter. *The Genius of the Place: The English Landscape Garden* (Paul Elek, 1975)

Lea, Raymond. *Country Curiosities: The Rare, Odd and Unusual in the English Countryside* (Spurbooks, 1973)

Lindley, Kenneth. *Of Graves and Epitaphs* (Hutchinson, 1965)

Vince, John. *Village Style* (Ian Allen, 1974)

Warren, Geoffrey. *Vanishing Street Furniture* (David & Charles, 1978)

# Index

Place-names listed in the Gazetteer (page 270) are not included in this index.